THE
VALUE
IMPERATIVE

Managing for Superior Shareholder Returns

James M. McTaggart
Peter W. Kontes
Michael C. Mankins

THE FREE PRESS
A Division of Macmillan, Inc.
NEW YORK

Maxwell Macmillan Canada
TORONTO

Maxwell Macmillan International
NEW YORK   OXFORD   SINGAPORE   SYDNEY

The Free Press
A Division of Macmillan, Inc.
866 Third Avenue, New York, N.Y. 10022

Maxwell Macmillan Canada, Inc.
1200 Eglinton Avenue East
Suite 200
Don Mills, Ontario M3C 3N1

Macmillan, Inc. is part of the Maxwell Communication Group of Companies.

Printed in the United States of America

printing number

1 2 3 4 5 6 7 8 9 10

Library of Congress Cataloging-in-Publication Data

McTaggart, James M.
   The value imperative: managing for superior shareholder returns/
James M. McTaggart, Peter W. Kontes, Michael C. Mankins.
     p.   cm.
   ISBN 0-02-920670-7
   1. Corporations—Valuation. 2. Corporations—Finance.
I. Kontes, Peter W.   II. Mankins, Michael C.   III. Title.
HG4028.V3M38   1994
658.15′54—dc20   93–50555
                                          CIP

TO BILL ALBERTS

Contents

PART 4: CREATING A HIGHER-VALUE ORGANIZATION

Acknowledgments

The authors owe a great deal to the work of our friend and colleague, Dr. William Alberts, to whom this book is dedicated. Both in his academic life at the University of Chicago and the University of Washington, and in his role as our partner at Marakon Associates, Bill has devoted his professional efforts almost exclusively to building an understanding of how managers' strategic and organizational choices can impact business performance and shareholder value. His always thoughtful and often brilliant work is the cornerstone of what many managers today consider "value based management." Without his patient teaching and inspiration over many years, this book could never have been written.

We also want to thank our colleagues at Marakon who devoted considerable time and energy to helping us complete the book. Particular thanks must go to Ron Langford and Ken Favaro, whose ideas and always constructive criticism have made this a much better book than it would have been otherwise. In addition, Ron has contributed directly to the substantial editing and reediting in the final days to completion, and his valuable input, particularly for Chapters Two through Nine, is deeply appreciated by all of us. Other partners who have served as readers and whose suggestions have been incorporated include John Kavanagh and Paul Favaro. We owe special thanks as well to Caryl Castellion, whose tireless efforts, through many long days and nights and endless redraftings, actually produced the manuscript, and to Ken Worzel, who served as editor, case researcher, and data checker through the final weeks of drafting. Other Marakon colleagues whose contributions can be found in the book include Lynn Tate Baldo, Paul Bridwell, Julio Farach, Dennis Hoffman, Nick Marsh, Dean Neese, Kevin O'Gorman, David Phillips, Troy Smeal, and Glenn Welling. To each of them, our thanks.

It has been our good fortune over the last twenty years to work with many executives who were and are pioneers of managing for shareholder value. While we cannot begin to name all of them, there are a few whom we would like to acknowledge for having afforded us special opportunities to teach a little and learn a lot along the way. They include Ernie Arbuckle, Roberto Goizueta, John Collings, Charlie Frenette, Chet Evans, Gary Wilson, Al Checchi, John Dasburg, Don Povejsil, Mel Goetz, George Kirk, John Powers, Alex Mandl, Bob Lanigan, Dick Lock, Paul Voight, John Buchanan, Phil Samper, Lee Horschman, Harry Shoff, Tony Carbone, Rick Gerardo, Chet Marks, Tom Burtch, Jim Forese, Fred Fassman, Sir James Blyth, David Thompson, Gordon Hourston, and Martin Bryant, who was also kind enough to act as a reader for this book.

We must also thank Robert Wallace of The Free Press, who stood by us when the demands of our business caused us to miss several deadlines extending over a number of years. Without Bob's encouragement, patience, sound advice, and, when that didn't work, gentle threats, we might not have persevered. Also, our thanks to Judith Eng, who had to overcome considerable odds to convert our writing into generally acceptable prose.

Finally, of course, we must thank our wives for their encouragement and support throughout the writing of the book. It is bad enough that they and our families must tolerate the professional demands on our time, especially the time we spend away from home. To ask for still more time to fit in the writing of the book was undoubtedly asking too much. But they all responded with grace and more understanding than we deserve. We promise, no more books for a while.

INTRODUCTION

The Value Imperative

Shareholders are restless. The past two decades have seen a dramatic increase in shareholders' concerns about the performance of the companies they own—performance that affects not only the economic welfare of the shareholders themselves but the welfare of nations, indeed, the entire world. When shareholders become frustrated or disaffected with the performance of companies, they naturally look to top management to reverse the declining fortunes of the firm or stand aside for others who will. In the 1980s, these frustrations were crudely, but effectively, expressed in the form of hostile takeovers. In the 1990s, they are more diplomatically expressed in meetings between top management and powerful institutional shareholders. But the message is the same: Performance must improve if top management is to justify its continued stewardship of the company.

What is at the root of shareholders' anxieties? Among the developments of greatest concern is the manifest inability of top management at some companies to act in the face of structural changes that pose a clear and present danger to the company's competitive and financial health. Even in those cases where action is finally taken, it often appears confused or panic-driven and rarely addresses the true causes of the company's problems. Another trend that worries shareholders is the proliferation of strategic objectives that companies proclaim as their top priorities, such as maximization of customer satisfaction, continuous quality improvement, and global market dominance. Shareholders understandably become anxious when objectives like

1

these, which are related only indirectly, if at all, to wealth creation, seem to preoccupy the chief executive and top management.

Chief executives and top management are also restless. Many view the shareholders and their concerns with suspicion and, occasionally, even intolerance. Others, more enlightened, recognize that the investors' expectation that managers will "create shareholder value" is hardly unreasonable. In our surveys of senior executives, we find the great majority in agreement with the proposition that creating shareholder value is a legitimate and important corporate objective. Some, although by no means the majority, even say it is the most important corporate objective. But there is widespread disagreement among executives about just what creating shareholder value means and, more important, how to accomplish it. Some see value creation as essentially a portfolio activity that consists of buying and selling the right businesses at the right time. Others see it as an activity that focuses on how the company can keep reported earnings per share rising inexorably at some minimum rate. Still others see it more clearly as managing the performance of individual business units with respect to the cash flow generated or rates of return earned over time. A small, but increasing, number see value creation as a governing objective and realize that building the capability to create wealth into the everyday management of the company can, itself, become a significant competitive advantage.

The frustrations of both shareholders and top management are certainly understandable. On one hand, we find that very few large, publicly owned companies are creating shareholder value at much more than half of their current potential to do so. And on the other hand, top management is finding it increasingly challenging to manage these huge, diverse enterprises so that they consistently perform at levels commensurate with investor expectations.

We have written this book to help professional managers deal with this challenge. In essence, *The Value Imperative* is an introduction to the subject of *managing* to create wealth, or shareholder value. We aspire to answer the questions often asked by those executives who agree that creating shareholder value is a high-priority objective: "So now what? What do we actually do to make the achievement of this objective a reality?" This is perhaps the hardest question for management. A company that cannot create new wealth cannot satisfy its customers for long, nor can it meet the expectations of more jobs and higher incomes for its employees. And yet, despite its importance, creating shareholder value remains the most elusive of management capabilities. We hope that this book provides a deeper understanding of how financial, strategic, and organizational decisions are likely to impact the value of the company, and how this understanding can help managers achieve superior performance for shareholders and all other stakeholders as well.

The Value Imperative is organized into four main parts. The first, "Managing for Value," lays the groundwork for setting the right corporate and business unit objectives and understanding the nature of the task of value creation. The second part, "Value Creation," sets out the fundamental linkages between shareholder value, as measured in the capital markets, and the financial and strategic performance of a company and its business units. The third part, "Creating Higher-Value Strategies," suggests how managers at the business unit and corporate levels can develop new strategic alternatives that are likely to increase the value of the company significantly and consistently over time. The fourth part, "Creating a Higher-Value Organization," develops the concept of institutional value drivers, the key management processes that can enable a company to build an organizational advantage for achieving superior performance for shareholders over time. Finally, the conclusion, "Making Value Creation a Core Competence," is a brief chapter focusing on the key factors that determine how effectively a company will respond to the "So now what?" question and begin to make the often-significant changes required to become and remain an exemplar of wealth creation.

Over the past 20 years it has been our privilege to work with some of the largest, most prestigious companies in the world, and many outstanding executives who have pioneered new management practices and new strategies for increasing shareholder value. This experience has produced a tremendous number of ideas to help answer the "So now what?" query, ideas covering the full spectrum of financial, strategic, and organizational management. One of our goals in writing this book was to provide managers with at least a few of these ideas that would be helpful immediately in improving the performance of their businesses. We hope that *The Value Imperative* passes this ambitious test.

PART 1
Managing Value

CHAPTER 1

The Governing Objective

We believe that all companies, especially publicly owned companies, should be managed to create as much wealth as possible. By this we mean that the company's resources should be managed to make them worth more than they would be if managed in any other way or by any other firm. This is an enormously demanding objective. To achieve it, management must focus on the continuous pursuit of opportunities to increase the value of the company's resources and establish maximizing wealth as not one of many equally important objectives, but as the preeminent or governing objective. Creating wealth is much more than a fiduciary responsibility, it is a hallmark of great management and great companies.

This book deals with the management of companies that are owned by private shareholders. For managers of shareholder-owned companies, maximizing wealth, or the worth of the company's human and financial resources, necessarily means the same thing as maximizing the value of the enterprise to its owners, or maximizing shareholder value. For the majority of companies with publicly traded shares, owners and managers have at their disposal a continuous objective appraisal of their success in wealth creation as reflected in the price of the companies' common stock. This assertion of the equivalence between the objectives of maximizing wealth and maximizing shareholder value is questioned by many managers who believe that investors typically undervalue, or fail to recognize, the wealth created by their companies. We will present considerable evidence to allay this

7

concern, but for now, those with misgivings about the validity of capital market valuations might remember Winston Churchill's observation about democracy: "... it has been said that democracy is the
worst system devised by the wit of man, except for the others."[1]

Today virtually all chief executives and directors of publicly traded
companies, especially in the United States, acknowledge that creating
value for shareholders is an important corporate objective. But they
face an awesome array of competing priorities, including other financial measures, such as earnings growth and return on investment; other
strategic objectives, such as global cost competitiveness and market
share leadership; and concerns for the welfare of their employees and
the communities in which they operate. Thus, the major problem they
face is not necessarily setting the objective itself but making it operational. One chief executive who obviously overcame this problem and
expressed his conclusions as vividly as anyone ever has, put it this
way:

> The objective of our company is to increase the intrinsic value of our
> common stock. We are not in business to grow bigger for the sake of
> size, not to become more diversified, not to make the most or best of
> anything, nor to provide jobs, have the most modern plants, the happi-
> est customers, lead in new product development, or to achieve any
> other status which has no relation to the economic use of capital. Any
> or all of these may be, from time to time, a means to our objective, but
> means and ends must never be confused. We are in business solely to
> improve the inherent value of the common stockholders' equity in the
> company.[2]

We recognize, of course, that not everyone agrees that the governing objective of a company should be to maximize wealth or shareholder value. For example, here is one unequivocal opinion to the contrary:

> Many managers in the United States still operate under the twin fic-
> tions that their most important stakeholders are shareholders, and that
> their primary purpose in management is to enhance shareholder value.
> Whether this is true from a legal perspective in the case of publicly
> traded firms is worthy of debate; but from a strategic and operational
> perspective, it is dead wrong for any firm—publicly traded or privately

held. A business does not exist for the benefit of investors, nor should it be run under that premise.[3]

This and other challenges to managing for shareholder value are not uncommon, and we will respond to them later in this chapter. But first we need to clarify the governing objective and what it means for managers of public companies.

Elaborating the Governing Objective

The phrase "maximizing shareholder value" is often interpreted to mean something different from what we intend here, carrying at times even a negative connotation. By maximizing shareholder value, we do not mean that managers should make uneconomic decisions to try to hype a company's stock price. The capital markets are much too astute to be fooled by any such maneuver, at least for long. Nor do we mean that managers should invest their time or energy in any sort of corporate image campaign designed to woo securities analysts to make "buy" recommendations or institutional investors to make "buy" decisions. The company's fundamental economic performance will speak for itself, and no amount of Madison Avenue spin control will have any but the most fleeting effect on a company's stock price. And finally, we do not mean to suggest in any way that corporations should become rapacious exploiters of their employees, customers, communities, or the environment.

In essence, the objective of "maximizing shareholder value" can only be achieved through a process of creating options and making choices. Every manager in every company is called upon to make thousands of decisions a year. All the most important decisions will involve making trade-offs, such as increasing R&D investments at the expense of current earnings, or increasing prices at the expense of volume growth, or investing to increase production efficiency at the expense of employment. On what basis are these decisions to be made, especially in huge decentralized organizations with operations spreading throughout the world?

Unlike very small companies, the modern corporation has no group of wise men and women at the top who can possibly oversee every decision and ensure that it complies with the company's objectives.

Large, complex companies need a set of principles that are understood by all managers and can be used to inform their judgments about which decisions or choices to make. To be consistent and effective, these principles must be linked clearly to a single overriding decision criterion, or governing objective. We will argue that maximizing shareholder value is superior to any other governing objective a company might adopt because it will lead managers to make the decisions most likely to increase the company's competitive, organizational, and financial strength over time.

To make this point more concrete, it is useful to consider the following situation. The general manager of a highly profitable business unit within a large global company has identified three alternative strategies the business could pursue: the "Deluxe" strategy, which would focus on offering a highly differentiated product to select high-end customers at a premium price; the "No Frills" strategy, which would focus on offering a good-quality but low-cost product at a low price to the mass market; and the "Everyman" strategy, which would serve all segments of the market by offering different features for the same basic product at attractive prices. Which strategy should the business pursue?

To answer this question, let us assume further that management has conducted a detailed analysis of each strategy, incorporating all the expected future benefits and costs to the business that would result from adopting any one of them. On the basis of this analysis, management has also estimated what the business would be worth if it were to implement any one of the alternatives successfully. The results of this analysis are shown in Exhibit 1.1.

With this information we can now rephrase the question to illustrate how the governing objective should be applied in this situation: Assuming that the business unit management team is capable of implementing each of these alternatives, are there any circumstances in which the general manager should choose either the Deluxe or the Everyman strategy?

We believe the answer is "No." The company's governing objective requires that choices of this type will be decided on the basis of maximizing value, which means in this case that management must choose to pursue the No Frills strategy. Note that this is true even when all

EXHIBIT 1.1

Applying the Governing Objective

Alternative Business Unit Strategies		Expected Wealth or Value Creation[1]
No Frills	⟶	$125 million
Deluxe	⟶	$100 million
Everyman	⟶	$ 85 million

[1]*Value in excess of investment needed to achieve strategy.*

three strategies in fact create value, because managing every business to create value is the *minimum objective,* not the governing objective, of a well-run company.

Experience tells us, however, that there are many instances where the No Frills strategy might not even have been identified, let alone selected, as the best strategy for this business. This is the central problem faced by all companies seeking to maximize wealth creation and, therefore, shareholder value: How can management ensure that each business in the portfolio will be able to identify, develop, and implement strategies to maximize the value of the resources with which it is entrusted?

We will deal with this question throughout the book. But we can begin to answer it by noting that managers must first overcome any hesitation they may feel about adopting wealth or value maximization as the governing objective of the company and every business, or business unit, within it. There are enormous internal and external pressures on management not to adopt such an objective, and many reasons are offered for not doing so. We address now the most commonly heard and accepted of these reasons and lay the groundwork for understanding why objectives other than wealth or value maximization will prove inferior in both the short run and the long run.

Addressing Challenges to the Governing Objective

The challenges to adopting value maximization as the company's governing objective generally fall into three camps. The first camp might be called the "capital market skeptics." This group, which includes many chief executives, generally accepts that increasing what they consider the intrinsic or warranted value of the company is an important objective. However, they argue, stock prices are such a poor measure of this warranted value that maximizing share price or shareholder value should not be the company's primary criterion for making important strategic and organizational decisions. The second camp takes the view that product market rather than capital market objectives should dominate decision making. This group of "strategic visionaries," which includes many academics as well as chief executives, argues that companies should focus on building market dominance or some specific competitive advantage in the product markets that will, by implication, also generate adequate financial performance. The third group argues that other stakeholders, such as employees and the community, have an equal or superior claim on the company's resources, and fairness mandates that management should make decisions to "balance" these competing interests. In this chapter we respond briefly to the challenge of the capital market skeptics and more fully to the strategic visionaries and those who argue for balancing stakeholder interests.

The Capital Market Skeptics

One of the most commonly heard objections to adopting maximization of shareholder value as the governing objective is that the prices set by investors in the stock market do not, on average, reflect what the company is really worth. Many believe that the stock market is guilty of "short-termism" or some other form of investor myopia that results in a persistent failure of stock prices to reflect the long-term value of the company. This argument was heard frequently in the 1980s as a management defense against hostile takeovers. For example, in 1986, when Champion International was rumored to be a takeover candidate, the company's CEO, Andrew Sigler, complained:

> There is intense pressure [from investors] for current earnings, so the message is: Don't get caught with major [long-term] investments. And leverage the hell out of yourself. Do all the things we used to consider bad management.[4]

The validity for capital market valuations is such an important subject that we will deal with it extensively, especially in Chapters Two, Four, and Five. We note here, however, that the claim that share price is not a good measure of value rests on the twin assumptions that (1) the capital markets systematically misprice (usually translated as underprice) the company's common stock, and (2) managers make strategic investment decisions using more robust, reliable measures of wealth creation than professional investors use. The evidence shows and our experience is, however, that both of these assumptions are wrong. We will demonstrate that in countries with reasonably wel-developed capital markets, share prices provide the most accurate and least biased appraisal of a company's true value over time. Further, managers are generally not better than investors at estimating value, even though they typically have better information. In fact, it is only by understanding how investors determine values and set share prices that managers can begin to ensure that their strategic investment decisions will lead to consistent and significant wealth creation. We will return to this theme repeatedly throughout the book.

The Strategic Visionaries

Setting a strategic rather than a financial governing objective has considerable appeal for managers. Product market goals such as increasing or dominating market share (in a niche or on a global basis), maximizing customer satisfaction, or producing at the lowest cost all seem more immediate, easier to relate to, and easier to manage than maximizing shareholder value. In one important sense, we agree that good strategic management is essential to creating wealth. But the problem with product market objectives, as we see it, is that they do not have the relationship to good financial performance that their supporters seem to assume. In fact, depending on the particular circumstances of a business, investing to increase market share, to increase customer satisfaction, or to lower relative costs might well *reduce* shareholder value rather than increase it. Conversely, there are times when reducing market share, reducing customer satisfaction, or increasing relative costs will *increase* shareholder value. These conflicts, or trade-offs, between product market and capital market goals are not rare.

Indeed, they are the norm, and managers need to have a way of deciding what to do when these trade-offs, must be made.

To illustrate the problem in using a strategic or product market goal as a governing objective, it is helpful to look at maximization of customer satisfaction, which many managers and academics favor over maximization of shareholder value. One often-quoted viewpoint was expressed a number of years ago by Theodore Levitt of the Harvard Business School: "The purpose of a business is to create and keep customers."[5] A very similar theme infuses the statements of many chief executives today, including this one from Paul Allaire, CEO of Xerox, who said: "I have to change the company substantially to be more market driven. If we do what's right for the customer, our market share and our return on assets will take care of themselves."[6]

It goes without saying that no company can create wealth for its shareholders without having very satisfied and loyal customers. But this result is by no means achieved automatically. It is quite possible to achieve high levels of customer satisfaction and yet be unable to translate this seeming advantage into adequate returns for shareholders, let alone great wealth. A very good, if unfortunate, example of this situation can be found at American Airlines (AMR). American is generally recognized as the leader among major U.S. airlines in customer service, producing such innovations as the SABRE reservations system and the now-ubiquitous frequent-flyer programs. The company's management is clearly working hard to satisfy its customers and create good returns for shareholders. And yet, the economics of the industry have been—and are currently—so unfavorable that $100 invested in AMR shares in 1983 would have grown to only $325 by the end of 1992, far better than the performance of competitors whose shares grew to just $255 on average, but much worse than the $449 investors would have earned from the Standard & Poor's 500 Index.

We address here these specific questions: Under what circumstances does the objective of maximizing shareholder value conflict with the objective of maximizing customer satisfaction? And when a conflict arises, how should management resolve it?

We begin by noting that every product and service generates a value to the customer, as measured by its utility in relation to its price, and a value to the shareholders, as measured by the financial benefit in the form of dividends they will eventually receive from their investment in the customer offer. As we illustrate in Exhibit 1.2, there are strategies (characterized by arrows #1 and #4) that can cause both customer satisfaction and shareholder value to increase or decrease simultaneously. In these cases, clearly, there would be no conflict of interest between the two groups. However, there are also strategies (characterized by arrows #2 and #3) that would cause a direct conflict of interest. We will consider all these cases to propose how conflicts between customer and shareholder interests should be resolved.

When management pursues strategies that increase both customer satisfaction and shareholder value, as characterized by arrow #1, customer and shareholder interests are favorably aligned. This occurs when a strategy succeeds in enhancing customers' satisfaction to such an extent that the increase in price they are willing to pay more than offsets the increase in resources invested, producing both happier customers and an attractive return on the required investment, thereby creating value for the shareholders. A recent example of this win-win strategy was Microsoft's introduction of Windows, a new software product, which was designed to offer the same type of user-friendly features pioneered by Apple's Macintosh. Since its introduction in 1990, Windows has received rave reviews from customers, quickly

EXHIBIT 1.2

Customer Satisfaction and Shareholder Value

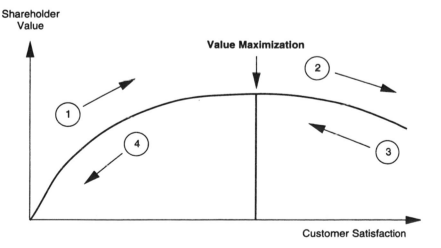

grabbing 20 percent of the market. It has helped propel Microsoft's market capitalization up by more than $10 billion, more than doubling its value for shareholders.

Strategies characterized by arrow #2 present a conflict. Here, management's investment has produced increased customer satisfaction, but the economic cost has exceeded the returns on the investment, producing a negative impact on value for the shareholders. An example of this strategy is General Motors' introduction of the Saturn car, which has consistently ranked high in customer satisfaction surveys and been so popular that the company has been unable to keep up with demand. The shareholders, however, have not done so well. Through 1992 GM invested nearly $6 billion to develop and manufacture the Saturn, an amount so large that the company would have to operate existing facilities at full capacity forever and earn more than double standard profit margins, keeping 40 percent of the dealer's sticker price as net cash flow, simply to earn an adequate return for its shareholders.

Within large companies, we generally find that a significant percentage of the products and services has overshot the peak of the curve, providing far more than the customer is willing to pay for. Can these strategies be justified on grounds that any resulting increase in customer satisfaction will be worth it in the long run? Basically, the answer has to be "No." Whenever shareholders subsidize customers in a significant way, the financial health of the company is diminished, ultimately to the detriment of all stakeholders. Not only is the company's cash flow lower than it would be otherwise, but its long-term competitiveness is also eroded by the increase in its cost structure and investment base. Over time, any company that pursues this type of uneconomic investment will undoubtedly face competitors that position themselves closer to the peak in Exhibit 1.2, offering somewhat less customer satisfaction at a far lower cost. These competitors will then find themselves with a cost advantage that may well be exploited either by lowering prices in a bid for market share or by investing in a type of satisfaction that is appropriately valued by the customer.

We believe the best strategy for any business that has overshot the peak is one that moves the business back up the curve, as illustrated by arrow #3. In many cases, this can best be accomplished by identifying and reducing those costs that contribute little or nothing to customer satisfaction. This was the course chosen by Compaq Computer in late

1991, when the board forced out the founding chief executive and abandoned its "follow and upgrade IBM" strategy. Through a combination of reengineering and outsourcing, management cut costs by more than 30 percent and introduced more than 70 new models at far lower price points. This change in strategy enabled the company to recapture more than the share it had lost previously and produced a 140 percent return to shareholders during a period when the market return was 25 percent.

Once near the peak, it is always possible to move to the left, as depicted by arrow #4. In these cases, both customer satisfaction and shareholder value are declining, sending the strongest possible signal that the company's strategy needs a major overhaul. Perhaps the most celebrated example of this is the decision by the management of The Coca-Cola Company to introduce New Coke in 1985. Customers immediately let it be known that they much preferred the "old" Coke and stayed away from the new product in droves. However, having made the mistake, management reacted very swiftly. Without hesitation, the old product was reintroduced as Coca-Cola Classic, while New Coke, renamed Coke II in 1992, gradually faded to a niche brand, leaving both customers and shareholders much relieved.

To summarize, as long as management invests in higher levels of customer satisfaction that will enable shareholders to earn an adequate return on their investment, there is no conflict between maximizing shareholder value and maximizing customer satisfaction. If, however, there is insufficient financial benefit to shareholders from attempts to increase customer satisfaction, the conflict should be resolved for the benefit of shareholders to avoid diminishing both the financial health and long-term competitiveness of the business.

This proposition for resolving trade-offs between maximizing customer satisfaction and shareholder value is pertinent for other trade-offs between product market, or strategic, objectives and value creation. When a strategy for increasing market share will increase shareholder value, it should be pursued, but if the opposite is the case and a strategy for reducing market share will create more value, this is the right decision for management to make. The same can be said of relative cost position or any other product market objective. Thus, these product market objectives should not be given the status of a company's governing objective, because to do so would as likely reduce shareholder value as increase it. Management cannot be indifferent to these outcomes.

The Balancers

The third common challenge to the objective of maximizing shareholder value is the claim that the interests of various stakeholders in the company somehow need to be "balanced." Until its acquisition by AT&T in 1991, NCR Corporation was one of the strongest advocates in this camp. In its last annual report, as an independent company, NCR described itself as follows:

> NCR is a successful, growing company dedicated to achieving superior results by assuring that its actions are aligned with stakeholder expectations. Stakeholders are all constituencies with a stake in the fortunes of the company. NCR's primary mission is to create value for our stakeholders.[7]

A recent survey of directors suggests that NCR was not alone in its views. The survey results led the authors to conclude that "boards of directors no longer believe that the shareholder is the only constituent to whom they are responsible." They state further that "this study reveals that these perceived stakeholders are, in the order of their importance, customers and government, stockholders, employees, and society."[8]

Balancing the interests of stakeholders is not a capital market or a product market objective, it is a social or political objective based on the presumption that there are fundamental conflicts between the interests of shareholders and other stakeholders. When these conflicts arise, fairness demands that management arbitrate between presumed adversaries without showing undue favoritism to shareholders. We believe this line of reasoning suffers from two problems. First, we do not see the relationships between shareholders and other stakeholders as essentially adversarial. Wealth creation is not a zero-sum game where an increment to shareholder value must somehow diminish the welfare of other stakeholders. Indeed, the reverse is true—increments to total welfare can come only from creating wealth. Second, balancing stakeholder interests is an impractical governing objective—it leads the company nowhere. We look briefly at each of these balancing problems.

First, to the extent that customers are sometimes referred to as stakeholders in the company, we have already shown that customer and shareholder interests are not inherently conflicting, although (subject always to protecting customer safety) when conflicts arise, the company must find a way to compete without consuming shareholder value. What about conflicts between employees, suppliers, the community, and shareholders?

In general, employees and shareholders share many similar interests in having a vital, profitable, and growing enterprise. Further, creating value for shareholders demands enlightened human resource management, since the company's work force is a potential source of significant competitive advantage that can be translated directly into superior value creation. Companies that attempt to pay their employees below-market wages, or churn the work force, or treat their employees in a manner that does not fully utilize their skills and talents are unlikely to create the maximum possible value for shareholders. On the contrary, we find that those companies with the best track records of value creation are also among the very best at human resource management. Not only do they recognize the crucial role their work force plays in creating and sustaining competitive advantage, which translates into value creation, but they can more easily afford to invest in education and training and share some of the benefits of their success with their employees. Further, in the event of a recession or other temporary downturn in business activity, these companies are better able to avoid layoffs and more likely to continue investing in their employees as resources to be retained and developed.

When a downturn in business is not temporary but structural, however, all companies face a shareholder-employee conflict. From the shareholders' perspective, the highest-value strategy will involve a permanent reduction in work force, probably accompanied by shutdowns of various facilities. From the employees' perspective, those who are likely to be let go would very understandably prefer that their colleagues and the shareholders accept lower incomes to keep them on the job. Those unlikely to be let go would, of course, feel sympathy for their colleagues but would also want the company to downsize and return to financial health as soon as possible, since this would enhance their own job security. Should management rank the objectives of those employees likely to be let go above those of the remaining workers and the shareholders? Again, as in the case of unprofitable investment in customer satisfaction, the answer is "No." Over time, the company that continuously transfers shareholder value to its employees in order to avoid difficult restructuring decisions will become less and less competitive as its wage costs per unit produced climb above those of competing firms. Rivals with substantially lower wage costs will either lower prices or use their cost advantage to increase investment in customer satisfaction in a bid for market share. Inevitably, the high-wage company will be forced to match the competition or face a steady decline in its fortunes. When this occurs, management usually faces a situation that forces it to restructure to survive, often involving a far greater reduction in work force than would have been required if top executives had acted sooner. In fact, those companies that manage for shareholder value tend to manage their employment levels so well that large-scale restructurings are very rare. Our conclusion: Pursuing the objective of maximizing value for shareholders also maximizes the economic interests of all employees over time, even when, regrettably, management is forced to downsize the company.

With respect to suppliers, we know of no one who seriously advocates that the governing objective of the corporation should be to maximize the economic interests of the company's vendors. Creating shareholder value requires treating suppliers fairly, meaning that as a customer, the business strives to pay "market" prices for its supplies, pay its bills on time, and generally treat its suppliers well. Switching suppliers frequently in an attempt to pay prices that are below market levels or delaying payment as much as possible will typically lead to supply disruptions or quality problems, which will damage the value of the business over time. Indeed, an important trend is for companies to view their suppliers as "business partners," working closely with them to improve quality and minimize cost. Such relationships are likely to help both the company and its suppliers create the maximum value for their shareholders.

As for reconciling the economic interests of the various communities in which it operates with those of shareholders, the objective of value creation does not preclude the company from making investments that enhance the environment for its employees and their communities. In fact, one could easily argue that these investments actually offer the prospect of creating value for shareholders since they reflect well on the company, enhance its image, improve the quality of life for employees, and make recruitment of talented people easier than it would be otherwise. Again, those companies that consistently create value for shareholders tend to be major contributors to improving the welfare of their local communities.

The second problem with the balancing argument is that it is an impractical governing objective. It offers decision makers no guidance to what the right "balance" is or how to achieve it. Faced with complex problems involving many trade-offs, managers can derive no guiding insight into how to resolve them. Thus every decision maker is left to rely entirely on his or her own personal instincts and judgment. In large organizations with thousands of decision makers, this would lead to complete chaos.

Concluding Remarks

Maximizing shareholder value is not an abstract, shortsighted, impractical, or even, some might think, sinister objective. On the contrary, it is a concrete, future-oriented, pragmatic, and worthy objective, the pursuit of which motivates and enables managers to make substantially better strategic and organizational decisions than they would in pursuit of any other goal. And its accomplishment is essential to the welfare of all the company's stakeholders, for it is only when wealth is created that customers will continue to enjoy a flow of new, better, and cheaper products and the world's economies will see new jobs created and old ones improved.

Maximizing shareholder value is also the most demanding objective management can set for itself. It requires great imagination and skill, as well as focus and determination, to create substantial new wealth consistently and over long periods of time. This is why it is the single achievement that most clearly distinguishes the great companies from the formerly great and the mediocre ones. In Chapter Two we look at some of these great (and a few of the mediocre) companies and explore the potential for value creation as well as the path for achieving the governing objective.

CHAPTER 2

The Potential
for Value Creation

For most large companies, maximizing shareholder value requires fundamental strategic and organizational change in every business unit and at the corporate center. Given the magnitude of the change required for a company to create value on a consistent and sustained basis, as well as the considerable organizational stress that these changes can cause, it is fair for managers to ask: "Is all this change likely to be worth it?"

In our view, the answer must be "Yes." The potential for value creation is so enormous that a considerable amount of organizational strain should be tolerated if necessary. In fact, a lesson repeated over and over again in our experience is that the potential for value creation almost always exceeds management's expectations—and usually by several orders of magnitude. In our work with over 100 large, publicly traded corporations in North America, Europe, and Australia, we find that most companies have the potential to increase their market value by 50 to 100 percent (over and above market expectations) within two to five years by undertaking a serious value creation program. Furthermore, while rates of increased value may slow somewhat with time (because some of the early gains may come from one-time changes), superior shareholder returns can often be sustained over many years.

This immense potential for improved performance is not limited to any single industry or type of company. We have observed the same untapped potential for value creation in industries as diverse as consumer products, retailing, integrated chemicals, financial services, and microelectronics. With individual companies, to the extent that we see any pattern at all, it is that the biggest improvements in shareholder returns are often achieved by firms that seem to have the fewest problems to begin with.

In this chapter, we present some of the evidence that points to the enormous size of the opportunity for value creation among large companies. In addition, we describe how a number of company leaders have created enormous wealth for shareholders over the years by formally and systematically managing for value creation.

The Size of the Opportunity

In order to describe the size of the opportunity, one must first determine how best to measure management's performance in terms of value creation. While no single measure is entirely free of problems, in our view the best external measure of company and management performance is *relative shareholder returns over time.* This is the total return (in the form of both dividends and share price appreciation) earned by the company's shareholders in relation to the shareholder returns generated by similar companies over any given time period. For example, if we look at Wal-Mart's performance for shareholders from 1982 to 1992, we see that the company's fortunate owners realized an average annual return of 36 percent.[1] As shown in Exhibit 2.1, this compares very favorably to the average shareholder returns earned by its peer group of other large U.S. retailing companies (23 percent) over this same period and by the overall market as measured by the S&P 500 (16 percent).

In monetary terms, this means that $100 invested in Wal-Mart at the end of 1982 would have had a value of $2,149 by the end of 1992. By comparison, that same $100 invested in a portfolio of other large U.S. retailers would have appreciated in value to only $773 by comparison (and $100 invested in the S&P 500 would have appreciated to an even lower $449). When these differences in shareholder returns are translated into market value differences, the results are staggering. As shown in Exhibit 2.1, Wal-Mart generated "excess" value for share-

EXHIBIT 2.1

Measuring Wal-Mart's Performance

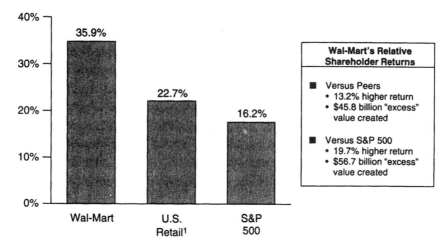

Annual Total Shareholder Returns (1982-1992)

[Bar chart:
- Wal-Mart: 35.9%
- U.S. Retail[1]: 22.7%
- S&P 500: 16.2%

Box labeled "Wal-Mart's Relative Shareholder Returns":
- Versus Peers
  - 13.2% higher return
  - $45.8 billion "excess" value created
- Versus S&P 500
  - 19.7% higher return
  - $56.7 billion "excess" value created]

[1]Comprised of the 11 largest U.S. retailers (except Wal-Mart) based on market values.

holders of $46 billion compared with peer companies (and nearly $57 billion of "excess" shareholder value compared with the S&P 500). This is a record that very few large companies have equaled or are ever likely to equal over such an extended time period.

The Wal-Mart example illustrates why we believe that the relative shareholder return measure has several characteristics that give it an advantage over any other single measure of a company's wealth creation performance. It is a direct market measure of a company's performance for shareholders, essentially unaffected by the company's accounting practices. It is indexed to eliminate the effects of overall market price movements and, to the extent possible, of industry-specific price movements. Thus, management need not worry about whether investors have made the right estimate of a company's absolute value (although we believe they do a pretty good job of this over time), but whether investors can evaluate changes in relative value of similar companies over time. In short, it is an unbiased estimator of how effectively the management of one company, in this case Wal-Mart, has developed and implemented strategies that have beaten the competition in *both* the product markets *and* the capital markets over the years.

Wal-Mart offers one example of the potential for value creation, but there are many more. Across a large universe of companies, there is wide variation in performance of shareholder returns. For instance, in Exhibit 2.2, we have plotted the distribution of annualized shareholder returns across all companies in the S&P 500 for the period 1982 to 1992. Wal-Mart's annual shareholder returns of 36 percent place them in the top 1 percent of all S&P 500 companies. At the very top end of the distribution was Circuit City Stores, a fast-growing speciality retailer of consumer electronics with an incredible 51 percent annual shareholder return over the ten-year period. At this rate of return, a $100 investment in Circuit City in 1982 was worth over $6,000 ten years later!

The wide variation in performance among companies highlights the

EXHIBIT 2.2

Total Shareholder Returns (S&P 500)

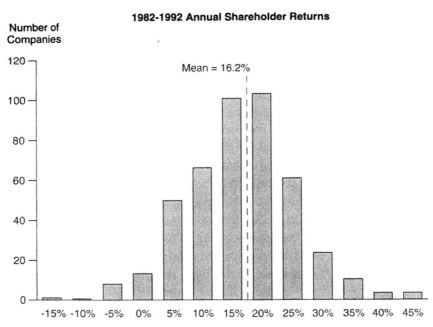

tremendous opportunity that exists for the vast majority of companies. Even in the middle of the distribution, the differences in performance are quite large. For example, the average difference in shareholder returns for companies in the second quartile versus companies in the third quartile is over 5 percent per year. For a company that has a $4 billion market value today, this difference between second-quartile and third-quartile performance would translate into a $3 billion difference in shareholder value created over the next ten years.

Perhaps even more interesting is the same type of information viewed on an industry-by-industry basis, as is illustrated in Exhibit 2.3. From an investor's perspective, companies such as Ford and General Motors, which compete in the same industry, have had significantly different performance over the 1982–1992 period. Had General Motors been able to perform at Ford's level of shareholder returns over the ten-year period, the company would have generated an additional $118 billion of shareholder value. Similarly, in each of the other industries, the top-tier performer significantly outperformed the bottom-tier performer, generating annual shareholder returns that were 16.5 percent higher on average.[2] Thus, even for companies in the same industry with similar value creation opportunities, we observe large variations in realized returns.

While these differences in shareholder returns are clearly quite large, it is difficult for data such as this to convince managers that the potential for improving performance at their own companies is of a similar magnitude. To be convinced, management must believe there is a link between company actions and shareholder returns, and that this linkage can be understood and used to make strategic and tactical decisions. Put differently, management must believe that the differences in shareholder returns among the peer companies shown in Exhibit 2.3 are not due entirely to company luck or random market movements.

There is a growing body of evidence that value creation, particularly in large public companies, is not a random or fortuitous occurrence and it can, in fact, be managed. The evidence comes from companies that have succeeded in linking their actions to the explicit objective of creating shareholder value. We describe here a number of these companies and illustrate the tremendous potential to create value that can be realized by skilled and determined managers.

EXHIBIT 2.3

Shareholder Return Performance Within Selected Industries

Industry	Representative Top-Tier (Quartile) Performers		Representative Bottom-Tier (Quartile) Performers	
	Company	1982-1992 Annual Shareholder Returns	Company	1982-1992 Annual Shareholder Returns
Aerospace	Boeing	17.8%	McDonnell Douglas	4.8%
Air Transport	Southwest Airlines	15.9	Delta Air Lines	3.5
Automobile	Ford Motor	23.2	General Motors	6.5
Banking	Banc One	21.5	Citicorp	7.0
Chemicals	Great Lakes Chem.	33.8	Olin	11.5
Computer	Hewlett-Packard	7.5	IBM	-2.5
Conglomerates	Berkshire Hathaway	31.2	ITT	12.4
Diversified Tech.	General Electric	17.3	United Technologies	9.2
Entertainment	Walt Disney	28.1	Time Warner	9.8
Food & Beverage	Coca-Cola	29.2	Borden	17.6
Grocery Store	Albertson's	26.3	Kroger	11.8
Insurance	GEICO	23.9	Travelers	7.9
Mass Retailing	Wal-Mart Stores	35.9	Kmart	17.2
Medical Products	Abbott Laboratories	22.8	Baxter International	5.2
Metals	Phelps Dodge	17.2	AMAX	-1.0
Natural Gas	Enron	19.4	Arkla	-2.0
Newspaper	Washington Post	16.7	Times Mirror	10.3
Office Equipment	Pitney Bowes	24.5	Xerox	14.0
Paper Products	Consolidated Paper	21.4	Champion International	4.1
Petroleum	Atlantic Richfield	16.7	Occidental Petroleum	7.1
Semiconductor	Intel	21.0	National Semiconductor	3.8
Shoe	Nike	24.4	Genesco	7.3
Specialty Retailing	Circuit City Stores	50.5	Tandy	-4.2
Steel	Nucor	23.4	Bethlehem Steel	-0.5
Telecommunications[1]	Southwestern Bell	22.0	NYNEX	18.6
Tire	Cooper Tire & Rubber	32.9	Goodyear Tire & Rubber	11.2
Tobacco	UST	32.1	American Brands	19.1
Toiletries	Gillette	29.7	Avon Products	14.6
	Average of Top Tier	**24.5%**	**Average of Bottom Tier**	**8.0%**

Excess value created by top-tier performers = $386 billion

[1] *Annual shareholder returns computed assuming reinvestment of all dividends. Returns for Southwestern Bell and NYNEX computed from AT&T breakup in January 1984.*

Realizing the Potential—
Evidence from Management Buyouts

Some of the best evidence of the potential for value creation can be found in the performance of once-public companies that were purchased by their own managements with the financial backing of private investors. Management buyouts are a textbook example of how a change in both strategy and organization can cause dramatic improvements in financial performance. Whenever a management team takes its company private, it acknowledges implicitly that a disparity exists between the company's near-term potential value and its current market value.

Duracell is a classic example of a successful management buyout. Until 1988, the batterymaker was part of Kraft's burgeoning consumer foods portfolio. While the market for dry-cell batteries had been expanding for most of the decade, management felt that rigid spending limits, tedious budgeting procedures and time-consuming capital approval processes—all of which may or may not have made sense for Miracle Whip® Salad Dressing or Cracker Barrel® Cheddar—unnecessarily constrained Duracell's growth and profitability. Fortunately, after Kraft sold the business for $1.8 billion to Duracell's management combined with the leveraged-buyout firm of Kohlberg Kravis Roberts & Co., decision making became simpler and less bureaucratic. Robert Kidder, Duracell's chief executive, maintains that investments that previously had required months for approval took only days after management bought the company. Kidder explains, "People could finally stop second-guessing Kraft management and worrying about 'What would the cheese people think?' "[3]

By focusing management more intensely on the battery business and aligning its incentives more closely with those of shareholders, the management buyout led to improvement of Duracell's market position and long-term profitability. In June 1991, exactly two years after management's buyout of the company and a month after Duracell had issued 34.5 million shares to the public, its market value had climbed to nearly $3 billion—or more than a 55 percent increase in value.

Duracell is not atypical. In fact, hundreds of management buyouts similar to the Duracell transaction have taken place in recent years. One Federal Government report estimates that from 1985 to 1987, management buyouts and third-party leveraged buyouts accounted for approximately 20 percent of all takeover activity in the United States.[4] Of particular interest to scholars were the 76 large management buyouts of publicly held companies that were subsequently taken public again. Since the market values of these companies can be observed before and after the transactions, it is possible to determine empirically whether value was created or destroyed as a result of changes in strategy and incentives. One study found that in the three years after the buyout these companies on average experienced significant increases in operating income decreases in capital expenditures, and improvements in cash flow. Not surprisingly, when these companies were later taken public, their shareholders did extremely well. In fact, the market value of these firms' common stock increased, by 96 percent, on average, from the two months before the buyout announcement to the post-buyout sale (adjusted for market returns). In other words, the managements of these companies nearly doubled their firms' market values—over and above what they would have been had they performed at parity with the market—by pursuing different business strategies and aligning the behavior of managers with the interests of the shareowners.[5] While these results may not tell the whole story (most have remained private and some have failed), the dramatic improvement in financial performance of these 76 companies stands as strong testimony to enormous benefits that can be realized if management begins to focus its energies on creating the maximum possible value for shareholders.

Realizing the Potential—Evidence from Exemplars

The performance of management buyouts is just one piece of evidence that points to the enormous potential for value creation. Our contention is further supported by the performance of a growing group of large public companies whose top management has a deep-seated commitment to shareholder value creation. Among those in the pantheon of companies that have clearly put wealth creation first and shown that basic management principles can be applied to achieve superior returns for their owners are the following: Berkshire Hathaway, The Coca-Cola Company, PepsiCo, Emerson Electric, The Walt Disney Company, and Lloyds Bank Plc. From the time their managements formally instituted the goals, measures, strategies, and processes consistent with maximizing shareholder value, the performance of these exemplars has been extraordinary by any measure.

Berkshire Hathaway

Arguably America's most "value based" chief executive (and also one of the wittiest), Warren Buffett has a track record that is unequaled in terms of earning consistently superior shareholder returns over an extended period of time. Since acquiring a small textile concern called Berkshire Hathaway for $22 million in 1964, he and his fellow shareholders have enjoyed an average annual return of almost 24 percent. This compares with an average annual return of little more than 10 percent for the S&P 500 over this same time period. To put this in perspective, an investment of $100 in Buffett's original acquisition would have appreciated to more than $40,000 by the end of 1992. What is remarkable about this performance is not only its scale but its duration. We are not aware of any other public company that has been able to perform at such high levels for nearly thirty years.

What explains Berkshire Hathaway's remarkable performance? In our view, the company's results are inextricably linked to Buffett's own management philosophy—a coherent set of "owner-related business principles" that focus exclusively on producing superlative results for shareholders.[6] These principles state explicitly how Berkshire management will evaluate business opportunities, make decisions concerning the firm's financial policy, and even how much information it will disclose to investors. Among the most central of Berkshire's owner-related principles is the company's governing objective. Buffett maintains:

> Our long-term economic goal . . . is to maximize the average annual rate of gain in intrinsic business value on a per-share basis. We do not measure the economic significance or performance of Berkshire by its size; we measure by per-share progress. We are certain that the rate of per-share progress will diminish in the future—a greatly enlarged capital basis will see to that. But we will be disappointed if our rate does not exceed that of the average large American corporation.[7]

Buffett has achieved the objective partly through excellence in investing and partly through excellence in managing. His investment choices have produced stunning results, including several of the companies listed as top-tier performers in Exhibit 2.3—Coca-Cola, Geico, the Washington Post, and Gillette. His operating portfolio of companies include a group of relatively small and diverse businesses—ranging from See's Candies to the *Buffalo News*—that have also realized superlative operating results.

Along with Charles Munger, Berkshire Hathaway's vice chairman,

Buffett chooses operating managers who possess unusual talent, energy, and character. Buffett then holds these managers accountable for producing exceptional financial results. As Buffett himself notes:

> . . . we had very high expectations when we joined with these managers. In every case, however, our experience has greatly exceeded those expectations. We have received far more than we deserve, but we are willing to accept such inequities. (We subscribe to the view Jack Benny expressed upon receiving an acting award: "I don't deserve this, but then, I have arthritis and I don't deserve that either.")[8]

These businesspeople are extremely well paid for producing their extraordinary results. Moreover, every one of them holds a sizable percentage of his or her net worth in Berkshire Hathaway common stock. While all this may seem simple enough, it obviously can't be that easy. Otherwise, many more companies would show similar performance.

Despite the common sense behind many of Berkshire's principles, Buffett feels compelled to repeat them over and over, year in and year out, with the most entertaining embellishments. Contrast this with companies where "creating shareholder value" is but one of several stated corporate objectives (usually qualified by the words "long term" to ensure that shareholders don't get too excited just yet), and where the day-to-day decisions that really determine the company's performance are made without any reference to value creation at all. Warren Buffett knows that continued commitment to value creation by the organization requires continued leadership on the part of the chief executive because the task is so difficult.

As impressive as the performance of Berkshire Hathaway has been, professional managers might argue that it is unrepresentative. After all, Warren Buffett owns over 40 percent of Berkshire's stock. Therefore, some may assert, he can afford to ignore Wall Street and "take a long-term view" or pursue other worthy objectives that, while obviously producing great value for the shareholders of Berkshire Hathaway, are somehow inappropriate for or denied to salaried managers—particularly managers of business units within large bureaucratic companies—who do not share in the ownership of the enterprise. While it is certainly true that ownership is a powerful motivator for concentrating one's energies on wealth-creating activities, we strongly believe that all managers should strive for this level of performance. Indeed, other companies have been successful in doing just that.

The Coca-Cola Company

One of the most stunning value creation success stories is that of The Coca-Cola Company. In 1990, a *Fortune* article reported:

> . . . the most noteworthy change under chairman Roberto C. Goizueta has been a shift in focus from boosting sales to maximizing shareholder returns . . . Goizueta says that he wrestles over how to improve value ". . . from the time I get up in the morning to the time I go to bed. I even think about it when I'm shaving."[9]

Under the leadership of Goizueta and Donald Keough, the company focused its energies on creating shareholder value through three broad initiatives. First, Coke has boosted its market share and gallon sales. This has been accomplished primarily through introductions of new products, such as Diet Coke®, and aggressive expansion in overseas markets, especially in Asia and Eastern Europe. Second, the company has focused its investment on the high-margin, high-return soft-drink business. Starting in the mid-1980s, Coke management divested most of the company's nonbeverage assets and has subsequently resisted diversifying into unrelated markets. Third, Goizueta's team has managed Coke's existing asset base to maximize productivity and efficiency.

The company's success in achieving these three goals has created enormous value for Coca-Cola's stockholders. In 1981, when Goizueta and Keogh became chief executive and chief operating officer, respectively, of the company, Coke's market value stood at $4.3 billion. By the end of 1992, The Coca-Cola Company had a total market capitalization of more than $59.3 billion—nearly a 13-fold increase in market value in just ten years.[10] What the Coca-Cola experience demonstrates so powerfully is that the potential for value creation is often enormous even for companies that are performing quite well to begin with.

PepsiCo

A longtime rival of The Coca-Cola Company, PepsiCo has achieved similarly superior performance for shareholders over the past decade, generating total shareholder returns of 29 percent per year from 1982 to 1992. The superior performance of both Coca-Cola and PepsiCo underscores the important point that value creation is not a zero-sum game. Even direct competitors that adopt similar management philosophies can, through different but almost equally effective strategies, each produce enormous wealth for their owners.

One of Wayne Calloway's, chairman and chief executive, fundamental management beliefs is, "If it ain't broke, fix it anyway." PepsiCo businesses are constantly challenged to identify alternative strategies to create more value. One example of a value-creating alternative strategy emerged in the late 1980s when Taco Bell, a subsidiary of PepsiCo, introduced the concept of "value pricing" (in this case, customer perception of the value of its food service offering, not shareholder value). The managers at Taco Bell became convinced that they had a significant competitive advantage over direct rivals due to the size of their stores and the way they had outsourced many of the traditional instore activities. They also believed that a significant reduction in menu prices would bring a large increase in their volume that competitors would find difficult to match and hold over time. Their analysis indicated that even though the move to lower prices would reduce margins and return on investment in the near term, it would enhance long-term growth and cash flow so that the value of Taco Bell would be substantially enhanced. In late 1988, Taco Bell introduced its new, value-priced menu to an enthusiastic response from customers. While margins were indeed squeezed somewhat in the first year, sales took off, rising 27 percent in 1989, thus validating management's assumption that the trade-off between near-term returns and future growth would be a net positive for shareholders. These accomplishments at Taco Bell are indicative of the kind of success that other PepsiCo businesses—from soft drinks to Frito-Lay—have achieved over an extended period of time.

PepsiCo's incredible returns have not gone unnoticed by its employees, as the company has been a leader in linking their rewards to shareholder value. To accomplish this, in 1989 PepsiCo implemented a program called SharePower, which awards stock options to all

300,000 full-time employees. As Wayne Calloway, chairman and chief executive of PepsiCo, states in his letter to shareholders, "Since we began SharePower, PepsiCo people have stepped forward with thousands of ideas to increase the financial performance of your company."[11]

Emerson Electric

Emerson Electric has put together a truly phenomenal record of consistent profitability and value creation for over three decades. Earnings per share and dividends per share have increased every year for the past 35 years. Over that same time, investors have been rewarded with annual shareholder returns of over 17 percent (which compares with roughly 11 percent for the S&P 500). Given the mature manufacturing markets in which Emerson competes, including a wide range of electrical, electromechanical, and electronic products, this record of superior performance underscores the point that management can achieve outstanding results even in a mature industry.

Charles Knight, chief executive of Emerson, attributes the company's success to management processes that are highly integrated, action-oriented, and focused on achieving superior economic profitability. Says Knight:

> We believe we can shape our future through careful planning and strong follow-up. Our managers plan for improved results and execute to get them. . . . We believe, for example, that profitability is a state of mind. Experience tells us that if management concentrates on the fundamentals and constantly follows up, there is no reason why we can't achieve profits year after year.[12]

More than at most companies, Emerson considers rigorous planning essential. As a sign of his commitment to planning, Knight claims to devote more than half of his time to this activity.[13] Planning is designed to be the core process for identifying and evaluating investment opportunities to create shareholder value. Says Knight: "In the process of planning, we focus on specific opportunities that will meet our criteria for growth and returns and create value for our stockholders."[14] Furthermore, the planning process is designed to produce concrete implementation plans that form a performance contract between corporate management and the business units. Because of this, Emerson's management processes are themselves a source of sustainable competitive advantage. Not only have these processes been instrumental in achieving high levels of performance in each existing business, they have also been instrumental in improving the performance of newly acquired businesses, successfully integrating more than 40 companies in the past twelve years. By using management processes to systematically improve the performance of acquired companies, Emerson has been able to consistently create shareholder value through acquisitions, a capability and record that very few other companies can claim.

Walt Disney Company

In 1984, with Disney's share price declining and its return on equity trapped in the single digits, the company was widely perceived as a sinking ship. A new management team—consisting of Michael Eisner, chief executive; Frank Wells, chief operating officer; and Gary Wilson, chief financial officer—was given the mandate to reverse the company's fortunes. One of the team's first steps was to orient Disney's corporate objectives toward shareholder value creation. The overriding financial objective of the company became "to maximize stockholder value" by consistently meeting two key financial objectives: (1) increase earnings per share at 20 percent annually over any five-year period; and (2) maintain high capital productivity with 20 percent return on equity through profitable reinvestment of cash flow. By imposing demanding growth and profitability objectives, Disney's new management hoped to reignite the creative spark in the company's core businesses (theme parks, filmed entertainment, and consumer products) and simultaneously build throughout the company a strong economic discipline, which Eisner calls the "financial box."[15]

Eisner, Wells, and Wilson soon discovered that Disney had been "underpricing its theme parks for years, under-exploiting its franchise consisting of the world's best-loved cartoon characters, and under-employing its film-making potential."[16] Working together, the three executives tackled all these shortcomings simultaneously. Within three years, after the price of admission tickets was increased, Disney's theme park revenues rose far faster than attendance. (The company increased prices faster than inflation until the real ticket price regained its levels of the mid-1970s.) The company's cartoon characters were sold more aggressively, both inside and outside the theme parks. Disney opened its own theme stores—designed to provide, in Eisner's words, "retail as entertainment."[17] Moreover, the scope of its mail order catalogues was dramatically increased by acquiring Childcraft from Grolier for $60 million in 1987. By 1991, the company was reporting more than $1.7 billion in revenues (over 28 percent of the company's total sales) from businesses that did not exist in 1984.[18]

Disney's filmmaking operations were also transformed during the early years of Eisner and Wells's tenure. Under the Touchstone label, Disney moved into movies for adults—films like *Splash, Ruthless People* and *Three Men and a Baby*. Moreover, in an industry proud of its profligacy, Disney's stinginess is legendary. The company has kept its costs of film production about 30 percent below those of competitors by "signing up actors temporarily down on their luck or up-and-comers who will work for less" and employing strict cost controls.[19]

Not every new strategy has been so successful, as the huge problems with Euro Disney have shown. Yet, from the shareholders' perspective, the company's performance on Eisner's watch has been nothing short of spectacular. A $100 investment in the Walt Disney Company in 1984 would have been worth more than $1,000 at the beginning of 1992—an average annual total shareholder return of more than 39 percent per year. Meanwhile, a comparable investment in the S&P 500 or a portfolio of other entertainment companies would have been worth less than $300 and $500, respectively.

Lloyds Bank Plc

Lloyds Bank, one of four major "clearing" banks in the United Kingdom, has been a consistent exemplar in terms of profitability and shareholder returns. Since taking over as chief executive of Lloyds Bank in 1983, Brian Pitman has systematically managed the company to create maximum shareholder value. Says Pitman: "We're not interested in chasing growth or size for their own sake, but in creating value for shareholders."[20] Over the period from 1982 to 1992, Lloyds generated annual shareholder returns of 31 percent, which is 19 percent higher than achieved by its peer group of U.K. clearing banks.

Lloyds' success is a result of management's commitment to creating value as well as its superior understanding of what drives value creation in financial services markets. For example, management recognizes that many financial services markets are economically unattractive, and therefore Lloyds has adopted a strategy of selective participation. Says Pitman:

> Profitability depends on selective market leadership. Profitability depends on sustainable competitive advantage; rigorous analysis of attractiveness and ability to compete; focus and hard choices.[21]

To accomplish this, Lloyds has been selective in entering markets on the basis of their ability to earn attractive returns, and it has been proactive in exiting markets that are destroying value. From 1987 through 1992, Lloyds successfully invested in life assurance and private banking, while simultaneously selling overseas operations that were more valuable to other companies than to Lloyds shareholders.

Lloyds also understands the drivers of value creation in each market it chooses to serve. For instance, Lloyds has been able to consistently identify changing customer needs well ahead of its competitors. Pitman recognizes that "we can only create value for our shareholders if we create value for our customers."[22] Lloyds has expanded services like asset management, which caters to its wealthier customers, and improved traditional branch services by reducing customer response times and providing greater availability to cashiers. At the same time, Lloyds has also been able to consistently identify the changes required in its operating configuration to consistently create value. For example, Lloyds anticipated faster than competitors the effects of computer technology on the traditional branch banking system. Responding to these changes, Lloyds has systematically reorganized its branch network, consolidating processing centers and reducing staff. In making all these changes, management recognizes that as the drivers of value change, so must Lloyds. It recognizes that to sustain consistently superior returns for shareholders, Lloyds must continue to make the right changes ahead of the competition.

Concluding Remarks

Our central point in this chapter is simple: All companies have an enormous potential to create higher value for their shareholders. By adopting maximizing value creation as the governing corporate objective and understanding how to manage relentlessly to achieve this end, we believe all companies can dramatically improve their competitive and financial performance, in both the near term and long term. Managers should be careful not to underestimate the magnitude of the task—after all, continuous and sustained value creation is hard work. Nevertheless, managers must never lose sight of the prize. As the experiences of the exemplar companies suggest, the upside benefits can be extraordinary.

CHAPTER 3

Value Based Management

Unlike the exceptional companies discussed in Chapter Two, the great majority of large corporations throughout the world are not managed with the objective of maximizing wealth or shareholder value. Not surprisingly, they show no particular capacity to sustain value creation or consistently achieve superior returns for their owners over time. In fact, many large corporations are voracious wealth consumers, draining resources and talent away from the comparatively few products and market segments in their portfolios that create substantial value and directing those resources and talent instead into the relatively large number of product market segments where the company's current strategies consume value. As we will demonstrate, today few large companies succeed in investing as much as half of their human and financial resources in strategies that even create, let alone maximize, shareholder value. Why is this so?

For many reasons, managers choose to invest in strategies with inadequate financial returns, but almost always these decisions reflect a lack of understanding or appreciation of the two forces all companies must overcome to achieve the governing objective. One force is *external:* It is the force of *competition,* which works relentlessly to drive investment returns down to levels where additional growth will produce no further value for shareholders. The other force, equally powerful, is *internal:* It is the force of the corporate *institution* itself that

41

works to direct the shareholders' funds into strategies and activities without regard for their value-creating potential. The best managers recognize these forces and exhibit an unswerving determination to defeat them. However, most managers fail to understand exactly what these forces are or to appreciate their huge impact in suppressing the company's value over time. In fact, managers often abet, however unwittingly, the institutional forces against wealth creation.

Achieving the governing objective to maximize wealth requires overcoming both the external forces of competition and the internal forces of the corporate institution. Indeed, the capacity to deal effectively with these two forces can be thought of as the single most important core capability a company can have. We call this core capability "value based management." Value based management is a combination of beliefs, principles, and processes that effectively arm the company to succeed in its battle against competition from the outside and the institutional imperative from the inside. These beliefs, principles, and processes form the basis of a systematic approach to achieving the company's governing objective.

The Forces of Competition

The dynamics of competition are straightforward. Where markets are competitive, value creation attracts imitators. Inevitably there is enough imitation, in the form of increasing capacity relative to demand, to cause most of the economic benefit to shift from producers to consumers in the form of ever-higher quality and wider availability at ever-lower real prices. Personal computer hardware and consumer electronics are among the most striking examples of this phenomenon in recent years—in each case, ever-higher quality and performance are delivered by companies that, on average, earn far too little on these products to meet investors' expectations. For most players, competition has driven out the ability to create new wealth within the existing market structure.

At the macroeconomic level, the power of competition, as embodied in Joseph Schumpeter's classic concept of "creative destruction," can be seen in the dramatic restructuring of the world's largest companies over the past forty years. For instance, of the top 100 firms on *Fortune's* list of America's largest corporations (in terms of revenues) in 1956, only 29 remained in that select group in 1989. And outside the United States, of the 100 largest firms listed by *Fortune* in 1956, only 27 remained on the list in 1989.[1] As *The Economist* aptly stated: "Within the span of one working life, well over two-thirds of the world's biggest companies were jostled out of the way by faster-growing [and more profitable] firms."[2]

At the individual business unit level, all products and services must cope with the incessant onslaught of competitive forces driving rates of return down to unattractive levels. This can be seen most vividly in technology-based products with short life cycles. For example, in Exhibit 3.1, we have plotted the return on investment for a highly popular disk drive product that was introduced several years ago.

The product was the technology leader of its day, providing a 20 percent improvement in data storage capacity and a 15 percent improvement in access time. During its first year on the market, revenues were $150 million, and because customers were willing to pay a 10 percent price premium for the superior performance of this product, the company was rewarded with a 28 percent return on its investment. However the reward was short-lived. Within 12 months, several competitors matched the performance advances and entered the market in force. Prices began to drop at a compound rate of 20 percent per year. Costs were also declining but not as fast as prices, with the result that

EXHIBIT 3.1

Return on Investment for Disk Drive Product

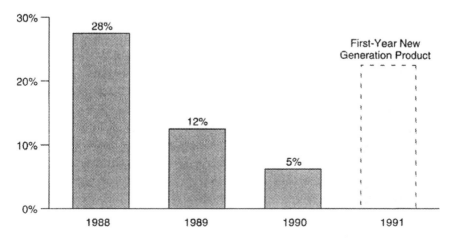

in its second year on the market this product generated peak revenues of $200 million but earned only a 12 percent return on the company's investment (about average for U.S. industrial companies overall). By the third year, two high-volume, low-cost producers captured a large share of the market, resulting in both a loss of the previous leader's share, with revenues falling to $100 million, and a still-further decline in its return on investment to a meager 5 percent—less than what could then be earned on Treasury bills. By this time, of course, a new product generation was emerging to start the process of innovation and competition for returns all over again. Thus, in less than 24 months, the forces of competition obliterated the new product's earning power. It generated a 15 percent average return for only three years and a zero return thereafter.

The forces of competition are, of course, acknowledged by all managers. In a general way, everyone appreciates that new product innovation, new capacity additions, lower-cost production processes, and challenges for market share through higher promotion or lower price can and do drive industry returns inexorably lower over time. The problem we see is that the strength of these forces, particularly the impact they can have on individual company returns, is greatly underestimated. There is considerable evidence that managers are much too complacent about how quickly, how dramatically and how permanently competition can force returns to levels that are too low to justify further investment. The great majority of strategic plans contain financial forecasts that, with their well-known "hockey stick" profiles of ever-higher market share and return on investment, implicitly assume only the most docile and congenial of competitors. These forecasts are based on denial of the forces of competition. Many managers assume that competitors will not match cost reductions, capacity additions, or product innovations; or competitors' currently "irrational" pricing behavior won't last; or business is so bad that one or more competitors will surely exit and suddenly allow the survivors to begin earning decent returns again. These and many other fantasies pervade strategic plans, especially the financial forecasts that go with them. Almost no denial argument is too silly to use in trying—usually successfully—to convince top management that the real problems the business faces are not with fundamental competitive challenges but with underinvestment "for the long term" by the corporate center.

Faced with the inevitability of the competition for wealth creation and the tremendous power of this force, managers need to raise their sights on what constitutes a good strategy. A good strategy is not one that is designed to achieve some product market objective such as greater share or a low-cost position or high customer satisfaction per se. A good strategy is one that "wins" by creating both competitive advantage in the product markets *and* increased value in the capital markets. Such strategies can be developed only if managers are highly knowledgeable and utterly realistic in their assessments of the impact of competition—direct and indirect, current and future—on the future financial performance of their businesses. Overcoming the forces of competition to create wealth will be our focus in Chapters Six through Ten.

The Institutional Imperative

The competitive forces working against wealth maintenance and creation, although easily underestimated, are fairly obvious. The institutional forces that work constantly to erode wealth are far more subtle. They might best be described by Pogo's classic comment: "We have met the enemy and he is us." These internal forces work just as relentlessly and effectively as a company's competitors to impede its value creation. They stem in part from what is sometimes called the "agency" problem: the potential conflict of interest that can arise between the company's owners and its nonowner managers and employees. They also stem, in our view, from the tendency of any large organization to move toward average performance—to drift in the direction of what seems safe and easy rather than to make hard decisions and challenge performance standards. Whatever the reason, the consequences are the same—there is extensive use of the shareholder's money to subsidize activities, practices, and business strategies that do not create new wealth.

We call this tendency to use the shareholders' money in ways that are contrary to their interests the *institutional imperative,* which is, in essence, the antithesis of the value imperative.[3] This calls attention to the reality that for many companies the governing objective is not to maximize wealth but to promote the growth, prestige, and survival of the institution or its parts, more or less regardless of the consequences to the shareholders over time. The symptoms of this corporate disease are many, including: customary reference to "the company" as something different and apart from what the shareholders own; a focus primarily on internal rather than external performance requirements; a focus on company size rather than value creation; a high tolerance for business units that consistently perform poorly; formulation of "strategic" rationales for obviously uneconomic acquisitions; buildup of excessive overhead; an organization matrix that promotes unclear or multiple responsibilities for performance; incentive programs with generous payouts regardless of performance; frequent use of terms like "synergy" and "world-class" as substitutes for competent strategic thinking; a purported need to "balance" portfolios or "smooth" earnings; and vacuous corporate mission statements. All these are symptoms of the institution attempting to put economic sheep's clothing on the political wolf of the institutional imperative.

The institutional imperative is widespread in the United States, United Kingdom and Japan, persisting even in well-managed companies. In many European companies the institutional imperative is actually revered as evidence of high-minded social behavior on the part of management—it would be politically incorrect to suggest that shareholders' claims are even equal, let alone superior, to those of other stakeholders, especially employees. But as these sorts of ideas continue to undermine competitiveness, changes are beginning to take place. German companies in particular are now starting to question whether they can continue to accommodate the institutional imperative and still compete effectively in the world economy. The answer must surely be "No," because global customers—including German consumers—have no desire or need to subsidize above-market benefits to any group of managers or employees.

The institutional imperative invades all companies at all levels. It is fiercely resistant to efforts to reduce its often-debilitating effects on a company's performance. And it is amazingly resilient. In one dramatic case, we worked with a company that was under severe competitive pressure and had to lower its costs substantially. Reluctantly, the chief executive decided it would be necessary to reduce the company's worldwide work force by 10,000 people. A generous early retirement program was implemented, and the targeted reduction was achieved. Only one year later, in a competitive environment that was even more severe, the head count was nearly back to its previous level. And a fair number of the new workers were actually former employees who had simply been hired back by a different part of the company! That was the institutional imperative at its finest.

Usually the institutional imperative is at work quietly inside the company and not particularly visible to the outside world. However, when its effects are most severe, companies can become so dysfunctional that the combination of rapidly deteriorating performance and management failure to take appropriate action becomes obvious to all. Unfortunately, the 1980s and 1990s have seen many instances of once-great organizations frozen in indecision, resisting the changes necessary to continue as the great engines of wealth creation they once were while trying to preserve an institutional memory that is no longer relevant or sustainable.

Faced with the twin forces of competition and the institutional imperative, management must be extremely disciplined and energetic to win simultaneously in the product and capital markets. The entire organization has to be geared to this task in order to succeed. Most large multibusiness corporations are unlikely to defeat the twin forces in order to achieve the governing objective unless there is a formal management approach designed for that purpose.

Value Based Management

The great majority of the exemplar companies cited in Chapter Two are managed formally to create shareholder value. For these companies, the objective of value creation is not simply a slogan appearing as the third or fourth important goal in the mission statement. It is the basis of all major decisions they make. While the degree of formality differs, each company shares a strong belief that managing for shareholder value is the right corporate objective, each has a good understanding of those aspects of its businesses that must be well managed to achieve the objective, and each has at least some processes, formal or informal, that provide effective support to management's efforts to create value. In other words, these companies and their managers are truly "value based" in their thinking and decision-making processes.

We use the term "value based management" to mean a formal, or systematic, approach to managing companies to achieve the objective of maximizing wealth creation and shareholder value over time. It is based on concepts we have developed and applied successfully during nearly 20 years of working with top management in many companies and industries all over the world. We believe it is generally applicable to any type of business, but the specifics of how an individual company adapts the general approach to its own circumstances are extremely important. Value based management offers no ideology that proclaims the one right way to run a company to create value or the best strategic theory for doing so. If we have learned anything, it is that creating value consistently over time is hard to do and does not lend itself very often to simple solutions, especially in complicated companies. Indeed, the creation of new wealth requires, by the very nature of the task and its rewards, a great deal of originality. This originality extends well beyond any new product or service concept: it is original in the very way in which managers choose to run the company.

Value based management has three main elements: *beliefs, principles, and processes.* The beliefs imbue the organization with a sense of purpose and a basis for decision making. The principles provide the knowledge and guidelines for making decisions consistent with the beliefs. And the processes provide the institutional capability to manage effectively within the framework of the beliefs and principles.

Beliefs

The basic beliefs behind value based management—managing for value is the best governing objective and companies can manage value creation in a systematic way—have been discussed in Chapters One and Two. An essential step toward making these beliefs work is for the company to specify value maximization as the objective of each business unit in its portfolio. The importance of this seemingly simple step cannot be overstated. It must be unmistakably clear to the business unit managers that their primary responsibility is to develop and implement the strategies that make the greatest possible contribution to the value of the corporation. It is not their primary responsibility to achieve any other predetermined financial or strategic goal, such as maximizing return on investment (ROI) or growth or customer satisfaction. These may or may not be important by-products of the best strategy, but they are not, and should not be treated as, adequate proxies for the governing objective itself.

Principles

In its simplest terms, managing to maximize shareholder value means generating, choosing, and implementing the best alternatives for any business strategy or organizational issue. One of its critical implications is that management must have a disciplined approach to generating alternatives and must be able to evaluate these alternatives in a rigorous way. This requires the basic principles of value based management to be integral to management's thinking at all times. These principles concern the financial, strategic, and organizational determinants of value as well as the relationships or linkages between them, as illustrated broadly in Exhibit 3.2.

Strategic effectiveness determines how well management will succeed in overcoming the external forces of competition, while organizational effectiveness determines how well management will cope with the internal or institutional forces that can limit wealth creation. Management's success at these tasks, in turn, determines the financial performance of the firm over time, which establishes the basis on which investors determine the value of the company's shares.

The principles of valuation concern the linkage between financial performance and shareholder value. Understanding of these linkages is essential for managers, enabling them to (1) become really committed to the idea that maximizing wealth and maximizing shareholder value are one and the same—i.e., accept that the governing objective is built on a solid foundation; and (2) be comfortable with utilizing capital market performance measures internally to make strategic and organizational decisions.

EXHIBIT 3.2

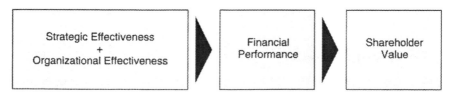

Understanding the principles of linkage between strategy and financial performance is, of course, essential to managing for value. It is not possible to do a consistently good job of developing great strategies or implementing them successfully without a well-grounded understanding of the impact they are likely to have on the company's financial performance and value.

The role of organization in value creation is no less important than the role of strategy, but because it involves human behavior, the principles we propose are derived more by induction than by deduction. Certainly these principles cannot be proved in the sense that one could "prove," for example, that a particular business unit structure would necessarily result in more creative or effective solutions to strategic issues. However, we have observed the kinds of organizational structures and capabilities that seem well suited to value creation over time, and from these observations we have developed a view of some general principles that seem to correlate with consistently superior performance for shareholders.

Processes

A belief in the governing objective and an understanding of the principles linking the company's value to its strategies and organization are necessary but not sufficient to achieve superior returns over time. The third element of value based management is management process. It can be an important factor in creating competitive advantage and wealth at many levels of the company.[4] But the specific processes we are emphasizing here are used by the company, in both the corporate center and the business units, to make key decisions on governance, strategy, resource allocation, performance targets, and top management compensation. These decisions are so important that we call the processes supporting them the company's *institutional value drivers*. The quality of their design and the skillfulness of their use will determine the company's propensity to create or consume wealth over time. We will detail these processes in Chapters Eleven through Sixteen.

Concluding Remarks

The beliefs, principles, and processes of value based management, taken together, form the basis of a company's capacity to create wealth over time. Appropriately tailored to the culture and needs of the company, value based management can become the foundation of its most important core competence—creating wealth. Value based management does not ensure that all of management's decisions will be wise or wonderful. It does, however, greatly improve the quality of decision making, by improving the quality of the alternatives that management has to consider as well as building into the organization a bias for choosing and implementing the best available alternatives. Further, it builds in a strong organizational counterpressure to decisions that would otherwise result in the perpetuation of value-consuming strategies and activities. We explore the principles, processes, and applications of value based management further throughout the balance of this book.

PART 2
Value Creation

CHAPTER 4

Linking Market and Management Values

In Chapter One, we discussed briefly the concerns of many managers that the company's share price is an unreliable, even biased, measure of warranted value, where warranted value reflects management's own valuation of the company. Unless such concerns can be alleviated, managers understandably will be reluctant to adopt the governing objective of maximizing value or have confidence that the financial consequences of their decisions will be reflected accurately in the price of the company's shares over time. The purpose of this chapter is to address these concerns and show how an understanding of valuation in the capital markets can be used to help develop an economic framework that links management decisions and actions directly to the warranted value of the company and its stock price. Specifically, we develop two related propositions:

- The capital market valuation of a company's common stock is not, as some have suggested, the product of some unfathomable mechanism manipulated at random by the forces of darkness but is generally an understandable, "rational," and unbiased measure of the company's worth, given its current strategies.
- Strategic and operating decisions can be linked directly to their likely impact on warranted value in such a way that any decision resulting in a material increase or decrease in the company's war-

55

ranted value will be translated relatively quickly and accurately into an increase or decrease in the company's market value.

On the basis of our experience in working with large, publicly traded companies around the world, we are convinced that these propositions are entirely sound. We have seen that once they are understood and accepted by managers, they form the basis for aligning the company's strategies and organizational structure with the objective of maximizing shareholder value.

The Relationship Between Cash Flow and Shareholder Value

The first, most fundamental economic relationship underlying value based management is that, in countries with well-developed capital markets, shareholder value (i.e., the market value of the company's common stock) is determined by discounting the cash flow investors expect to receive over a long-time horizon at the minimum acceptable rate of return they require for holding equity investments, also known as the cost of equity capital. If the expected cash flow to investors increases, or the cost of equity capital declines, stock prices will go up. Conversely, if expected cash flow falls or the cost of equity capital rises, stock prices will go down.

To demonstrate the validity of this important relationship, we begin by examining how investors value and set the prices of corporate bonds. We will then demonstrate that the same approach is applied to the valuation and pricing of common stocks.

Determining the Value of Corporate Bonds

For all the difficulty managers sometimes find in accepting the idea that an essentially rational mechanism guides the valuation of their company's common stock, they typically have little problem accepting that a rational pricing mechanism exists in the corporate bond market. The process of bond valuation is well understood. Three basic factors determine the value of any standard corporate bond: (1) the cash flow that investors anticipate from holding the bond, namely, its coupon and principal payments; (2) the term of the bond, i.e., the number of years to maturity; and (3) the interest rate, which investors use to convert the stream of future coupon payments into a present value by "discounting" them—each coupon payment is divided by an interest rate factor that increases geometrically over time (e.g., for a 10% interest rate, a payment received in one year is divided by 1.10, in two years by 1.10 squared, and so forth); the present value, of course, is the sum of these "deflated" payments.

As an illustration of how the U.S. capital markets value corporate bonds, consider a series issued in 1992 by Minnesota Mining and Manufacturing (3M). This series consisted of 10,000 bonds with a face value of $1,000 each, or a total of $10 million face value. They were your basic, "plain vanilla" bonds, with no unusual terms or features, offering investors coupon payments of 9 percent, paid semiannually, and maturing in the year 2007.

How should investors have valued these bonds? Well, from the information contained in the description of the bonds, investors knew that they had been promised future cash payments of $45 every six months until December 31, 2007. Consequently, investors knew the coupon payments, or future cash stream that they would receive, and the term, or principal repayment date, of the bond. To estimate the third factor, the investor's required interest rate, or rate of return, it is important to understand the risk associated with 3M's bonds. In 1992, 3M's bonds were rated AAA, signifying a very low probability of default. Moreover, in the month prior to the issue of these bonds, most AAA bonds were yielding approximately 9.5 percent, representing a premium of one percentage point over U.S. Government bonds of similar maturity. Thus, to convert the semiannual cash payments of $45 to a price that would yield the required return, investors would have to "discount" the payments at 9.5 percent. The resulting calculation suggests that, on average, investors would have been willing to pay a price of $950.92 per bond.[1]

If the capital markets operated in an efficient manner, the actual trading price of the bonds should have been very close to this "discounted cash flow" value. Indeed, when 3M's bonds were sold to the public, they began trading at an average price of $951.00. Coincidence? Certainly not. It is now generally accepted that bond prices are determined by using a discounted cash flow approach. If one compares the present value of other corporate and government bonds to the actual prices investors pay for these bonds, the relationship is nearly one to one, a correlation that testifies to the widespread application of the discounted cash flow model for pricing bonds.[2]

As a final point, bond prices are dynamic—typically fluctuating daily, if not hourly. This does not mean, however, that the bond market is shortsighted or irrational. Price fluctuation is a natural result of new information about inflation expectations or credit quality being processed as soon as it is received, causing buy or sell orders to move prices quickly to new discounted cash flow values. The bond market is dominated by a large number of well-heeled institutional investors looking for ways to create value for themselves or their clients by buying (or selling) bonds that yield a bit more (or a bit less) than the investors' required return. Since virtually every one of these institutional investors uses the same discounted cash flow approach to calculate prices, market competition always acts to drive each bond's price to within a fraction of its discounted cash flow value.

Determining the Value of Common Stocks[3]

The rational pricing mechanism so clearly evident in the valuation of bonds is essentially the same that investors use to value common stocks. In the abstract, it is easy to see why this is the case—the stocks and bonds of most large companies are traded in similar markets, by predominantly the same investors and, in many cases, are held in the same institutional portfolios. With all the apparent interrelations between stocks and bonds, it is difficult to understand why the owners of these two kinds of securities would apply a rational model to value bonds and not apply the same basic model to value common stocks. Yet many executives imply a belief in this inconsistency when they assert that the stock market is short-term-oriented, capricious, or in some other sense, irrational in its pricing behavior.

As with bonds, investors value common stocks by discounting expected future cash flow. However, despite the similarities in the approaches used to value bonds and common stocks, there are several important differences.

First, a bond's coupon represents a legal obligation to pay some specified amount of cash in the future. Common stocks carry no such promise. Thus, the expected cash flow to investors, defined as the expected "equity cash flow," must be estimated. Equity cash flow is a residual payment. In its simplest form, it is the portion of earnings paid out to investors rather than reinvested (or retained) by the company.[4] In a year when a company neither issues nor repurchases common stock, equity cash flow is simply the dividend paid to the stockholders. Most investors speak in terms of dividends, not equity cash flows. Thus, when the discounted cash flow model is applied to stocks, the investment community usually refers to it as the dividend discount model.

The forecast of equity cash flow will, of course, be influenced by investor perceptions of the general economy and how the company's strategies are likely to affect future earnings and investment streams. The brighter the prospects for the future, the higher the anticipated equity cash flow and, therefore, the higher the valuation of the company's common stock. Alternatively, the gloomier a company's prospects, the lower the anticipated equity cash flow and the lower the stock valuation.

A second key difference between the valuations of stocks and bonds involves the term over which cash payments will be made. Bonds typically have a specified term. For most U.S. corporate debt, this term is not longer than 30 years. Stocks, on the other hand, have no finite term. Instead, common stock values *must* be determined by discounting a forecast of equity cash flow over an indefinite, or infinite period, assuming that there is no reason to expect the company to terminate its operations. In practice, this means that investors must explicitly forecast equity cash flow over some forecast horizon, say, five or ten years, and then capture the remaining cash flow in the form of a post-forecast-period, or "continuing," value.[5]

Finally, the cost of equity capital is more difficult to estimate than the observable discount rate for bonds. However, the estimation process is not overly difficult. For most publicly traded companies, the cost of equity can be estimated quite easily within acceptable levels of accuracy. As a benchmark, between 1980 and 1992, the cost of equity capital in the United States was approximately 4 percent above the long-term U.S. Government bond rate. For most large companies, the cost of equity capital fell within a range of 2 percent to 6 percent above the long-term Government bond rate, depending on how investors perceived the risk of holding the company's shares relative to the average risk for the market as a whole.[6]

These three differences make the valuation of common stocks more complicated and challenging than that of bonds. Nonetheless, as we shall demonstrate, the same basic process of determining the present value of a security by discounting expected cash flow at an appropriate cost of capital is at work in both the stock and bond markets.

To illustrate how investors value a common stock, let us revisit Minnesota Mining and Manufacturing. In the spring of 1992, 3M's stock was trading at approximately $92 per share. With the company coming off a somewhat disappointing year in 1991, most Wall Street analysts were forecasting a rebound in 3M's earnings for 1992 and significant growth for the company throughout the remainder of the decade. For instance, one representative investment firm projected the dividends and estimated the 1996 value of 3M's shares as shown in Exhibit 4.1.

Since the cost of equity capital for 3M was 13 percent at the time, approximately equal to the average cost of equity in the United States, the discounted present value of forecast dividends per share and the estimated value per share at the end of 1996 would have been $91⅛, or just a bit less than 3M's actual market price of $92 per share at the time.

The close relation between 3M's discounted cash flow value per share and the actual market price of the company's stock is not unusual. Indeed, applying the same analysis to many common stocks, we find that the correlation between the "predicted" values per share, estimated by discounting expected equity cash flow, and actual share prices is usually quite high. Each observation in Exhibit 4.2 represents the discounted cash flow value per share and market price for a com-

EXHIBIT 4.1

Projected Dividends for 3M[7]

Year	Dividends per Share	Projected Value-per-Share
1992	$3.20	
1993	3.36	
1994	3.70	
1995	4.08	
1996	4.50	$144

EXHIBIT 4.2

Predicted vs. Actual Market Prices (S&P 500)[8]

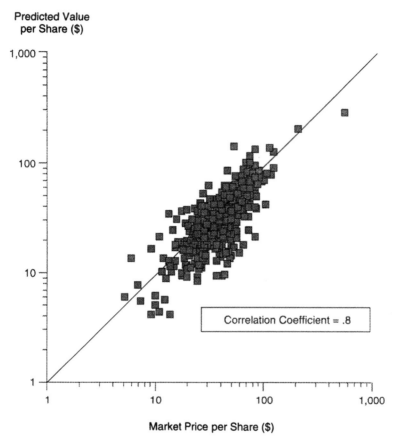

Source: Value Line Investment Survey (1993); Marakon Associates analysis.

pany listed in the S&P 500 Index. And while the "fit" for individual companies is not always as close as in the 3M case, the data in Exhibit 4.2 suggest a strong relationship between discounted cash flow values per share and actual market prices.

Do the results of this correlation prove that all—or even most—investors actually engage in this formal discounted cash flow procedure when making their decisions to buy or sell common stocks? The answer is mixed. Many investors use comparative ratios, such as price/earnings or price/book, to gauge relative values when making buy and sell decisions, where these ratios essentially perform a function quite similar to discounting expected cash flow over time. However, most sophisticated institutional investors especially in the United States and increasingly in the United Kingdom and Europe, employ the dividend discount model or some other form of discounted cash flow analysis in making investment decisions. The close correlation between discounted cash flow values per share and actual market prices suggests that the values investors place on companies are generally consistent with what we would expect if, in fact, all investors were to use the discounted cash flow approach.[9]

What About Short-Term Earnings?

When we discuss the economics of equity valuation with a group of executives, most find the argument that the stock market takes a long-term view of their business persuasive and perhaps a little reassuring. Nevertheless, the discussion rarely goes on for long before someone asks: "If stock prices are driven by long-term forecasts of equity cash flow, why do securities analysts seem to focus so intensely on short-term earnings?" The short answer to this question is simply that appearances can be deceiving. Indeed, while it is true that the market often responds to quarterly earnings announcements, the level and trend of current earnings are not the primary determinants of shareholder value and stock prices.

Contrary to popular belief, the stock market as a whole places considerable weight on long-term performance. In fact, most of a company's market value is embedded in investors' expectations of the earnings it will generate and the investments it will make in the distant future. Typically, more than 50 percent of the present value of a company is captured by discounting the cash flow expected more than five years into the future. This is true not only for high-technology or exotic new businesses but for old-line, established companies as well. Exhibit 4.3 displays for the Dow Jones 30 Industrials Average, the percentage of each firm's stock price that comprises its next five years' estimated dividends per share. For these companies, projected performance over the next five years accounted for roughly 20 percent of their market value at the end of 1991 on average—ranging from less

EXHIBIT 4.3

Percentage of Stock Price Due to First Five Years' Dividends

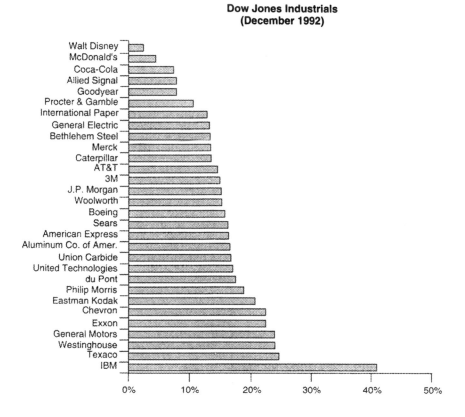

**Dow Jones Industrials
(December 1992)**

than 10 percent for companies like McDonald's and Allied Signal to over 40 percent for IBM.

The fact that shareholder value is determined by a forecast of equity cash flow over an indefinite time period rather than the level or trend in current earnings can be seen even more clearly when one considers companies that generate little or nothing in current sales, let alone earnings. If investors looked only at current earnings when determining values and setting prices, why have companies in the cellular phone, biotechnology, and cable television industries commanded such high market values in recent years—before many of these firms generated even a penny in current earnings for their shareholders?

One timely example of the market valuing long-term cash flow rather than short-term earnings can be seen in McCaw Cellular Communications. While a giant in the cellular communications industry with 1992 revenues of $1.7 billion, McCaw has not made a profit or paid a cent in dividends since going public in 1987. Despite this lack of earnings, the market valued the company at nearly $9 billion at the end of 1992, and in August 1993 AT&T agreed to buy McCaw (subject to U.S. Government approval) in a stock swap valued at $12.6 billion.

Even though the level and trend of current earnings are not primary determinants of shareholder value, they play an important role. As noted earlier, equity cash flow consists of earnings less the amount of equity reinvested in the company or business unit. Thus, annual earnings account for a significant portion of the equity cash flow generated by most companies. In addition, quarterly earnings announcements contain information that sheds light on the firm's prospects for the future and can cause changes in investors' long-term forecasts of both earnings and equity cash flow. Quarterly earnings announcements provide a continuous check that investors use to verify that their expectations are being realized. In many cases, poor results today may signal poor results tomorrow. If management's strategy has failed to produce satisfactory returns in the near term, it is only natural for the market to question the strategy's viability over the long term. Like dedicated news reporters, the capital markets probe for information from any source. Thus, quarterly earnings announcements are an important source of information for investors in making or revising long-term forecasts. But shareholder value is not determined by the level and trend of current earnings, it is determined by discounting expected equity cash flow.

The Relationship Between Shareholder Value and Warranted Value

We now turn from the external valuation that shareholders place on the company to an internal measure of the company's value—what we call its warranted value. This is the present value of the company based on the current cost of equity capital and *management's best estimate* of the expected equity cash flow that each business unit, and therefore the company as a whole, will generate over the long term.[10]

As shown in Exhibit 4.4, the consolidated equity cash flow stream generated by the business units can and should be specified so that they equal the equity cash flow stream projected by management in the form of dividends and share repurchases, less any share issuances.[11] Thus, as long as management's best-estimate forecast of equity cash flow is similar to the forecast made by investors, the company's warranted value and its market value will be approximately equal.

We will discuss how managers should develop this best-estimate forecast in Chapters Five and Six, so they can avoid the common tendency to submit upward-biased financial projections, or "hockey sticks." At this point, however, we simply note that management's *best* estimates of expected equity cash flow should reflect an objective assessment of the likely profitability and growth of each market the company serves, its competitive position in those markets, and the strategies of the business units. When the forecasts of expected equity cash flow have been "grounded" in this way on market economics and

EXHIBIT 4.4

Cash Flow and Value Linkages

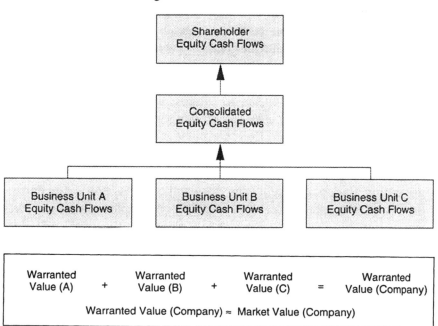

competitive position, we can say with confidence that maximizing the company's warranted value will also result in maximizing shareholder value.

This is an extremely important conclusion for top management. We assert it confidently because our experience has taught us over and over again that when forecasts of each business unit's equity cash flow *are* properly grounded on an unbiased assessment of its market economics and competitive position, the sum of the business unit warranted values will seldom deviate by much from the company's actual market value. Indeed, in our analysis of over 100 companies during the past 15 years, we have found only three instances of significant divergence between market and warranted values, and in each case there was a major market correction toward the warranted value within a few months.

This close relationship between warranted values and market values attests to the impressive ability of investors to ferret out information and process it quickly to arrive at pricing decisions. And it holds important information for management. On one hand, it is highly unlikely that investors will place a value on any company that is based on what they perceive as unrealistic expectations of future performance. Despite the hopes and dreams that management may harbor for its businesses, investors will value the company only on the basis of the future equity cash flow that the current strategies are likely to produce. Thus, the often-heard claim that the stock market systematically undervalues any particular company is, in our experience, completely unfounded. This is not meant to suggest that investors never make forecasting errors—they certainly do, but the errors are not systematically biased and the corrections are made quickly. On the other hand, this close relationship between warranted value and shareholder value is extremely good news. It enables top management to internalize the governing objective by requiring that each business unit in the portfolio as well as the corporate center identify and implement those strategies that maximize its contribution to the company's warranted value. To the degree that management at all levels succeeds in making strategic and organizational decisions that increase the company's warranted value, there is a high probability that the increase will be reflected in the company's market value as soon as investors learn of the decisions or see the results. Of course, the converse is also true. When strategies are implemented that reduce warranted value, odds are high that investors will reduce the value of the common stock as well.

Before summarizing our key conclusions, two further points should be made. First, both warranted values and market values are dynamic and should be expected to change considerably over time. While it might simplify decision making if both warranted values and market values were to appreciate along a nice, smooth path, this would be the exception rather than the rule. Neither markets nor managers are prescient. Current values and prices reflect fairly well all that is known but not what is unknown—such as future changes in interest rates and oil prices, or a blockbuster new product that a competitor is about to launch, or discovery of a new process technology. These are the unexpected events or shocks that can cause huge changes in values and prices, and both managers and investors have to live with them. Second, the close correlation we find between warranted values and market values does not mean that investors actually develop forecasts for the company's individual business units (although some do)—it means that with the information that is available to them about individual business unit strategies, corporate strategy, and the capabilities of the company's management team, investors are able to develop a remarkably good sense of the company's overall ability to generate equity cash flow over time.

Concluding Remarks

In the first part of this chapter we described briefly how investors value a common stock by discounting, at the cost of equity capital, the expected equity cash flow they believe the company will generate over an indefinite time horizon. We then introduced the concept of warranted value, which we define as an internal valuation of a business unit or the company based on management's best estimate of the expected equity cash flow, discounted at the cost of equity capital.

In our experience, when management's best estimate of expected equity cash flow is grounded on an unbiased strategic assessment of each business unit, the company's warranted value and its actual market value will seldom differ by much over time. This equivalence between warranted value and market value enables management to establish maximization of shareholder value as the governing objective for the company as a whole and every business unit within the company's portfolio. It also provides a foundation for building an economic framework that explicitly links strategic and operating decisions to their likely impact on warranted value over time, a subject we will detail further in Chapter Five.

CHAPTER 5

Financial Determinants of Value Creation

Most managers find it an intuitively appealing proposition that the value of a business or company is determined by expected equity cash flow over time. After all, companies have been using discounted cash flow models to evaluate discrete investment projects for several decades. Most managers are also comfortable with the proposition that when confronted with a range of strategic options, they should choose the one that makes the largest contribution to the company's warranted value. Nevertheless, in our experience, few line managers understand how the conventional financial ratios used to measure performance relate to cash flow over time and warranted value. Without this understanding, however, it is difficult, if not impossible, to develop value-maximizing strategies for all of the business units within a large organization.

This chapter focuses in particular on three measures of financial performance which are the primary financial determinants of value and value creation: return on equity (ROE), the rate of growth in equity capital (g), and the cost of equity capital (K_e). Our general aim is to describe the relationship between these three measures of financial performance and warranted value as well as value creation. This latter term is measured by both the *difference* between the warranted value of a business unit or company and the amount of capital invested and the *ratio* of warranted value to the amount of capital invested. Our specific aim is to advance two important and related propositions about these three primary determinants:

- Value is created only when a business unit or company can earn a return on equity over time that exceeds its cost of equity capital; when ROE consistently falls short of the cost of equity, value is destroyed.
- There are two kinds of growth—good growth, which magnifies value creation, and bad growth, which magnifies value destruction—a distinction that plays a crucial role in strategy development.

As the reader will see, understanding and acceptance of these propositions plays a crucial role in development of the capability to link strategic decisions directly to their likely impact on shareholder value.

The Financial Determinants of Value Creation

In Chapter Four, we showed that both warranted value and shareholder (or market) value are determined by expected equity cash flow over time and the cost of equity capital. But simply knowing the magnitude of equity cash flow in any year provides an uncertain signal about the strengths and weaknesses of a business. And without further analysis, a simple measure of annual equity cash flow cannot possibly suggest ways to improve performance. Further, if managers are thinking about the important problems facing their businesses, translating possible solutions quickly and intuitively into a discounted cash flow analysis is a somewhat forbidding mental feat. Therefore, managers need a reasonably reliable "shorthand" for thinking about how specific decisions might impact the warranted value of their business in terms that are more familiar than those used to perform a discounted cash flow analysis. Such a shorthand exists in the form of the relationships between ROE, growth, the cost of equity, and value creation.

Recall from Chapter Four that for any particular year, equity cash flow (ECF) is the difference between earnings, or net income, and the amount of equity reinvested in that year. This definition implies that the linkage between ROE, the equity growth rate, and ECF is given by the equation

$$ECF = [Equity\ Investment] \times [ROE - growth\ rate],$$

where the first term refers to equity capital at the beginning of the year.[1] This equation tells us that for high-ROE companies that are growing slowly, such as Philip Morris, the difference between ROE and growth in any year is quite large, implying that the company will generate a huge equity cash flow that year. Alternatively, with low-ROE companies that are growing rapidly—as was the case with McCaw Cellular—the difference is small, or negative, implying that these companies will generate little or no equity cash flow until ROE increases, growth slows, or both occur.

As shown in Exhibit 5.1, return on equity and equity growth over time determine the stream of equity cash flow, which means that they also determine the warranted value of a company or business unit, both absolutely and relative to the beginning equity investment. It turns out that if ROE and equity growth are assumed to be roughly constant, or sustainable over time, this framework can be expressed with two useful equations. We call the first one the constant growth value equation and the second, the value-to-book equation.[2] These two equations appear in Exhibit 5.2. Note that the first equation clearly

EXHIBIT 5.1
Financial Determinants of Value

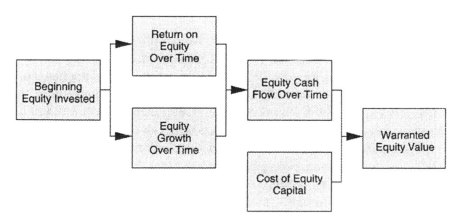

EXHIBIT 5.2

Constant Growth Value and Value-to-Book Equations

$$V \ = \ B \ \times \ \frac{ROE - g}{K_e - g} \quad \text{and} \quad \frac{V}{B} \ = \ \frac{ROE - g}{K_e - g}$$

V = Equity value of common stock
B = Beginning book value of equity investment
ROE = Expected long-term return on equity
g = Expected long-term growth in equity ($\leq$ GNP growth)
K_e = Cost of equity capital

Note: If management's estimates for ROE and g are used, equity value becomes warranted value;
If investors' estimates for ROE and g are used, equity value becomes market value.

shows that value is driven by ROE and equity growth over time, given the beginning equity and the cost of equity, while the second equation shows that the value-to-book ratio is driven by ROE, growth and K_e.

For mature companies and business units that can be expected to grow at a sustainable rate less than that of the economy, the constant growth value equation can be used to make a rough estimate of value without going through a formal discounted cash flow exercise.[3] By forecasting a company's sustainable return on equity and equity growth, and by determining the cost of equity capital, the value can be calculated literally on the back of an envelope. Returning to our earlier example of 3M, we can see in Exhibit 5.3 that this shorthand technique works fairly well.

Looking a bit deeper into the relationships shown in Exhibit 5.1, it is easy to see that if expected ROEs increase or the cost of equity capital declines, then as long as the sustainable growth rate is unchanged, value and value-to-book will increase. Further, when management or investors expect ROEs over time to be greater than the cost of equity, the business unit's or company's warranted value and market value will be greater than its book value, and value will have been created in the sense that the unit or company is worth more than what shareholders historically have invested in it. When this occurs, we describe the business unit or company as economically profitable and earning a positive "equity spread," our aim being to capture with these terms the

EXHIBIT 5.3

Valuation of 3M Stock

$$\text{Estimated Value per Share} = \frac{\text{ROE} - g}{K_e - g} \times \text{Book Value of 3M per Share}$$

$$= \frac{24\% - 7.5\%}{13\% - 7.5\%} \times \$28.72$$

$$= \$86$$

$$\text{Actual Value per Share} = \$92$$

Source: Forecasts based on Value Line Investment Survey (1992); Marakon Associates analysis.

fact that ROE is expected to exceed the cost of equity over time and the company is creating value for shareholders. In the 3M case, where investors are projecting future ROEs that average about ten percentage points more than the cost of equity capital and an equity growth rate of 7.5 percent over time, the company's market value is three times higher than its book value.

There is, of course, a negative side to these relationships. Whenever a business unit or company is expected to earn a sustainable ROE that averages less than its cost of equity capital (a negative equity spread), it is economically unprofitable and is destroying value in the sense that it is worth less than the shareholders' investment. For example, if investors were to wake up tomorrow convinced that 3M's sustainable ROE would fall to 10 percent, the company's market value would fall to $13 per share (10 percent less 7.5 percent, divided by 13 percent less 7.5 percent, multiplied by $28.72). If this unlikely event were to actually occur, 3M would be economically unprofitable (even though it would be reporting an accounting profit), earning a negative equity spread of 3 percent and destroying somewhat more than $15 per share of value.

At this point, we should note that in certain circumstances the signal about economic profitability and value creation can be vulnerable to accounting distortions, even though these distortions do not affect equity cash flow or value. If, for example, a company took a large write-off last year, both ROE and the value-to-book ratio would probably increase temporarily as a consequence of the reduction in book equity.

Over time, however, as equity is reinvested in the company, ROE and the value-to-book ratio would both recede toward the level they would have had if the write-off had not been taken (or if they had been calculated with the write-off added back). Thus, when using equity spreads as a performance measure, it is important to calculate these spreads over a long enough time horizon to minimize the potential impact of any accounting distortions, or make adjustments to the equity account so that the distortions never emerge. For example, deducing that a business is economically profitable or unprofitable based on the equity spread for one year may prove misleading relative to the signal that management might get from a multiyear perspective.

In addition to the equity spread of a business or company over time, there is a second measure that signals whether value is being created or destroyed. This measure is the "economic profit" generated by the business unit or company. While equity spread measures profitability in percentage terms, economic profit measures it in dollar terms. Economic profit is defined in two equivalent ways, as shown in Exhibit 5.4. First, it is the difference between earnings and the dollar cost of invested equity capital—where this dollar cost is obtained by multiplying the percentage cost of equity by the amount of equity invested in the business unit or the company. In other words, while accounting earnings reflect a deduction for the dollar cost of debt capital (i.e., interest expense), economic profit reflects an additional deduction for the implicit cost of employing the shareholders' capital. Second, economic profit is equal to the equity spread in any year multiplied by the amount of book equity at the beginning of the year.

From this second definition, it is easy to see that in any period when economic profit exceeds zero, the company or business unit has earned a return on equity that is greater than the cost of equity capital. Con-

EXHIBIT 5.4
Two Equivalent Definitions of Economic Profit

1. Economic Profit = Earnings - Equity Capital Charge,

Where Equity Capital Charge = Cost of Equity x Equity Invested

2. Economic Profit = Equity Invested x Equity Spread

EXHIBIT 5.5

3M Economic Profit

3M Economic Profit = Earnings - Equity Capital Charge

$$= \$1.23B - (13\% \times \$6.3B)$$

$$= \$1.23B - \$819M$$

$$= \$411M$$

versely, when economic profit is less than zero, ROE will also be less than the cost of equity.[4] For example, Exhibit 5.5 shows that 3M had accounting earnings of $1.23 billion in 1992 and an ROE of 19.6 percent. Since this ROE was greater than its 13 percent cost of equity capital, 3M was economically profitable in 1992; its economic profit equaled $411 million, $1.23 billion in earnings less an $819 million capital charge for its $6.3 billion in equity capital.

The use of economic profit as a measure of business unit and company performance has become increasingly widespread in recent years. In the United States, it has been adopted in various forms by a number of large companies, including Coca-Cola, AT&T, Kellogg, and Scott Paper, as their principal measure of profitability, replacing operating income and net earnings as the focus of management's attention. The use of economic profit has two virtues. First, it is a single monetary measure that can be linked directly to value creation. Second, it is easy to understand, particularly for non-financial managers who are accustomed to various ways of measuring profit. Further, it is fairly easy to incorporate measures of economic profit or loss into most management financial reporting systems, provided the company has developed full income statements and balance sheets for each of its business units and has an estimate of each unit's cost of equity. As we shall see later, economic profit can also be measured at the product line and customer level, providing useful signals about value creation and destruction within a business unit.

Good Growth and Bad Growth

The proposition that value is created by earning sustainable positive equity spreads or positive economic profit over time is usually accepted by most managers with whom we have worked. They recognize that these measures are much better indicators of performance than simple accounting earnings. Somewhat less intuitive is the insight the value-to-book equation gives us about growth. As can be seen from the example in Exhibit 5.6, growth is very much a double-edged sword. For economically profitable businesses, as is the case for business unit A, increasing sustainable growth by one percentage point increases value from $1,040 million to $1,200 million, or more than 15 percent. For economically unprofitable businesses, however, increasing sustainable growth by one percentage point causes value to fall by $40 million, or more than 16 percent.

From these relationships we can draw the distinction between good growth and bad growth. Good growth results when the shareholders' money—the equity capital supporting a business unit or the company—is invested in strategies that earn consistently positive equity spreads and, thus, positive economic profit over time. This economically profitable growth will increase both warranted equity value and value creation. Further, good growth acts as a powerful magnifier— the more good growth investments a business unit or company can make, the more value it will create. Bad growth, of course, is just the opposite. It occurs when the shareholders' money is invested in strategies that produce consistently negative equity spreads and, thus, economic losses over time. The more investments a business unit or com-

EXHIBIT 5.6

Only Profitable Growth Creates Value

	Business Unit A (Economically Profitable)	Business Unit B (Economically Unprofitable)
Book Equity Investment	$400M	$400M
Sustainable Return on Equity	20%	10%
Cost of Equity Capital	12%	12%
Sustainable Equity Spread	8%	-2%
Economic Profit	$320M	-$80M
For Sustainable Growth = 7%		
• Warranted Equity Value	$1,040M	$240M
• Value-to-Book	2.6x	0.6x
For Sustainable Growth = 8%		
• Warranted Equity Value	$1,200M	$200M
• Value-to-Book	3.0x	0.5x

pany makes in bad growth, the more value it destroys. This economically unprofitable growth may well increase sales and earnings, but it will always cause value to be destroyed.

There are many examples of good and bad growth. Exhibit 5.7 illustrates the contrasting experiences of General Electric and General Motors from 1982 to 1992. Both GE and GM experienced considerable growth over this period, as reflected by the total equity investment the companies made (of approximately $16 billion by GE and $11 billion by GM). However, with average equity spreads of nearly 4 percent, GE's equity investment of $16.3 billion produced an enormous increase in value for the company's shareholders. In fact, between 1982 and 1992, GE's market value increased by more than $51 billion as the company entered new markets, divested several unprofitable businesses, and aggressively managed its costs and assets.

EXHIBIT 5.7

Good Growth vs. Bad Growth

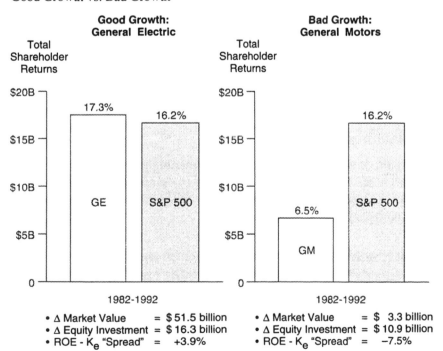

- Δ Market Value   = $ 51.5 billion
- Δ Equity Investment = $ 16.3 billion
- ROE - K_e "Spread"   =   +3.9%

- Δ Market Value   = $ 3.3 billion
- Δ Equity Investment = $ 10.9 billion
- ROE - K_e "Spread"   =   −7.5%

On the other hand, GM managed to invest its shareholders' funds quite unprofitably over this same time period. Indeed, between 1982 and 1992, GM invested nearly $11 billion of equity in acquisitions, automation, and new plants at an average spread of −7.5 percent, with the result that GM's market value increased by only $3.3 billion over this time period—causing a loss of over $7 billion of value to the company's stockholders. In hindsight, GM's strategy between 1982 and 1992 appears to have been a classic example of a management team pursuing bad growth.

The idea that growth can be bad is not always immediately obvious or acceptable to managers. After all, they are paid, essentially, to grow their businesses and are accustomed to thinking that adding any sales and earnings is good for the company. Further, as we noted in Chapter Three, the institutional imperative to grow largely ignores how such growth impacts shareholder value. The combination of these emotional bonds to growth and short-term economic incentives to grow at almost any cost exists in virtually all large companies, often with very negative consequences for the company's product market and capital market performance over time. GM is a particularly striking example, but the recent history of decline at other once-great wealth-creating enterprises such as IBM, Sears, Eastman Kodak, and Philips Electronics makes it clear that there are many other companies that have not understood the distinction between good and bad growth.

Profitability Principles

An understanding of the financial determinants of value and value creation leads directly to two profitability principles that can be used to help analyze business performance and develop strategic options for increasing value:

(1) If a business unit or company earns a return on equity that is consistently greater than its cost of equity capital (i.e., if it consistently generates an economic profit over time) it creates value for its shareholders. To the extent that new investment consistently earns a positive spread and, thus, positive economic profit, the resulting growth is good and will magnify value creation.

(2) If a business unit or company earns a return on equity that is consistently less than its cost of equity capital (i.e., if it consistently generates an economic loss over time) it destroys value for its shareholders. To the extent that new investment consistently produces a negative spread and economic losses, the resulting growth is bad and will magnify the amount of value destroyed.

These two principles have an obvious implication for strategy formulation and evaluation that we will explore more fully in Chapters Seven through Ten. For an economically profitable business unit, a fundamental strategy question should be: "What avenues are available to expand the business?" On the other hand, for an economically unprofitable business unit, growth should be discouraged until the business is capable of producing consistently positive equity spreads. Note that for businesses in the early stage of their product life cycle and for capital-intensive businesses in markets such as commodity chemicals or cable television, the return on equity must be measured over a time period that is long enough to capture the expected increase in ROE in the distant future. Failure to calculate the *average* ROE over time, or the *average* ROE over a product life cycle or business cycle, may lead to systematic underinvestment in businesses with long-term payoffs, assuming that the payoffs are large enough to compensate for the wait and the financial sacrifice required to produce them.

These basic principles can be seen in Exhibit 5.8, which plots the equity spreads of the Dow Jones Industrials—based on four-year forecasts of ROE and estimates of the cost of equity capital for each company—versus each company's market value-to-book ratio. As this exhibit shows, those companies that are expected to generate positive equity spreads (ROE > K_e) over time have market value-to-book ratios greater than 1.0.[5]

Differential growth rates are the primary reason for the scattering of the observations in Exhibit 5.8. Boeing and Disney, for example, have equity spreads that are expected to be within a percentage point or so of one another, yet Disney's market value-to-book ratio is near 4.5, while Boeing's is 2.0. The major factor driving this difference is expected growth. Disney's growth is expected to be in the range of 15 to 20 percent, while Boeing's growth is expected to be considerably lower—near 5 percent. Consequently, despite the fact that both com-

EXHIBIT 5.8

Profitability of Dow Jones Industrials[6]

Market Value-to-
    Book Ratio

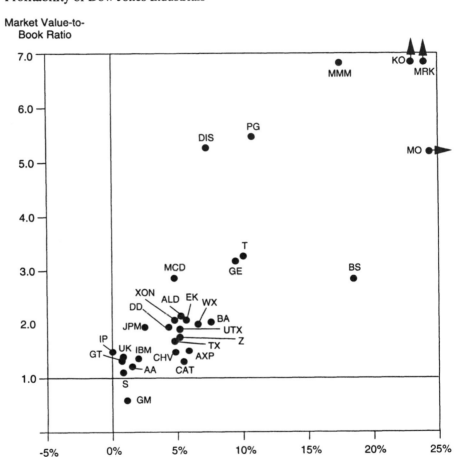

Forecast Equity Spread (ROE - Cost of Equity)

ALD	Allied Corp	
AA	Aluminum Co. of America	
AXP	American Express	
BA	Boeing	
BS	Bethlehem Steel	
CAT	Caterpillar	
CHV	Chevron	
DD	du Pont	
DIS	Walt Disney	
EK	Eastman Kodak	
XON	Exxon Corp.	
GE	General Electric	
GM	General Motors	
GT	Goodyear Tire	
IBM	Int'l Business Machines	
IP	Int'l Paper	
JPM	J.P. Morgan	
KO	Coca-Cola	
MCD	McDonald's	
MRK	Merck & Co.	
MMM	3M	
MO	Philip Morris	
PG	Procter & Gamble	
S	Sears, Roebuck	
T	AT&T	
TX	Texaco	
UK	Union Carbide	
TUX	United Technologies	
WS	Westinghouse	
Z	Woolworth (F.W.)	

Source: Value Line Investment Survey (1992); Marakon Associates analysis.

panies are economically profitable, Disney has created 165 percent more value per dollar of invested equity than Boeing has.

Uses of Profitability Measures

Measures of economic profit and equity spread can help managers at all levels of the company to discriminate between good growth and bad growth. Within a business unit, the profitability of individual products and customers can be measured to identify those that are contributing to value creation and those that are just breaking even or destroying value. For the senior management responsible for a business unit, the profitability of entire product lines and customer groups can be measured, as a means of flagging critical strategic issues and stimulating the development of alternative strategies. For corporate management, an unbiased assessment of the amount of value created and destroyed by individual business units is a crucial prerequisite for developing portfolio strategy and allocating resources.

An example of a corporate value assessment is shown in Exhibit 5.9. For this large company, the variability of profitability and value creation across business units is quite large. At one end of the spectrum, business unit A has a value-to-book ratio of about 4.0. At the other end, business unit J actually has a negative value, which we term a "black hole" in the portfolio. This can occur when sustainable ROE is less than sustainable growth, thereby causing equity cash flow to become negative over time, or when management simply overinvests in a low-return business in which the impact of the near-term negative cash flow outweighs the positive cash flow expected in later years. Note that since investors would never finance a negative cash flow stream on a continuing basis, a public company can never have a negative value. However, black holes are frequently discovered within large corporations because of a capital allocation process that does not discriminate effectively between value-creating and value-destroying business units. In contrast, the corporate center within a value based company manages an internal capital market that works to direct resources to only those businesses that are likely to create value for shareholders. We will return to this subject in detail in Chapter Fourteen. At this point, the key message is that a thorough understanding

EXHIBIT 5.9

Business Unit Profitability and Value Creation

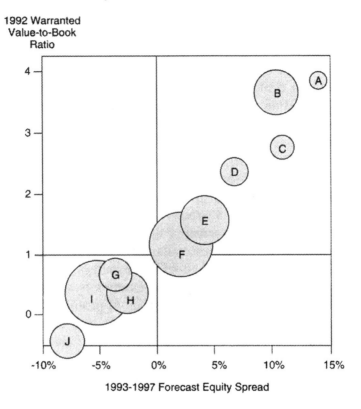

1992 Warranted
Value-to-Book
Ratio

1993-1997 Forecast Equity Spread

Note: Circle size proportional to equity interest.

of the profitability principles and the ability to measure equity spreads and economic profit over time at various levels within the company are crucial prerequisites for effective strategy development and re- source allocation.

We should emphasize that despite the considerable benefits the profitability principles and related financial measures bring to strategy development and resource allocation, they should serve only as guide- lines, or signals, and should not be used as a basis for making choices among competing strategic options. While they can be very useful in helping managers formulate alternative strategies, the task of selecting the best option must be left to a more thorough evaluation of the likely impact of each strategy on warranted value. For example, when deciding whether an aggressive growth strategy is a better option than a "hold market share" strategy, one must compare how each option would affect the warranted value of the business. The function of the financial determinants and profitability principles is to act as a bridge between valuation based on discounted cash flow and traditional accounting measures of performance. That is a fair task as is, and the measures should not be stretched to do more.

Concluding Remarks

This chapter has three important implications. First, management must develop much better internal financial information than it normally has. The great majority of companies do not even have proper business unit income statements and balance sheets, let alone the capability to generate reliable measures of economic profit and value creation across and within business units. This means that corporate and business unit managers are flying blind more often than not when it comes to knowing how or where to look for strategies to increase warranted value.

A second implication is that managers would benefit enormously by adopting economic profit instead of operating income or reported earnings as their basic measure of business performance. While it might be disconcerting to discover suddenly (as some companies have) that as many as half the business units in the portfolio are no longer "profitable" once forced to recognize their full economic cost, this gives a much more reliable signal of the true economic health of a business than conventional measures do. Changing the accounting system and educating managers in the use of these new profitability measures may require a bit of time and effort, but this investment will certainly generate excellent returns for the company.

The third implication, of course, is that managers must learn to discriminate carefully between good growth and bad growth. The difference between the two cannot be emphasized too often or too strongly. Most companies must grow to create value, and achievement of the governing objective will require that the company constantly seek out and invest in all new opportunities for good growth. But as we shall see, if management does not at the same time control and eliminate bad growth investments, much of the value created by its good growth strategies will be wasted or destroyed.

CHAPTER 6

Strategic Determinants of Value Creation

Most managers have learned from direct experience how quickly competitive forces can decrease profitability. We hear frequently about specific competitor actions (occasionally characterized as "irrational") that have had a significant negative impact on the revenue growth or economic profit of a business. Yet again and again, we see managers producing financial forecasts that significantly underestimate the negative impact that competitive forces are likely to have on the future financial performance of the businesses they manage. Consequently, many businesses invest too much in attempting to build competitive advantages that never materialize and invest too little in defending their most profitable products and markets against competitive attack.

In addition to underestimating the impact that competitive forces have on profitability, most managers lack an economic framework that explicitly links the forces of competition and a business unit's competitive position directly to value creation. This leads to two common problems. First, most managers have no clear understanding of the competitive advantages that are likely to create value and those that are unlikely to do so. As a result, most businesses invest as though all competitive advantages are equally likely to create wealth and, therefore, underexploit their most valuable assets. Second, in the absence of an economic framework that clearly delineates the strategic determinants of value creation, many large, diversified companies seize upon the latest ideas for building competitive advantage (e.g., global market leadership, customer satisfaction, cycle time compression, process reengineering) and mandate that every business unit pursue the same general strategic direction, even though these businesses compete in very different product markets, with very different competitive requirements.

In our view, having an economic framework that explicitly links competitive forces directly to value creation is not just a good idea, it is a necessity. In order to systematically create value, managers must understand how their business unit's competitive performance in the product markets impacts its value in the capital markets. In Chapters Four and Five we described the financial determinants of value creation. We outlined how a business unit's long-term returns and growth drive its warranted value. In this chapter, we describe the strategic determinants of value creation. Specifically, we detail how the forces of competition in the product markets, impact its long-term financial performance and value. We use this relationship to support two important and related propositions:

- The two primary strategic determinants of value creation are market economics, and a business unit's competitive position; and accordingly,
- There are only two ways to defy competitive forces and sustain value creation in any business: participate in economically attractive markets and/or build and maintain a competitive advantage.

Once managers thoroughly understand both the strategic and financial determinants of value creation, they can use the resulting economic framework to assess their business unit's current strategic position and begin to develop and evaluate strategic options that will create more value over time.

Overview of the Strategic Determinants

While competitive forces are constantly working to erode any firm's capacity to create value, a great many companies—and even some entire industries—succeed in resisting these forces. For example, we estimate that the average equity spread earned by the U.S. ethical drug industry was roughly 12 percent between 1976 and 1991—compared with the 1 percent spread generated by the U.S. economy as a whole.[1] Over the same 15-year span, the industry's top performer, Merck, earned an average spread of 24 percent (reflecting an average return on equity of 36 percent and cost of equity averaging 12 percent). Of course, not all businesses have been able to sustain this level of profitability. For instance, from 1976 to 1991, America's semiconductor industry earned an average return on equity that was seven percentage points less than its cost of equity capital, while its revenues grew more than fourfold. Given this poor overall performance, it should come as no surprise that the industry's laggard, National Semiconductor, earned an average equity spread of −16 percent. On the other hand, the industry's leader, Intel Corporation, managed to earn an average equity spread of +3 percent over this time period, while growing from a little more than $200 million in sales in 1978 to nearly $4.8 billion in 1992.

What explains these dramatic differences in profitability? Put simply, the wide variation of financial performance is caused by significant differences in the two primary strategic determinants of value creation: *market economics* and *competitive position.* As Exhibit 6.1 shows, market economics encompasses the structural factors or com-

EXHIBIT 6.1
Strategic Determinants of Value Creation

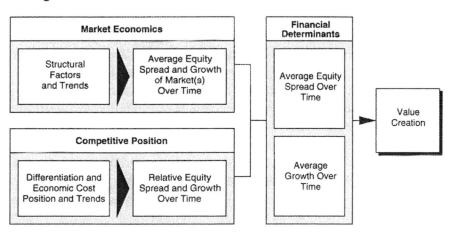

petitive forces, that jointly determine the *average* equity spread and growth rate over time for all competitors in a particular product market. Competitive position encompasses the factors, or forces, that jointly determine a specific competitor's equity spread and growth rate over time *relative* to that of the average competitor in its product market—where a company's competitive position is defined in terms of its combined product differentiation and economic cost position. By implication, market economics and competitive position determine a business unit's long-term profitability and growth.

Market Economics and Value Creation

The "attractiveness" of any market depends on the profitability of the average competitor in the market, as measured by spread between the return on equity earned over time and the cost of equity capital or by the level of economic profit earned over time. We specify a market as attractive only if the equity spread and economic profit earned by the average competitor is positive. If the average competitor's equity spread and economic profit is negative, the market is unattractive. Put simply, *an attractive market is one in which the average competitor is creating value for shareholders, and an unattractive market is one in which the average competitor is destroying value.*

Unlike many of the other techniques used to determine market attractiveness, this approach reserves judgment as to whether growth is likely to be good or bad. In markets where the average participant is economically profitable—as in soft drinks and consumer foods— growth makes the market even more attractive by magnifying value creation. On the other hand, in markets where the average participant is destroying shareholder value—as in consumer electronics or textiles—growth makes the market even more unattractive by magnifying value destruction. In short, the average profitability of competitors over time defines whether a market is attractive, and growth defines the *degree* of attractiveness.

As Exhibit 6.2 suggests, there has been a wide variation in the equity spreads across industries in the United States. In fact, between 1976 and 1991, equity spreads ranged from −17 percent per year for the average oil field service operation to more than a positive 13 percent for the average soft-drink concern. In addition to the wide vari-

EXHIBIT 6.2

Historical Equity Spreads Across Industries (1976–91)

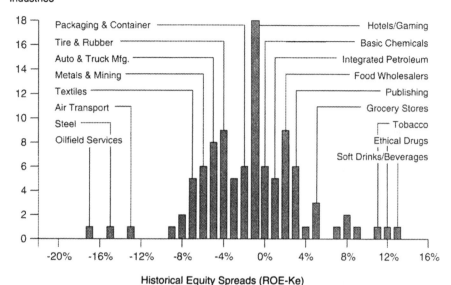

Number of
Industries

Source: Value Line Investment Survey; Marakon Associates analysis.

ation in equity spreads, one must be impressed by the average, or mean, of the distribution of historical equity spreads. During this 15-year period, the largest, most successful companies in the United States managed to generate a return on equity approximately equal to the cost of equity capital—a testimonial to the ability of competitive forces to drive returns toward the cost of equity capital over time.

The wide variation in equity spreads shown in Exhibit 6.2 leads directly to an important question: What determines the profitability and thus attractiveness of an particular market? As Exhibit 6.3 shows schematically, the profitability of any market is determined by two *direct forces* and four *limiting forces*. The two direct forces are the *intensity of direct competition* and *customer pressures*. Since the economic profitability of a market is the direct result of the market's prevailing price level and its cost structure, including the cost of capital, typically the more intense the competition between rivals in a given market and the higher the level of customer pressure, the lower the market's pro-

EXHIBIT 6.3

Determinants of Market Economics (or Profitability)

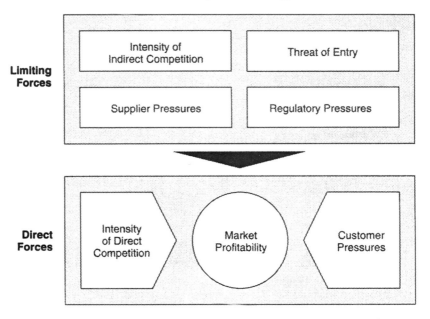

fitability will be. In fiercely competitive markets with powerful customers, for example, prices rarely keep pace with inflation and returns are typically below the cost of capital.

In addition to these two direct forces, four limiting forces also impact the profitability of most markets: the *intensity of indirect competition,* the *threat of entry, supplier pressures,* and *regulatory pressures.* As their designation implies, the limiting forces do not impact directly the average equity spread in a market.[2] Instead, they act primarily to restrict the ability of any competitor to increase prices and economic profit, effectively limiting the amount of value that can be created. Thus, these limiting forces place a ceiling on the level of prices and economic profit in a market, while the direct forces determine how low the floor is likely to be.

The intensity of direct competition and customer pressures have several underlying determinants. By quantifying these determinants, it is possible to make accurate estimates of the equity spread or economic profit that the average competitor in any given market is likely to earn. More important, an understanding of these underlying determinants allows us to compare average profitability across the product markets in which a business participates and assess likely changes in average profitability over time.

The intensity of direct competition in any market is typically explained by four underlying determinants.[3] The first is the *amount of excess production capacity* in the market. The greater the amount of excess capacity, the greater the likelihood that competitors will engage in volume-oriented pricing in order to increase utilization—thus driving down margins and equity spreads. Excess capacity is an especially important driver of profitability in capital-intensive businesses, such as airlines and basic chemicals. The second determinant of the intensity of direct competition is the degree of *standardization of the product or service being offered.* The more standardized a product or service, the greater the likelihood of price-based competition and low to average profitability. The third determinant is the *number and concentration of rivals* in a particular market. The higher the concentration of rivals in a given market, the greater the odds that competitors will find a way to tacitly cooperate with one another, setting prices high enough to earn handsome equity spreads but low enough to deter entry. For many years, the automobile market under GM's leadership appeared to be highly cooperative and largely free from volume-oriented pricing.

The fourth determinant influencing the intensity of direct competition is *growth in demand.* In markets experiencing rapid growth, the intensity of competition is reduced, since each rival can satisfy profitability and growth goals without having to take share away from one or more competitors. As growth slows, however, its impact on profitability usually swings from positive to negative. Typically, producers interpret the slowdown as merely a pause rather than a structural change. By the time they recognize what has happened and reduce the growth rate of their capacity additions, the market is awash in excess capacity and profitability tumbles. The petrochemical industry in Europe is a classic example of how growth affects profitability. In the late 1980s, growth in demand outstripped available supply, causing prices and economic profits to skyrocket. Rising profit, in turn, led to a large increase in capacity additions. When growth finally declined in the recession of 1991, excess capacity increased significantly, causing huge declines in both prices and industry profitability.

Perhaps no single market demonstrates more vividly these secondary forces at work than the U.S. airline industry. For nearly two decades, the industry has been saddled with immense overcapacity. Since 1970, industry capacity utilization—as measured by the ratio of total revenue passenger miles to available seat miles—has rarely exceeded 65 percent. Accordingly, each airline fights intensely for incremental passengers in order to improve its passenger load factors and amortize its immense base of fixed operating and capital costs. In addition, air travel has become increasingly standardized, with few companies able to differentiate their service offering in any meaningful way. The combination of tremendous excess capacity and a standardized service offering has led to volume-oriented pricing and frequent fare wars. The predictable result of the market's fierce rivalry has been extremely poor financial performance. Indeed, the average equity spread for the airline industry has been −13 percent for the past two decades.

Within the airline industry, different geographic markets have different levels of competitive intensity. In the northeastern United States, for example, the intensity of direct competition is fierce, with nearly every major air carrier vying for passengers. In the southwestern United States, however, direct competition is less intense, due to higher competitor concentration and fewer air transport alternatives. As a result, the average airfare in the Northeast is significantly lower than in the Southwest, and the nation's only consistently profitable air carrier—Southwest Airlines—participates predominantly in southwestern markets.

The level of customer pressures, the second direct force, reflects two underlying determinants: the *price sensitivity of customers* and their *negotiating leverage*. Both are critical in setting market prices and determining the level of product quality and service that a company must provide to compete effectively. When customers are highly price-sensitive and have a strong negotiating position, they typically prevent most, if not all, suppliers from earning a positive economic profit over time. When customers are price-insensitive, or price-sensitive but have a poor negotiating position, it is far easier for suppliers to operate profitably. In most industrial markets, price sensitivity can be estimated directly by determining, first, the percentage of the customers' total costs that are represented by the market's product and then the profitability of the customers being served. The lower the product's cost, as a percentage of the customer's total cost, and the higher the customer's profitability, the lower the price sensitivity. In most consumer markets price sensitivity is determined by the ratio of the product's cost to the customer's disposable income and by the absolute magnitude of disposable income. The lower the product's cost and/or the higher the customer's income, the lower the price sensitivity.

The degree of customer negotiating leverage depends on: customer concentration (the higher the concentration of customers, the greater their negotiating leverage); the propensity for customers to integrate backwards (the higher the propensity for backwards integration, the greater their bargaining leverage); the extent to which the product is used by customers to gain a competitive advantage (if the product is essential to the customer's competitive position, the producer will have a stronger negotiating position); costs of switching suppliers (the lower the switching costs, the greater the customer's leverage); and the number of alternative suppliers (the greater the number, the greater the customer's leverage).

Typically, as markets mature, customer pressures play an increasingly important role in determining market profitability. In emerging markets, for example, customers tend to be uninformed about different product attributes as well as the cost of providing additional services. As a result, during this phase the market's product and service providers have a negotiating advantage over their customers and can therefore price to earn large equity spreads. Over time, however, as customers learn more and more about individual product characteristics and the costs of incremental services, their negotiating position strengthens considerably, thus putting downward pressure on prices and equity spreads. Indeed, in those markets where this increase in negotiating leverage coincides with high price sensitivity, customer pressure can cause profitability to vanish for all but the lowest-cost competitors.

Along with the direct forces that impact the economic profitability of any market, four limiting forces act, with one exception, to constrain a market's capacity for value creation. These forces include the *intensity of indirect competition,* the *threat of competitor entry, sup-*

plier pressures, and *regulatory pressures.* Each of these forces impacts the profitability potential of a market in a different way. Indirect
competition from substitute products, for example, places a ceiling on
prices. In markets where substitutes that offer comparable performance are readily available, prices often are set to discourage customers
from switching to these substitutes. Thus, the availability and performance of substitute products acts to place a ceiling on prices which
constrains profitability. Likewise, the threat of entry also places a ceiling on market profitability. In markets with low entry barriers, incumbents typically set prices in order to protect market share by making
entry economically unattractive to outsiders. Thus, the lower the entry
barriers, the lower the ceiling on prices and profitability. Growth tends
to encourage competitor entry. Thus, in addition to its favorable impact on the intensity of direct competition, growth tends to have a
negative impact on a market's profitability by encouraging entry and
inducing downward pressure on price ceilings. Suppliers limit a market's profitability to the extent that they drive up input costs faster than
a market's customers will allow these costs to be passed on. Thus, in
many industries—particularly those where access to raw materials or
labor is restricted—supplier pressures limit returns. Regulatory pressures are the only exception to the rule that limiting forces constrain
profitability. These pressures can have both positive and negative impacts on market profitability, depending on the form of government
intervention and its impact on customers, suppliers, and substitute
products.

In summary, these direct and limiting forces all work *jointly* to determine the average profitability of a market. The intensity of indirect
competition, the threat of competitor entry, and supplier pressures
place an upper limit on market profitability. The intensity of direct
competition, customer pressures, the threat of entry and regulatory
pressures, in turn, work to determine what the average market profitability will be relative to the upper limit. Growth in market demand
affects the degree of market attractiveness, making profitable markets
more attractive and unprofitable markets even less attractive. Growth
also impacts profitability indirectly by reducing the intensity of direct
competition and increasing the threat of competitor entry. How these
two effects net out depends on where the business stands in in its product life cycle. In embryonic markets, the reduction in the intensity of

direct competition tends to dominate any increases in entry risk. As markets mature, the threat of competitor entry becomes a larger and larger factor in limiting profitability.

Competitive Position and Value Creation

We have often heard it said that "picking the right horse" is more important than the "skill of the jockey." Managers of businesses that participate in unattractive markets, for example, frequently maintain that their business cannot possibly produce an economic profit over time due to the powerful direct and limiting forces at work in their product markets. While seemingly reasonable, in many cases they are wrong. Indeed, we have found that for most businesses, competitive position has a far greater impact on profitability than market economics do. In nearly every market, no matter how unattractive, there are businesses that are able to build a competitive advantage large enough to more than offset the poor market economics, enabling them to earn a positive economic profit consistently over time. Nucor Steel and Cooper Tire, for instance, are exemplary performers despite the fact that both companies compete in unattractive markets characterized by persistent excess capacity and price-based competition. Looked at another way, the distribution of economic profit and equity spreads across companies *within* a market is much wider than the distribution *across* markets. Not only are many companies quite profitable in unattractive markets, many companies are unprofitable even though they participate in *attractive* markets.

For example, as Exhibit 6.4 illustrates, the U.S. chemical industry, which includes a broad cross-section of chemical markets, produced an average equity spread of just under 1 percent between 1976 and 1991. Nevertheless, while industry spreads were near economic breakeven for this period, several companies were very profitable. As one example, WD-40, a small, single-product company with an extraordinary brand franchise, managed to produce an average equity spread of greater than 30 percent over this 15-year period. Conversely, Olin, a diversified company with roughly half of its assets invested in basic chemicals, generated equity returns that averaged eight percentage points less than its cost of equity capital over the period. These differences in profitability reflect to some degree the differences in the at-

EXHIBIT 6.4

Historical Equity Spreads within the Chemicals Industry (1976–91)

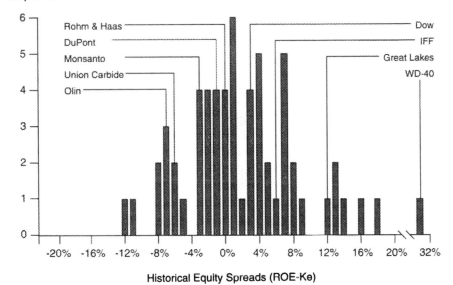

Source: Value Line Investment Survey; Marakon Associates analysis.

tractiveness of served markets, but for most businesses they reflect differences in each company's competitive position relative to the average participant in its markets.

From an economic perspective, competitive advantage can take either or both of two forms. The first is an offering, or *differentiation advantage,* based on customer perception of a superior product or service offering, resulting in a willingness to pay a premium price relative to the prices of competitive offerings. The second is a *relative economic cost advantage,* which is gained when total economic costs (operating plus capital costs) are lower than those of the average competitor. Thus, like an attractive market, an advantaged competitive position also has a precise definition when used in a value based context. *A business is competitively advantaged if, as a by-product of its offering or relative economic cost position, it generates over time a level of economic profit, or equity spread that is higher than that of the average competitor in its markets.*

Offering Advantages

In strategic terms, differentiation occurs when customers perceive a business unit's product offering (defined to include all attributes relevant to the customer buying decision) to be of higher quality, incur fewer risks, and/or perform better than competing product offerings.[4] This difference in customer-perceived benefits enables a business to price its offering at a premium to its competitors and maintain market share or, alternatively, to gain share by holding price at the same level as competitors.

It is important to understand the distinction between products or services that are merely different from those of competitors and those that have a differentiation advantage. In our experience, there is a marked tendency for managers to overestimate the uniqueness of their products. While their perceptions of differences between competing offerings can be important, they do not determine whether their offerings are or are not differentiated. Differentiation of a particular offering occurs only when *customers* perceive a significant difference in quality or benefits, with the result that *the offering is capable of commanding a price premium relative to competitor offerings.* In other words, if customers will not pay a premium price for the improvement in the offering, differentiation has not occurred. We should note here the importance of the word "capable." Once an offering has been successfully differentiated, management may choose to exploit the advantage in two ways: by increasing price to the point where it just offsets the improvement in customer benefits, leaving market share unchanged; or by pricing below this "full premium" level with the goal of building market share. By defining differentiation this way, the magnitude of a differentiation advantage can be measured explicitly over time by (1) the size of the price premium—if market shares are stable; (2) the increase in market share—if pricing is at parity with competitors; or (3) the combination of price premiums and share gains. These measures, not management "impressions," should be used to determine whether the offering is significantly differentiated.

For example, a few years ago, we worked with a business unit whose general manager was adamant about the wisdom of pursuing a differentiation strategy. In the manager's view, the business unit's products were technically far superior to all competing offerings.

However, as shown in Exhibit 6.5, only two of the unit's five product lines commanded a price premium in their respective markets without loss of market share. Thus, while clearly different from competing offerings, the business unit's products were not differentiated in the eyes of the customer. In reality, customer research (rather than the internal views of management) revealed that this particular business was actually at a substantial offering disadvantage in most of the major market segments it served. Customers had become quite sophisticated in the use of the products and were simply unwilling to pay for many of the new features that the client's engineers had developed.

We also must emphasize that building an offering advantage does not always result in value creation. As noted in Chapter One, to create shareholder value, a differentiation effort must generate a price premium over time that exceeds the costs and investment required to dis-

EXHIBIT 6.5

Measuring Differentiation

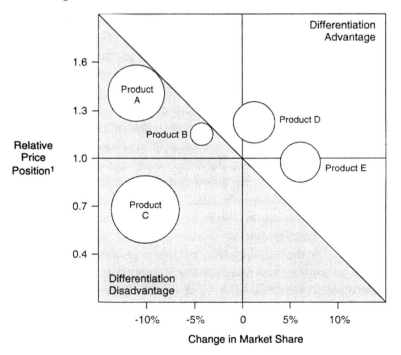

[1]Client price ÷ average price.

tinguish the offering or gain enough market share to cause an increase in revenues that exceeds both the costs of differentiation *and* the costs of expansion. By recognizing the distinction between a differentiated offering and one that is merely different, providing no additional benefits to the purchaser, managers can more easily avoid the "different but not differentiated" trap. This trap tends to be sprung when no effort has been made to determine the likely impact of a differentiation program on economic profit over time.

There are many ways to achieve higher customer benefits. Initially, most of us think of manufacturing and selling a product or service that is clearly superior to all competitive offerings in terms of perceived quality. For years, the Mercedes-Benz automobile accomplished this feat so well that its name became synonymous with the highest level of quality—people would describe a product as "the Mercedes-Benz" of its category. The American Express Card is another clear example of this type of differentiation advantage. AmEx has established a unique reputation for reliable, high-quality travel and financial services. For many years, this quality image has allowed the American Express Company to command a significant price premium in the highly competitive financial services market—a premium that reflects, in its words, the "privileges of membership."

In addition to improving the actual quality of a product or service, it is also possible to differentiate by enhancing the customers' perception of quality through superior advertising. Advertising has been a key driver of differentiation in consumer goods markets for many years. The producers of Clorox Bleach and Absolut vodka, for example, have maintained an image of higher quality than competing products—allowing each to be priced at a significant premium to its competition—despite the fact that these products are chemically indistinguishable from competing brands. The customer's perception of superior performance provided by these products has been created almost entirely by effective advertising.

While less common, explicit attempts to reduce the customer's perceived risks can also be an effective means of differentiation. For several decades, superior service capabilities and high vendor switching costs produced by proprietary architecture and software enabled IBM to build and maintain a commanding leadership position in the mainframe computer industry. Until the era of open systems dawned in the mid-1980s, risk-averse customers were very reluctant to make large capital and conversion outlays for mainframe computer systems without strong assurance of reliability on the part of the manufacturer. As a result, more than seven out of ten customers bought "Big Blue." In fact, many of the company's rivals complained that in the Management Information Systems departments of large companies it was an unwritten rule that "nobody ever got fired for buying IBM." Ironically, the move away from proprietary architecture to open systems enabled thousands of small companies to specialize in key activities, such as the manufacturing of disk drives or the writing of applications software. These companies effectively created merchant markets in these activities, destroying the economic argument for vertical integration and weakening IBM's differentiation position. As a result, IBM's huge overhead and service infrastructure, once the engine of enormous wealth creation, is now one of the focal points of management's strenuous race to improve the profitability of the company.

Economic Cost Advantages

For some products and services, particularly those viewed as commodities, building a cost-effective offering advantage can be very challenging. We acknowledge that in principle it is always possible to differentiate any product by providing *augmented* benefits, for example, extra services sold in conjunction with the product. Nonetheless, in many markets, it can be *very* difficult, if not impossible, to convince customers to pay enough of a price premium to more than offset the cost of the augmented benefits. In these markets, superior profitability will have to come from a relative economic cost advantage.

As is the case with an offering advantage, a relative economic cost advantage has a very precise definition when used in a value based context. *A business has a relative economic cost advantage if it has lower total economic costs per unit than the market average.* By total economic cost we mean the sum of total operating costs and a charge for capital, where this charge, again, represents the amount of capital employed in the business multiplied by the pretax cost of capital.

As most managers readily appreciate, this definition of a relative cost advantage is considerably different from the conventional definition, which is based only on differences in operating costs. Without full recognition of the charge for capital, investing heavily to reduce operating costs can actually increase the economic cost per unit if the investment increases the capital charge by more than the reduction in operating costs. A particularly striking example of this is the case of General Motors. Over the course of the 1980s, the company spent billions on automation and robotics, only to find itself with a much higher total economic cost per vehicle than its crosstown rival, Ford, which spent those years implementing programs designed to increase the efficiency of its work force. This broader definition of cost not only increases line management's awareness of the amount of capital invested in the business but also makes it easier to link the business unit's competitive position directly to value creation.

A relative economic cost advantage enables a business to price its product or service lower than competitors in order to gain market share and still maintain the same level of profitability, or, alternatively, to price its offering at parity with competing products or services and increase profitability. Note that while the magnitude of an offering advantage can be measured in several ways, there is only one way to measure the magnitude of an economic cost advantage, and that is by comparing the total economic cost per unit of a business against the comparable cost of its competitors—through direct observation or benchmarking.

Exhibits 6.6 and 6.7 characterize the economic cost position of two businesses from our client work. Exhibit 6.6 shows a "supply curve" designed to depict the total economic cost per unit for all competitors in a basic manufacturing market relative to each competitor's unit volume. The graph portrays clearly the client's business unit, represented by the shaded bar, as 10 percent disadvantaged relative to the average producer's economic cost and more than 20 percent disadvantaged relative to the low-cost producer. Exhibit 6.7 shows a comparison of the total economic cost of a medical equipment company, broken down into major activities, and the average competitor's total economic cost. In this case, the client has a competitive advantage, due primarily to its low-cost selling, equipment servicing, and overhead activities.

There are many sources of an economic cost advantage: access to low-cost raw materials; innovative process technology; low-cost access to distribution channels or customers; and superior operating

EXHIBIT 6.6

Market Supply Curve

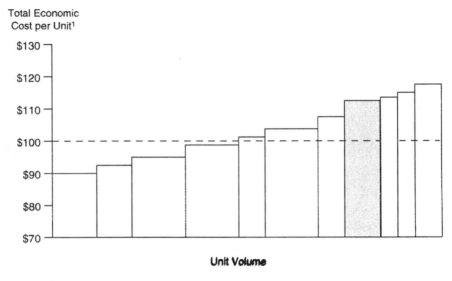

Total Economic
Cost per Unit[1]

Unit Volume

[1]*Indexed: Competitor average = 100.*

management. In addition, it may be possible to gain a relative economic cost advantage by exploiting economies of scale in some markets.

Access to low-cost raw materials usually reflects serendipity, vision, or the use of superior negotiating skills. Many of the Organization of Petroleum Exporting Countries (OPEC) producers, for example, have constructed petrochemical plants in close proximity to low-cost natural gas that they had been flaring. As another example, movie studios for years restricted their competitors' access to top box-office stars by signing these artists to long-term, exclusive contracts. For the most part, however, it is difficult to create the advantage of low-cost access to raw materials, since it is almost always in the interest of raw material suppliers to sell to as many competitors as possible.

Superior process technology is another major source of relative economic cost advantage. The best process technology, of course, is one that has a large impact on total economic cost and is proprietary. In the 1970s, for example, a new generation of catalyst technologies was introduced into many chemical refineries. For those firms that

EXHIBIT 6.7

Total Economic Cost by Activity

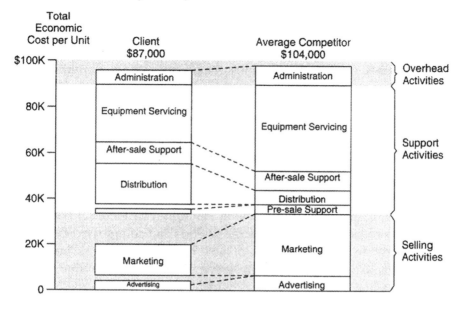

were quick to invest in the new technologies, the energy cost savings were considerable. However, those marginal players that lagged in utilizing the new catalyst technologies saw the profitability of many of their basic chemicals erode as more energy-efficient facilities began passing the cost savings on to their end customers. Eventually, any chemical producer that did not implement the new process technology became so cost-disadvantaged that it could not operate at accounting breakeven, let alone earn an economic profit.

Low-cost access to distribution or customers can be a source of great advantage in many markets. Proprietary mailing lists in the catalogue industry, access to broadcast frequencies, or having the best locations in a given retail market are examples of advantaged access to customers. In many ways, the strategy common to most packaged-food companies, namely, branding their products and advertising to create consumer demand, is an attempt to gain shelf space in grocery stores and other retail stores that provide primary access to customers.

Perhaps the most important source of a sustainable cost advantage is simply superior operating management. There are numerous examples of companies with significant and sustainable cost advantages that stem from their managements' unique abilities to run their purchasing, manufacturing, marketing, and distribution activities more efficiently than competitors do. As has been widely noted, Honda Motor Company has taken the art of manufacturing cost management to new heights. Once viewed by most Americans as nothing more than a low-end motorcycle manufacturer, Honda today is a major automotive powerhouse and a credible threat to Ford and GM worldwide. Over the course of two decades, Honda has built significant manufacturing cost and design advantages into engines and power trains, which it has exploited by rapidly expanding its share in automobile, lawn mower, marine engine, and generator markets worldwide. A key success factor for Honda has been the firm's ability to manage manufacturing costs. Low-cost assembly, combined with carefully considered product design, has reduced the firm's operating costs and compressed the cycle time between the introduction of new car models. The reduction in cycle time has purged excess inventory from its system—thus reducing its capital costs—and also provided an advantage on the offering side.

Every business is made up of a chain of activities. The product or service is developed, raw materials are procured, the product or service is produced, marketed and sold, customers are serviced, and bills are collected. For each of the activities in a business unit's chain, there is a possibility of achieving a relative economic cost advantage from economies of scale. Economies of scale can produce an economic cost advantage in three major ways. First, the business unit or the parent company is able to procure components, parts, services and/or financing in such large quantities that a discount can be negotiated with suppliers. Second, increasing scale and volume reduces the economic cost per unit by increasing capacity utilization. This type of scale economy, however, diminishes rapidly as utilization approaches 100 percent and typically works to make a business unit only less disadvantaged rather than more advantaged. Third, large businesses can use their high production volume to acquire and substitute efficient technologies that are inefficient at smaller volumes. In some markets, particularly those subject to rapid change in demand, this scale-based substitution can actually lead to an increased economic cost per unit relative to a smaller-scale, more flexible manufacturing facility. In others, particularly those where the minimum efficient scale is large relative to the size of the market, the first mover in the market can gain a significant economic cost advantage.

A good example of this third approach is Hillenbrand Industries, a Batesville, Indiana, manufacturer of caskets and hospital beds. Hillenbrand has spent millions on robotized production facilities and just-in-time inventory management systems. Both investments have given Hillenbrand a significant total economic cost advantage per unit relative to its less-automated competitors. The key to sustaining this cost advantage, however, has been the large size of the investments needed to reap the economies of scale relative to the size of the market. Once Hillenbrand preempted its competitors and made these investments, no other manufacturer could justify matching the company's capital spending, given the high odds that the volume required to make such an investment pay off could not be attained without a bloody price war. If the investment were smaller, or alternatively, if the casket market were larger, Hillenbrand's rivals would have been able to match its investments and minimize or eliminate the company's cost advantage.

Like a differentiation advantage, a relative economic cost advantage does not necessarily create value for a company's shareholders. Indeed, to create value, the investment required to drive down economic costs must be more than offset by the improvement in profitability over time or the gain in market share, depending on how management chooses to exploit the advantage. Many companies have overinvested in an attempt to gain a cost advantage, only to discover that the advantage could not be sustained long enough to produce the first dollar of return on their investment.

In summary, a business unit's competitive position in its product markets ultimately determines its profitability relative to its competitors. Businesses that have built a cost-effective competitive advantage are capable of earning equity spreads that are above the average for their market or earning average spreads and increasing their market share over time. Conversely, disadvantaged business units generate equity spreads *below* the average spread for their market. A competitive advantage can take one of two forms—an offering advantage or a relative economic cost advantage. Finally, creating a sustainable competitive advantage is not enough to ensure value creation. The advantage must produce an increase in economic profit over time that is large enough and lasts long enough to more than offset the investment required to gain the advantage in the first place.

Implications for Managing Shareholder Value

By understanding the key factors determining market economics and a business unit's overall competitive position, management can assess the current and expected profitability of the business. As shown in Exhibit 6.8, there are four general relationships between market economics, competitive position, and profitability over time.

Business units with sustainable competitive advantages in attractive markets will always be profitable—their economic profit will be substantial, their ROEs will exceed the cost of equity capital, and their market values will be greater than their book values. Coca-Cola and Merck are clear examples of companies with competitively advantaged businesses participating in attractive markets. Both are immensely profitable, and both have created enormous value for their respective shareholders.

Business units with weak competitive positions in unattractive markets will always be unprofitable—they will produce economic losses,

EXHIBIT 6.8

Linking Strategic Position to Value Creation

Market Economics	Disadvantaged	Advantaged
Attractive	Uncertain, Usually Unprofitable	Always Profitable $(ROE > K_e)$
Unattractive	Always Unprofitable $(ROE < K_e)$	Uncertain, Usually Profitable

Competitive Position

their ROEs will be less than the cost of equity capital, and their market values will be less than their book values. Bethlehem Steel holds such a position in the U.S. steel industry. Therefore, at the two extremes of market economics and competitive position, the linkage to profitability over time and value creation is direct and powerful.

In the remaining two cases, however, the linkage is less clear. As noted earlier, competitive advantage tends to have more influence on a business unit's profitability than market economics do. As a general rule, when a business has a significant competitive advantage and participates in unattractive markets, it typically is able to generate economic profits over time and, therefore, create value—but its long-term profitability obviously depends on the size and sustainability of its advantage. Boeing is a good example of a company that finds itself in this position. Finally, businesses operating with competitive disadvantages in attractive markets are usually unprofitable. Even when these business units generate positive economic profits and equity spreads, they are highly vulnerable to a deterioration in market economics, which is usually beyond management's control.

Concluding Remarks

When we first began our journey in the development of value based management, we recognized that understanding where value was being created and destroyed within a company and an individual business unit was a crucial first step in maximizing shareholder value. The first problem that we ran into was lack of forecast credibility. Since managers are not taught how to make realistic financial forecasts, and most tend to be inherently optimistic anyway, nearly all projections of financial performance are upwardly biased. Without some way of grounding the forecasts on market economies and competitive position, determining the warranted value of a business unit or company is a "garbage-in, garbage-out" process of little value to managers. The linkage between the strategic and financial determinants of value creation provides a practical economic framework for making grounded financial forecasts and accordingly, for making accurate estimates of the warranted value of a business or company. This linkage provides a foundation for undertaking a strategic position assessment, the subject we examine in Chapter Seven.

PART 3

Creating Higher-Value Strategies

CHAPTER 7

The Strategic Position Assessment

The governing objective of maximizing value requires every business unit to have a process that enables management to formulate strategic options, evaluate the impact they will have on warranted value, and effectively implement the highest-value strategy. In our view, this process has three prerequisites. First, management must have the best possible *information* about the sources and drivers of value creation in its business. Second, managers must use this information to make the best possible *choices* concerning which markets to serve and how to compete effectively in each served market. Third, the organization must possess the talent, skills, and processes needed to achieve the best possible *execution* of these strategies over time.

The best possible information results from a careful analysis of the strategic and financial determinants of value for a business. This can be obtained most effectively through what we call a *strategic position assessment*. The best possible choices result from the formulation and rigorous evaluation of creative strategic options. These two tasks comprise the strategy development process. Finally, the best possible execution can occur only if an organization's key management processes are designed to support the effort required to carry out the highest value strategy within each business unit.

This chapter focuses on the first task in the strategy development process—generating the best possible information through a strategic position assessment that delineates the key sources and drivers of value creation for a business. Chapter Eight will describe how this information can be used to help management make the best possible choices about competing effectively in each served market. Chapters Nine and Ten will outline how this information can be used to make the best possible choices about which markets to serve at the business unit and corporate level. Chapters Fourteen through Sixteen will delineate some of the key management processes necessary to ensure the best possible execution of the company's strategies over time.

Elements of the Strategic Position Assessment

In our experience, most companies are data rich but information poor. Inside most large companies are volumes of data about customers and competitors and a treasure trove of detailed financial data. This data is rarely analyzed and integrated in a way, however, that enables managers to make an accurate determination of a business unit's market economics and competitive position. Nor is the analysis routinely done in sufficient detail to derive insights into how the business might create more value. For example, conventional assessments of customer needs frequently profile what is required of a business in order to build volume but do not delineate the product or service attributes with the greatest impact on profitability. Competitor information typically benchmarks the technical or functional capabilities of rivals but often fails to provide managers with a detailed economic profile of the competition—including each competitor's relative economic cost, price, and share position by market. Finally, profitability information almost always excludes capital costs and is generally not available at the product and customer level, where it is needed most to help managers allocate time and resources within the business unit to their highest-value use.

The strategic position assessment has two primary aims. First, it generates the strategic and financial information that managers need to produce an accurate baseline valuation of the business under its current strategy, as well as a quantification of the contribution that individual products and customers make to the unit's warranted value. Second, this assessment lays the groundwork for formulating strategic

EXHIBIT 7.1

Outputs of a Business Unit Strategic Position Assessment

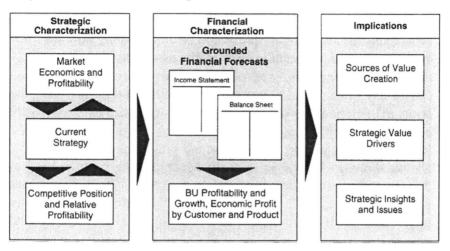

options. It enables management to identify and prioritize the key issues facing the business and quantifies the potential upside value to be realized from resolving these issues effectively.

As shown in Exhibit 7.1, a comprehensive strategic position assessment of an individual business unit has three major components: first, a *strategic characterization* of each product and customer segment—including a fact-based assessment of the attractiveness of each of its product markets as well as the unit's competitive cost and differentiation position in each of these markets; second, a *financial characterization* of each product and customer segment—including an assessment of likely future growth and profitability that is linked directly to the strategic characterization of each product and customer segment; and third, the major *implications* of both characterizations—including the sources of value creation or destruction under the business unit's current strategy, the unit's strategic value drivers, and the major issues and insights that should serve as the basis for developing alternative strategies.

In sum, a strategic position assessment provides a basis for gathering and organizing both external and internal information, and then analyzing this information in a systematic and rigorous way.

The Strategic Characterization of a Business Unit

The strategic characterization begins with an assessment of market economics to determine whether the product markets in which a business competes are currently profitable or unprofitable, how fast they are growing, and how market profitability as well as growth are likely to change over time. This is accomplished by gathering information on competitor strategies and economic profitability and by analyzing the structural determinants of market attractiveness, such as the intensity of direct competition, customer pressure, and the four limiting forces. In most cases, since the profitability and growth rates of competitors are not directly observable, in-depth benchmarking must be used to deduce each competitor's financial performance. While this strikes many managers as an almost impossible mission, the task is generally quite feasible. By thoroughly understanding the profitability and growth rate of their own business, managers can identify the specific information required to deduce each competitor's likely economic profit and growth rates. In fact, in many cases much of the information already exists within the company somewhere. Where there are information gaps, we have found that a series of third-party interviews with customers, suppliers, and employees who interact with certain competitors, coupled with an in-depth literature search, can provide the missing pieces of the puzzle. When these estimates of competitor profitability are combined with a thorough assessment of market growth, the resulting profile of market economics provides a detailed understanding of where value creation is likely to occur in all product markets the business serves.

Exhibit 7.2 illustrates the results of this process for a basic materials company. Each chart within the exhibit displays the economic profit per pound by product (designated A, B, C, . . .) versus the number of pounds sold. The chart in the upper left corner of the Exhibit is the client's profitability profile in 1992 (not a particularly good year). By benchmarking relative prices, costs, and assets, the economic profit of each of the client's four major competitors was estimated. The five profiles were added to develop a profitability profile for the market as a whole. As can be seen readily, only Products A and B produced an economic profit in 1992. Next, the underlying determinants of market economics were analyzed to identify the structural forces responsible

EXHIBIT 7.2

Strategic Characterization: Market Economics

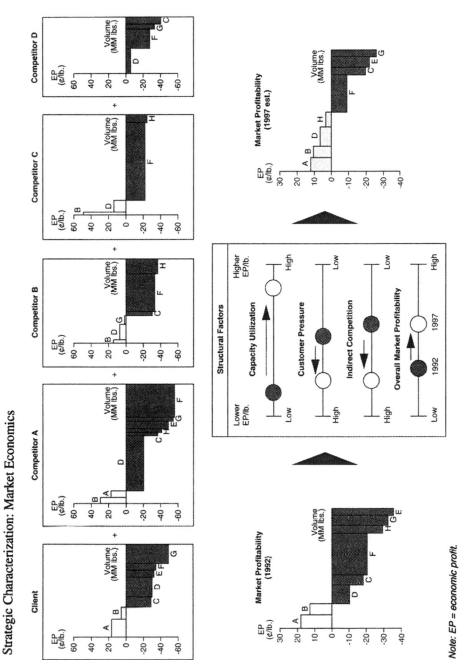

Note: EP = economic profit.

for producing the economic profit and loss in each product market segment during 1992. In this case, excess capacity created by the recession was the primary culprit. More worrisome, however, was a substantial increase in customer pressure, caused by a wave of consolidation among customers, and the introduction of a new substitute product. Finally, forecasts of each structural factor were made, so that a profile of likely market profitability and growth over the next five years could be constructed. As the profitability chart in the lower right corner of the exhibit shows, market economics were expected to improve with increasing capacity utilization but nowhere near as much as the client's management had forecast. Indeed, fundamental changes in customer pressure and the intensity of indirect competition were likely to cause continued economic losses in half of the market's segments.

The next stage in the strategic characterization focuses on developing an accurate assessment of the business unit's competitive position. Recall that competitive position is defined by relative product and service differentiation and relative economic costs. As with market economics, an accurate assessment of competitive position should be comprehensive and rely on quantitative analysis in order to build the foundation for developing alternative strategies. An accurate assessment of a business unit's differentiation position, for example, typically requires information on relative pricing by product market and changes in market share by competitor over time, along with data on customer needs and competitor offerings. Similarly, a business unit's relative economic cost position can be assessed only by benchmarking its economic costs relative to those of competitors at each major stage of its activity chain. The combination of a business unit's differentiation and economic cost position determines whether, and more important, why it will be more or less profitable than the average participant in each product market over time.

In Exhibit 7.3, we have illustrated the results of a competitive position assessment. The two bubbles represent the combined differentiation and economic cost position of this particular business unit for the current year (1992) and a forecast for 1997. The smaller triangles represent the current combined position of each major product market in 1992 and the forecast position for 1997. Note that the current disadvantaged position is expected to improve to near-competitive parity in

EXHIBIT 7.3

Strategic Characterization: Competitive Advantage

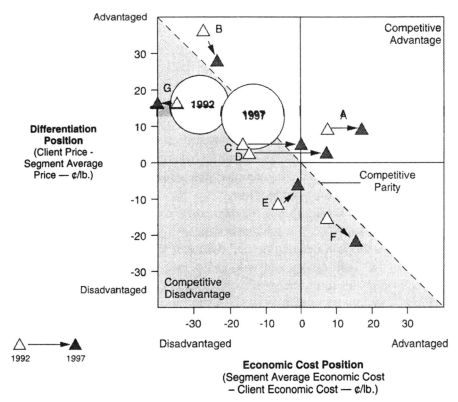

1997 as a result of management's efforts to reduce economic cost per pound in each product.

The final component of the strategic characterization is a concise description of the business unit's current strategy. This includes a clearly defined statement of the product markets that the business serves currently and plans to serve in the future as well as the competitive position the business seeks to achieve in each of these markets over time. By describing the current strategy in this way, managers can often find inconsistencies between what the strategy is designed to do and what the strategic characterization suggests may be appropriate. For example, the business may be planning to grow aggressively in markets that are unprofitable and in which the business unit does not have a sustainable competitive advantage.

The results of a detailed strategic characterization nearly always bring to light valuable insights into a business. For example, consider the characterization of a specialty chemicals business shown in Exhibit 7.4. As the left hand graph indicates, the business produced two primary product lines—Product Line X (low-density resins) and Product Line Y (high-density resins). In terms of profitability, these two product lines differed substantially. Initially, the market for the low-density resins was awash in excess capacity. As a result, competing producers had bid down prices significantly and the average producer barely broke even on an accounting basis. Superior capacity planning enabled this business to operate its facility at a much higher utilization rate than its competitors. As a result, while the market for low-density resins was unattractive, the company was able to generate a small economic profit from its product line.

The market for high-density resins, on the other hand, was near economic breakeven for the average competitor. The specialized nature of the production process, combined with extensive environmental regulations that historically had worked to limit entry, made the market more profitable on average for high-density resins than for the low-density products. In addition to enjoying more favorable market economics, the high-density product line was significantly advantaged. The company's technical support capabilities were far superior to those of its competitors, which enabled management to price its offer-

EXHIBIT 7.4

Strategic Characterization for a Specialty Chemicals Producer

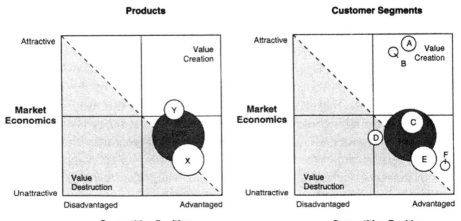

ing at a significant premium and still capture a significant share of the high-density market. The combination of breakeven market economics and a highly differentiated offering produced a substantial economic profit for the parent company.

This strategic characterization of the business varied across customer segments as well. Some customer segments were enormously profitable, while others were producing economic losses. For example, in Segment B the primary customer was a large pharmaceutical company. Since the business unit's product represented a small percentage of the total cost of manufacturing this customer's end-product—treatment for hypertension—customer price sensitivity was very low and the business was able to obtain very high prices. Furthermore, the company had a modest cost advantage, which was based on its unique manufacturing process and a highly efficient sales and customer service organization. Thus, the market was structurally attractive and the business had an advantaged competitive position, a combination that produced an ROE in this particular customer segment that consistently exceeded 25 percent.

This strategic characterization had a major impact on management's perception of the business unit and its strategy. First, the information contained in the strategic characterization enabled management to forge a consensus around the need to search for alternative strategies. Prior to the assessment, there had been a strong aversion to even considering such alternatives. Second, while the business as a whole was economically profitable, management recognized that profitability was quite vulnerable to further deterioration in market economics. This caused management to ask: "What steps can we take to improve the profitability of the market overall?" Later, when management turned to developing strategic options, several opportunities to improve industry capacity utilization through consolidation and joint venture strategies were explored. Third, the current strategy did not effectively address the fact that economic profitability varied dramatically across the unit's two product lines and six market segments. This observed inconsistency in profitability spurred management to develop options for altering the mix of products it sold to various customer segments, improving its offering (especially to its most valuable customers) and reducing the cost of serving its unprofitable customers.

The strategic characterization of a business always produces a fact-based assessment of both market economics and competitive position. As noted at the end of Chapter Six, this information and analysis can be linked directly to the likely profitability and growth rates for a business unit, enabling management to develop credible financial forecasts.

The Financial Characterization of a Business Unit

The purpose of the financial characterization is to develop a credible financial expression of the business unit's likely performance under its current strategy. This requires that a business have complete income statements and balance sheets in order to measure its returns, growth, and cash flows. Since many companies do not have complete financial statements at the business unit level, this information—particularly the balance sheet data—often has to be created. Appendix B outlines many of the issues involved in creating these management accounts for the first time. Once a business unit is able to generate these statements, financial forecasts should fully reflect the expected profitability of its product markets as well as its competitive position in them. More briefly, the unit's financial forecasts should be grounded on strategic reality.

The experiences of a specialty metals producer illustrate how the strategic characterization of a business can help managers develop more realistic financial forecasts. In 1991, the business had a broad participation in several specialty metals markets. Unfortunately, the markets were all plagued by tremendous overcapacity and limited opportunities for product differentiation. The strategic characterization of the business suggested that the average producer in the market was not earning its cost of equity capital—in fact, the average equity spread in the market was estimated to be around –4 percent. Furthermore, detailed benchmarking of the unit's economic costs relative to competitors suggested that it was significantly disadvantaged—due in large part to the age of its production facilities and the outdated process technology employed at several sites. Given the business unit's disadvantaged competitive position in an extremely unprofitable market, the strategic characterization suggested that its current strategy would probably never earn a return equal to its cost of equity capital.

EXHIBIT 7.5

Linking the Strategic Characterization to Financial Forecasts

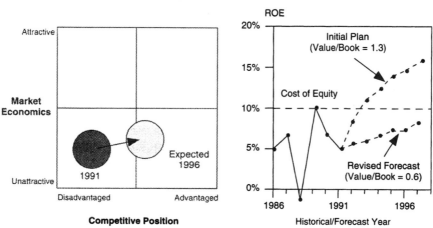

Specialty Metals Illustration

After complete income statements and balance sheets were developed for the business, these suspicions proved to be justified. In fact, as Exhibit 7.5 suggests, the business unit's returns were well below the cost of equity—averaging approximately 7 percent between 1986 and 1991 relative to a cost of equity capital of more than 12 percent.

The business unit's management team, however, was determined to turn the business around. In fact, the strategic plan called for a complete overhaul of its production processes—including the modernization of several plants and a number of other manufacturing initiatives designed to reduce costs. Management contended that these actions would dramatically improve competitive position and lead to an equally dramatic rebound in profitability. As Exhibit 7.5 shows, management forecast that the unit's ROE would improve substantially—from less than 7 percent in 1991 to more than 17 percent in 1996.

While management's financial forecasts seemed reasonable enough from a purely internal perspective, they were clearly inconsistent with the strategic characterization of the business. Indeed, a careful assessment of competitor strategies revealed that each and every one of the business unit's rivals was also modernizing its production facilities and instituting similar manufacturing programs. Thus, the fiercely competitive nature of the specialty metals market suggested that much, if not all, of the resulting cost savings would be passed on to the customer in the form of lower prices. In short, the structure of the market made it highly unlikely that anyone in the industry—even its most advantaged player—would ever generate the kind of returns that management forecast.

This information, combined with a reassessment of the capital investment needed to implement management's plans, led to a sharp downward revision in the financial forecasts—thereby producing a financial characterization of the business that was consistent with the strategic characterization. More important, however, the strategic and financial characterization encouraged management to think more creatively about its current strategy. Once the poor structural conditions present in many of the business unit's markets were quantified, management began to consider alternatives that would reduce capital spending far more than assumed in the initial plan and minimize the business unit's participation in markets generating the largest economic losses.

In addition to producing credible forecasts of future performance, the financial characterization generates valuable information about the economic profitability of individual products and customers within a business unit. For example, Exhibit 7.6 displays the strategic and financial characterization from a position assessment of a large manufacturing business. In this case, the business unit in question was very profitable overall—generating an average return on equity of more than 25 percent and growing 7 to 8 percent per year. Nevertheless, when profitability information was developed for each product, management discovered that nearly half of the business unit's products were generating economic losses. This relationship is not uncommon. In fact, we frequently find that 100 percent of a business unit's economic profit is produced by as little as 30 percent of its products and customers. Understanding the concentration of economic profit and value creation within a business unit (or within the company's portfolio of business units) is extremely important for making better choices concerning the markets a business should serve and the business units a company should keep in its portfolio. We will return to these topics in Chapters Nine and Ten.

EXHIBIT 7.6

Product Profitability Profile

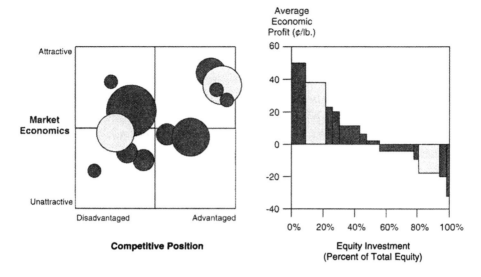

Competitive Position

Equity Investment
(Percent of Total Equity)

The concentration of economic profit across products highlighted two crucial issues that were later embodied in alternative strategies for the business. First, management realized that many of the business unit's products were inappropriately targeted for growth. Because the company used margin data to measure product profitability (and, accordingly, ignored differences in overhead and capital intensity), management was misinformed about the true economic profitability of its products. As a result, many products that appear at the left-hand side of the profitability distribution (bar chart) in Exhibit 7.6 were actually being targeted for elimination as part of a rationalization plan. Moreover, two products on the right-hand side of the profitability distribution, which had been part of the business unit's heritage, were being positioned and priced for high volume so they could absorb a larger portion of the unit's fixed operating costs. Further analysis revealed that these products were actually being priced at or below the variable economic costs required to produce and market them. As a result, the higher volumes produced ever-larger economic losses. Once management quantified the true economic profitability of each product, it moved quickly to increase prices in order to rationalize many of these products.

Second, management realized that the business had opportunities to manage product substitution more effectively. For example, each of the two light-shaded products in Exhibit 7.6 was a substitute for the other. The profitable product on the left-hand side of the bar chart was new and preferred by customers because it had several features that were missing from the older version. The sales force viewed the product as less profitable on a direct margin basis and was reluctant to push it extensively. This margin-based view had led management to conclude that it should phase in the rate of substitution over the longest time period possible by pricing the new product at a substantial premium to the old one—resulting in substantially lower economic profits from the combination of the two products than an alternative pricing strategy would have produced.

As these examples illustrate, the financial characterization of a business involves far more than simply extrapolating line items within a business unit's income statement and balance sheet. If management is careful to link the financial characterization to a robust strategic characterization, the information and analyses produced by this process can be invaluable in guiding the search for more valuable strategic options.

Implications

In studying a great many business units over the years, we have found that managers typically point to three important benefits that accrue from a thorough strategic position assessment.

First, the position assessment provides an unbiased, baseline valuation of the entire business unit under its current strategy and clearly delineates which products and customers are creating value, which are destroying value, and why. This appraisal of the business provides management with a standard for comparing alternative strategies. Moreover, as noted earlier, the valuation itself can motivate the entire management team to strive for better performance or, alternatively, fight to sustain superior performance. In those areas of the business that are not generating an economic profit, management is usually energized to identify strategies that can restore profitability. On the other hand, in those areas of the business that are economically profitable, most management teams are challenged to identify ways to leverage their favorable market economics or competitive advantages to the fullest.

The second benefit of a strategic position assessment is the identification of a business unit's *strategic value drivers.* In brief, these are the "organizational capabilities" that are controllable by management and have the greatest impact on the business unit's future competitive position and potential for value creation. They are identified by carefully analyzing the fundamental sources of competitive advantage and understanding the implications of these advantages for the business unit's warranted value.

As we outlined in Chapter Six, a business unit's overall competitive position is determined by the degree to which its product offerings are differentiated and by its relative economic costs. These determinants explain a business unit's profitability and growth relative to those of its competitors. Peeling away a bit more of the onion, we find two fundamental sources of differentiation or economic cost advantage. First, a business can own proprietary *strategic assets*—consisting of both tangible and intangible forms of property—that provide the ability to earn an equity spread greater than that of competitors. There are many familiar examples of strategic assets: the trademarks and brand names of Coca-Cola, Marlboro, and Kellogg; the purchasing volume and access to shelf space that Procter & Gamble and Unilever have built over the years; Arco's crude oil reserves in Alaska's North Slope; the superior site locations of McDonald's restaurants; Merck's portfolio of ethical drug patents; and Microsoft's installed base of MS-DOS software. Each of these assets can be considered a form of "inherited wealth" that is difficult, if not altogether impossible, for competitors to duplicate.

Second, many business units have unique *organizational capabilities* that enable them to earn an equity spread above those of their competitors. In contrast to a business unit's strategic assets, which often generate an economic profit over time regardless of the skills of the current management team, its organizational capabilities must be enhanced continuously to ensure that they remain a source of meaningful competitive advantage. Examples of superior organizational capabilities include new product development at Intel and Microsoft; Wal-Mart's extraordinary processes for restocking its stores; Nordstrom's legendary customer service; Goldman Sachs's management of client relationships; Merck's extremely productive research and development process; Hanson Trust's ability to make profitable acquisitions; and Emerson Electric's planning and acquisition integration processes. It is important to note that many of these organizational capabilities can actually produce strategic assets—as when an R&D capability produces a patented product, or a capability in new product development produces a valuable new brand. In addition, an organizational capability may be the ability to manage more effectively another business unit's strategic assets—for example, Gillette's management of Braun small appliances and Paper Mate pens.

While both strategic assets and organizational capabilities are sources of competitive advantage and help to explain a business unit's *current* level of profitability and growth in a market, the strategic value drivers consist solely of those sources that are controllable by management and have the greatest impact on *future* value creation. Since a business unit's strategic assets already produce a stream of economic profit and, thus, a contribution to warranted value, they cannot make a large impact on future value creation on their own. Looking out in time, large increments of value creation can be generated only by using unique organizational capabilities to build and sustain competitive advantage and, possibly, create new strategic assets for future generations of managers to exploit. For example, Kraft's Velveeta Cheese brand—a strategic asset to the company—may produce economic profit that makes the cheese business worth five times the amount of capital invested. Over the next five years, however, the brand itself will not cause the unit's warranted value to double or triple; these levels of performance can be attained only through superior capabilities in strategic planning, brand management, and new product development. In short, while both strategic assets and organizational capabilities influence a business unit's current level of value creation, only its organizational capabilities can generate significant growth in warranted value over time.

There are two reasons why identifying these controllable, high-impact capabilities is important. First, the process of identifying strategic value drivers correctly prioritizes the characteristics of the business that are likely to have the greatest impact on competitive advantage and, therefore, profitability and growth relative to competitors. In our experience, most management teams can produce a lengthy list of what they perceive to be the value drivers, based on their intuition and experience, but they seldom agree on how to prioritize them. Reaching consensus on the organizational capabilities likely to have greatest impact on relative profitability and growth nearly always produces fresh thinking about alternative strategies. For example, management at one specialty chemicals company discovered that the most important strategic value driver for its business was on-site technical services. These services were highly valued by customers and had enabled the company to capture a significant price premium for many of its products. While management had been aware of the importance of these services, they had not been given the resources necessary to defend the advantage or exploit it more fully. In fact, by comparing the economic profit generated by each customer account with the level of spending on customer services, management found that many of the unit's most profitable customers were woefully underserved, an observation that led to development of several options for redirecting resources.

Identifying a business unit's strategic value drivers can also stimulate management to consider bold changes in strategy. At one large technology company, for example, management found that the strategic value drivers were shifting inexorably from engineering skills to distribution capabilities as customers learned more and more about how to use the product. The business unit's competitive advantage had always been built around excellence in engineering, not the capability to deliver products through low-cost distribution channels. Thus, the shift presented management with a major threat to the business unit's profitability. To counter this threat, several options for acquiring low-cost distribution capabilities were developed—ranging from a series of start-ups, using distribution capabilities transferred from other business units within the company, to an all-out search for outside distributors that might be profitably acquired.

Second, identifying a business unit's strategic value driver is important because it can often be leveraged in order to enter new markets profitably. This was the situation that Michael Eisner and Frank Wells found at the Walt Disney Company in 1984, when they were put in charge of one of the world's greatest collection of strategic assets—

the company's beloved cartoon characters. By leveraging these strategic assets, management was able to enter a number of new businesses profitably—including retailing, publishing, and the hotel development business—and add roughly 28 percent to the company's revenue base in just five years. Seen in this light, strategic value drivers can be invaluable to the development of product and market extension strategies at both the business unit and corporate level, a subject we will address in greater detail in Chapters Nine and Ten.

Finally, in addition to identifying the sources and drivers of a business unit's warranted value, the position assessment also generates a large volume of strategic information that can be used to develop insights, identify key issues and stimulate the search for options. For example, the assessment of customer needs and buying behavior is often a real eye-opener. Many longstanding beliefs about the features or attributes that customers value most can turn out to be erroneous. Benchmarking the business unit's offering accurately against competitive offerings nearly always reveals a surprise or two about differentiation of offerings from the customer's viewpoint. Benchmarking against competitor costs and assets usually offers additional insight into sources of value creation and destruction. We have also found that once managers accept the fact that a long-standing rival has managed to reduce costs and asset intensity below those of their own business unit, they become highly motivated to seek out ways to match or better the competitor's performance.

Detailed knowledge of likely competitor strategies is also prized information that can play a large role in identifying issues and generating creative strategic options for the business. When the strategic information is thoughtfully integrated with the information about product and customer profitability, most managers quickly develop a list of ideas for reallocation of their time and energy, as well as capital, to enhance good growth and minimize or eliminate bad growth.

Concluding Remarks

The strategic position assessment for a business unit has three major components: the strategic characterization, the financial characterization, and the implications of these characterizations for the major sources and drivers of value creation or destruction under the unit's current strategy. This assessment has two aims. The first is to generate the strategic and financial information necessary to determine the contribution that each of the unit's products and customers makes to warranted value. The second is to lay the groundwork for the next task in the strategy development process: formulating and evaluating strategy options. We turn our attention to this task in Chapters Eight, Nine, and Ten.

CHAPTER 8

Competitive Strategy

In nearly all competitive situations, there is a wide range of alternative strategies that a business could pursue. The best managers understand this and work hard to continuously formulate and evaluate alternative strategies for their businesses. They realize that unless the current strategy is challenged by new ideas about how to compete more effectively, their businesses can become ossified and vulnerable to the forces of competition. In our experience, however, many managers within large companies do not routinely develop and evaluate alternative strategies that are meaningfully different from their current strategy. Moreover, in those cases where several alternatives are developed, usually only one is truly viable. Henry Kissinger, former U.S. secretary of state, reportedly complained of a similar problem. Whenever he asked for foreign policy options, the story goes, his staff always produced three: the first would invariably lead to thermonuclear war, the second would result in unconditional surrender to the Soviet Union, and the third option was the one that his staff really wanted to pursue.

There are many reasons that managers do not routinely develop strategic options. For some, the strategic planning process itself is an obstacle, since in most companies it neither requires nor encourages the formulation of meaningful alternatives. For others, top-down goals for achieving a target earnings per share or growth forecast constrain the development of alternative strategies designed to achieve some other objective such as value creation. The most common deterrent to development of alternatives, however, is that management lacks *both* the necessary information and an effective framework for formulating and evaluating strategic options.

In Chapter Seven, we described how an integrated strategic and financial characterization of a business can produce the best possible information concerning the sources and drivers of value creation. This chapter will focus on how managers can use this information to formulate and evaluate strategic options that represent fresh thinking about how the business can compete most effectively and create additional value for the parent company. Initially we outline the two key elements of business strategy: participation strategy, focusing on which markets to serve; and competitive strategy, focusing on how to compete in each served market. We then describe the three related components of competitive strategy and highlight some issues managers should consider in formulating competitive options. Finally, we show how to evaluate integrated competitive strategies that involve complex trade-offs between profitability and growth over time.

Two Key Elements of Business Strategy

In many companies, the process of strategy development is loosely defined and applied in different ways by different people. In some cases, strategy development simply involves a statement of intent or the desired direction in which management wants to guide the business. In other cases, strategy development is narrowly focused on specific actions required to improve current operating performance. In only a few instances have we seen a strategy development process that facilitates the *formulation, evaluation,* and *implementation* of options that are likely to increase the value created by each business within the company. The process involves three major tasks:

- First, to facilitate the *formulation* of meaningful options, management should undertake a detailed strategic position assessment of the business, specifying its market economics, competitive position and current strategy, as well as the profiles of product and customer profitability and the unit's strategic value drivers.

- Second, to facilitate the *evaluation* of alternatives, each feasible strategic option must be converted into a grounded financial forecast so that it can be valued. These options cannot be just qualitative statements of direction, they must include specific quantitative profitability and growth targets over time and describe the resources necessary to reach these targets.
- Third, to facilitate the *implementation* of the highest-value strategy, the strategy development process must result in a business plan that includes the specific initiatives and actions required for the business unit's success.

On the basis of these considerations, we define a business strategy as a predetermined sequence of actions designed to change the competitive environment in a way that creates the highest possible value for a business.

As we noted at the beginning of Chapter Six, a business can create value in two ways—participate in attractive markets or build and sustain a competitive advantage. Accordingly, the options formulation process centers on two questions: "In which markets should the business participate?" and "How should the business compete in each of its markets?" The answers to these questions form the basis of a business unit's *participation strategy* and its *competitive strategy,* as illustrated in Exhibit 8.1.

A firm's participation strategy is a statement of the product markets in which it will compete. In essence, participation strategy draws the boundaries around the customers the business will serve, and consequently, those it will not serve. There is a wide spectrum of possible participation options for most businesses—ranging from very broad participation (similar to that pursued by Goodyear in the worldwide tire market) to highly focused, or niche, participation (such as Cooper Tire's strategy to compete only in the replacement auto tire market in the United States). At the corporate level, participation strategy concerns itself with entry into new businesses and exit from existing ones, which we will cover in Chapter Ten. At the business unit level, participation strategy focuses on entry into unserved markets and exit from currently served markets, which is the subject of Chapter Nine.

A business unit's competitive strategy spells out the means that management will use to build and sustain competitive advantage

EXHIBIT 8.1

Elements of Business Strategy

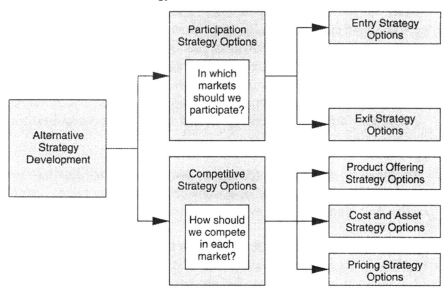

and/or reduce competitive disadvantage in a particular served market. Development of a competitive strategy involves three related tasks: determining how best to differentiate the *product and/or service offering,* how best to configure and manage the business unit's *costs and assets,* and how to *price* the product or service offering. The first two of these tasks address this question: "What combination of product offering and economic costs is likely to create the largest, most sustainable advantage relative to competitors?" In contrast, pricing strategy addresses a separate question, namely, "What is the best way to exploit our advantages or cope with our disadvantages so that the combination of all three components of competitive strategy yields the highest warranted value for the business unit?"

Product Offering Strategy

The primary goal of product offering strategy is to build, maintain, or defend a differentiation advantage profitably. More specifically, the goal is to identify opportunities to improve differentiation where the price premium created by increased customer benefits exceeds the total economic cost of providing the incremental improvement in the product offering. Development of profitable differentiation options obviously requires a thorough understanding of current and future customer needs and buying behavior, as well as an objective assessment of how customers perceive the business unit's current offerings in the market. This can be accomplished with a variety of techniques, including surveys, focus groups, and conjoint analysis (a sophisticated research tool that quantifies customer preferences). With this type of information, we have found that managers can easily begin to formulate a variety of product offering options with potential for enhancing differentiation.

All differentiation options involve an improvement of the product offering position as viewed by customers. This can be accomplished by improving the product offering itself, by improving how the product is promoted, or by improving both (see Exhibit 8.2). Improving the product offering typically involves identifying customer needs more effectively than the competition does and tailoring the attributes, or features, of the offering to satisfy these needs. Gillette's 1990 introduction of the Sensor razor, for example, represented a dramatic improvement in the company's core product line. After investing $200 million in product development, Gillette was able to mount its twin

EXHIBIT 8.2

Formulating a Product Offering Strategy: The Starting Point

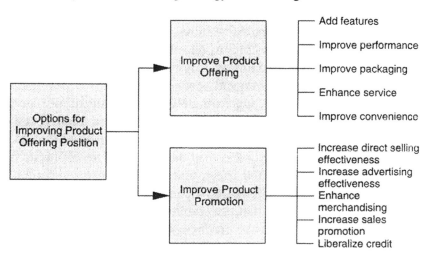

shaving blades on an independent suspension system that vastly improved the "closeness" of the shave without sacrificing "comfort". Within two years, the Sensor product line was producing $500 million of revenue at a 40 percent operating margin, which was largely responsible for increasing the company's return on investment from 20 to 26 percent and nearly doubling Gillette's stock price.

In some cases, the best way to improve a business unit's offering position is to change the promotion of an existing product instead of physically changing the product itself. The shirtmaker Van Heusen, for example, significantly improved its product offering by simply changing its approach to advertising. Instead of matching the likes of Arrow and Hathaway with ads targeting male readers of such magazines as *Esquire* and *Gentlemen's Quarterly,* Van Heusen aimed its advertising at women—recognizing that as many as 70 percent of all men's clothing purchases are made by women—and developed a successful print campaign in women's magazines.

As emphasized earlier, management's search for product offering alternatives should reflect the information and analyses provided by the strategic position assessment. For advantaged businesses competing in attractive markets, for example, increasing growth will almost always create more value, assuming that profitability is not severely penalized. Accordingly, management should focus on identifying all offering options capable of increasing profitable growth. Frito-Lay, for example, has been able to maintain differentiation and build market share by aggressively developing new products, more attractive packaging, and more efficient distribution. After an in-depth analysis of customer needs, management introduced several line extensions—new varieties of its existing Doritos, Lays, and Fritos brands—to expand its market share in the frequent-snackers segment (i.e., one-third of U.S. consumers, who buy approximately three-fourths of all snack chips). At the same time, management introduced more than 20 new brands of snack food to meet the preferences of medium to light snackers. As a result, in 1992, Frito-Lay had the largest share of the U.S. snack chip market, nearly four times that of its nearest competitor, while maintaining an ROE above 20 percent.

In the case of businesses that are currently destroying shareholder value, management's search for product offering alternatives should focus primarily on ways to increase profitability over time. The Gap, for example, has completely revamped its product offering and positioning strategy over the past ten years. Back in the early 1980s, the company's common stock was trading at a slight premium to its book value and consumers viewed the retailer as "a schlocky, just-jeans chain catering to teenage shopping mall groupies." In 1983, with the jeans craze fading, Donald Fisher, founder of the company, plucked Millard Drexler from the president's post at Ann Taylor to take over operations at The Gap. Upon his arrival at the company, Drexler changed practically everything—putting more emphasis on profitable, private-label goods and reducing the proportion of sales generated by Levi Strauss products from nearly 25 percent to less than 5 percent. The Gap's new focus has produced record profits for the company and paid off handsomely for shareholders as well. Back in 1983, The Gap's return on equity was below 10 percent. By 1990 it had ballooned to over 35 percent, and the firm's earnings growth rate had more than doubled.

In most businesses, profitability varies considerably across product lines and customer groups, requiring a highly tailored mix of product offering and promotion strategies. A large department store chain, for example, recently conducted a strategic position assessment that led to consideration of some significantly different product offering and promotion strategies for its portfolio of merchandise categories and stores. While the retailer as a whole was very profitable, earning a return on equity of more than 30 percent, profitability varied dramatically in various merchandise categories. In fact, as Exhibit 8.3 shows, more than 50 percent of the retailer's product lines, representing about 30 percent of sales, did not earn a positive economic profit. This meant that in individual stores about half of the average floor space was devoted to product categories that the company was unable to differentiate successfully. Further detail in the position assessment showed that even in very profitable departments, some products were not creating value, while departments earning low returns had some very profitable products. Further, with customer buying patterns differing considerably by regional market area, there were marked geographic differences in store and product economic profitability. Not surprisingly, it turned out that other retailers aimed their sharpest competitive attacks against the product groups earning the highest economic profit.

From this information, management identified four key strategic is-

EXHIBIT 8.3

Merchandise Positioning Strategy for a Department Store Chain

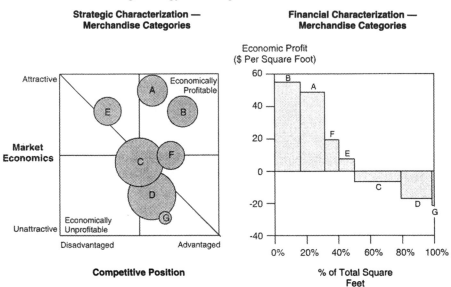

sues—all interrelated—that appeared to offer the greatest potential for value creation: (1) finding the optimal product mix to achieve the highest economic profit per square foot rather than the highest revenue per square foot in each store; (2) finding an effective strategy to counter competitive threats to the highest-value product groups; (3) finding the best store operating configuration, including department layouts, to generate the maximum customer purchases of the most profitable goods; and (4) finding the optimal regional product offering and configuration strategies to accommodate geographic differences in customer preferences.

A number of high-potential alternatives were developed to address each issue. This was followed by thorough field trials of each potential product mix alternative, each potential store configuration alternative, and several new approaches to serving different regions of the country. In addition, a number of very aggressive marketing alternatives were developed to blunt competitive incursions into the retailer's most profitable product groups. The resulting strategy, designed to double the value of this already very successful business in three to four years, included significant changes in all four areas. The product offering was simplified and stripped of value-consuming products, with a re-

EXHIBIT 8.4

Alternative Department Store Layouts

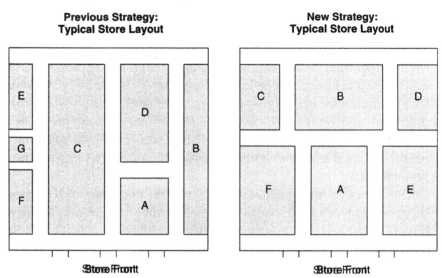

sulting reduction of operating complexity and overhead costs. Most stores were reconfigured to increase customer awareness and purchases of high-value goods, as illustrated in Exhibit 8.4. In addition, market share erosion was arrested through much more precisely targeted advertising, which was possible only because of the detailed product profitability and competitor strategy information developed in the position assessment. In fact, in a number of regions, market share losses were actually reversed.

Development of creative product offering options is only one of the three related components of competitive strategy. For many businesses, as with the department store chain, finding cost-effective ways to differentiate their offering will have the greatest impact on value creation. For other businesses, the greatest impact will come from establishing and maintaining the lowest economic cost per unit, our next subject.

Cost and Asset Strategy

The goal of cost and asset strategy is to build and sustain an economic cost advantage. The relative importance of an economic cost advantage depends, of course, on the particular forces that determine market profitability and, even more, on the willingness of customers to pay price premiums for differentiated products. In pure commodity markets, where competition is focused primarily on price, only the most cost-advantaged competitors are likely to be economically profitable. On the other hand, in markets with highly differentiated product offerings and limited price competition, a business unit's relative economic cost position may not play as critical a role in its ability to generate substantial economic profits over time. Therefore, as in product offering strategy, a detailed understanding of market economics and competitive position is essential to the formulation of cost and asset strategy options.

There are two fundamental ways to improve the economic cost position of any business. First, as Exhibit 8.5 shows in summary form, a business can reconfigure its activity chain and change the degree to which it is vertically integrated. Chrysler, for example, in an attempt to improve its disadvantaged cost and asset position has significantly decreased the percentage of internally manufactured automobile parts. In effect, the company has become less vertically integrated over time. IBM, on the other hand, increased the percentage of personal com-

EXHIBIT 8.5

Formulating a Cost and Asset Strategy: The Starting Point

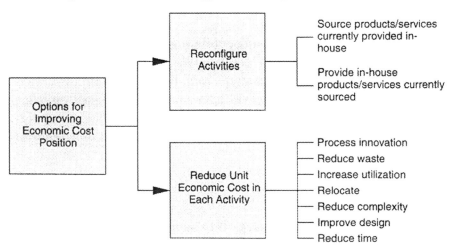

puter parts produced internally during the 1980s in an attempt to lower its manufacturing costs. These two examples illustrate the kinds of configuration alternatives that all businesses (especially those that are already vertically integrated) should consider in the search for the highest-value cost and asset option.

Second, a business unit can exploit opportunities to reduce operating costs, capital costs, or both, for each activity it performs internally. There are many ways to reduce economic costs, including employment of more efficient process technology; reducing waste; increasing utilization by reducing excess capacity; relocating product and/or supply activities; reducing complexity through better facility loading; improving product and process design; and, compressing production cycle time. Whether or not any of these options are appropriate for a particular business will depend on a wide variety of considerations, including the nature of its competition and its own capabilities. In the end, the goal for each option is to produce a sustainable reduction in economic costs that exceeds any loss in customer benefits.

The current strategic position and profitability of the business should play an important role in guiding management's search for value-creating cost and asset options. For profitable businesses, management should focus on delivering the lowest total economic cost consistent with maintaining (and even increasing) profitable growth. For example, H.J. Heinz has gained a significant cost advantage in ketchup production by developing a higher-yielding (plumper) tomato. In addition, the company has reduced its tomato-to-ketchup manufacturing time from 11 hours to an average five hours, decreased the thickness and weight of its ketchup containers, and shifted from two labels to one on each container. These seemingly minor adjustments, combined with cultivation techniques that cut the company's water use by some 10 percent, have saved Heinz millions of dollars without altering its basic product quality in the eyes of the consumer.[1] In essence, Heinz has identified the strategic cost and asset drivers at each stage of its activity chain and has exploited its capability to increase raw materials yield and reduce both cycle time and packaging weight to enhance its economic cost position. In contrast, for a lesson on how not to reduce costs for a profitable product, consider the case of Schlitz Beer, which reformulated its product to reduce operating expenses and in so doing alienated all but its most loyal customers—a strategy change from which the company never recovered.

For unprofitable businesses, management should focus on ways to reverse the unit's economic loss. John Deere & Company—a Moline, Illinois-based manufacturer of farm equipment—has fought tenaciously to slash manufacturing costs in its five operating units. In its axle spindles division, for example, Deere has used cellular manufacturing techniques—the grouping of machinery to cut manufacturing time and the overhead costs associated with work in process—to cut production costs by 15 percent. Deere management has also worked hard to cut labor costs by gradually reducing the company's work force. Hans Becherer, the company's Chief Executive Officer, notes that Deere produced the same tonnage in 1990 that it did ten years earlier—but with one-third fewer workers. "We've cut costs 2 percent to 2.5 percent a year for the past five years," Becherer asserts, "and that should continue."[2]

The most valuable cost and asset options typically will be those that combine changes in the configuration of the activity chain with changes in techniques that work to lower the economic cost of each activity. For example, a recent position assessment for a large glass container business found that its current strategy—based on years of following "tried and true" industry practices—would probably never produce an economic profit. To begin with, the glass container market is fiercely competitive, with intense direct competition and strong customer pressures. The assessment of market economics suggested that the average competitor was earning a return on equity well below the cost of equity capital. Further, while this particular business unit had a high market share, its relative economic cost position was poor in many geographic markets. In fact, when the business was benchmarked against its principal rivals, its economic cost per unit was estimated to be 15 percent higher than that of the average competitor in the market. Thus, the business unit's disadvantaged competitive position in a structurally unattractive market fully explained the fact that its return on equity had hovered around 4 percent during most of the preceding decade. More important, the position assessment revealed that profitability was unlikely to improve without a dramatic change in strategy.

Based on the strategic and financial characterization of the business, management concluded that options to differentiate its containers were unfeasible. This reinforced the need for a quantum reduction in economic costs. A detailed study identified the two most important strategic cost and asset drivers: plant siting, which determined the maximum shipping distance (MSD), and capacity management, as measured by production scale and capacity utilization. Because glass containers are fragile and bulky, transportation costs tend to be quite high. All things being equal, a competitor would prefer to minimize shipping distances in order to reduce its transportation costs. At the same time, however, the glass production process is extremely capital-intensive. In fact, as much as 75 percent of the average competitor's economic costs are fixed. As a result, manufacturing scale and capacity utilization are the two economic factors that most heavily influence production costs. Assuming equivalent capacity utilization, for example, a manufacturer would prefer to have large facilities in order to gain economies of scale. Alternatively, assuming equivalent production scale, a producer would prefer to have higher rates of utilization in order to amortize fixed costs.

Once management determined exactly how these strategic drivers affected economic cost, it was possible to formulate alternative strategies for improving both its competitive position and profitability. As Exhibit 8.6 illustrates, the business unit's current plant configuration for one region (the Northeast) was designed to minimize transportation costs. To keep shipping distances under 200 miles (which the industry had always assumed to be the maximum distance at which it was profitable to serve customers), the business operated six plants, each running at an average capacity utilization of approximately 60 percent. Another configuration—Alternative A in Exhibit 8.6—called for closing two plants and operating four, raising the average capacity utilization to approximately 85 percent. This alternative enabled the business to serve all its existing customers but required an increase of the maximum shipping distance to just over 300 miles. Finally, a third configuration—Alternative B—was developed. Under this configuration, the business would operate only two plants at 90 percent capacity utilization and the maximum shipping distance would be increased to approximately 500 miles. To implement Alternative B, five plants would have to be closed and one new facility built. However, the two remaining production facilities would use the latest technology and be

EXHIBIT 8.6

Configuration Strategy for a Glass Containers Manufacturer, Northeast Region

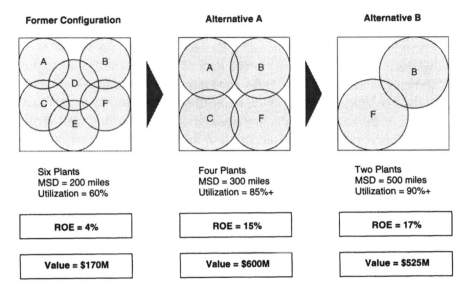

Former Configuration

Six Plants
MSD = 200 miles
Utilization = 60%

ROE = 4%

Value = $170M

Alternative A

Four Plants
MSD = 300 miles
Utilization = 85%+

ROE = 15%

Value = $600M

Alternative B

Two Plants
MSD = 500 miles
Utilization = 90%+

ROE = 17%

Value = $525M

Note: MSD = maximum shipping distance.

much larger than any other plant in the system, thereby reducing economic cost per unit well below those of any competitor in the market.

When the three options were evaluated, management discovered that the two configuration options had such a large impact on economic cost that the business could afford much higher transportation costs and still earn an economic profit. The cost savings provided an opportunity to reengineer and invest additional capital in the business unit's entire logistics activity, further reducing operating costs and improving delivery times. While both options were clearly more valuable than the existing strategy, selection of the best option involved a detailed assessment of the likely profitability and growth that each would produce. While the current configuration produced a return on equity averaging around 4 percent, Alternative B offered the prospect of increasing ROE to roughly 17 percent—more than five percentage points above the cost of equity. Alternative A was deemed likely to increase ROE to 15 percent. Only after management looked at the value impact was it convinced that Alternative A was the clear winner. By reducing the business unit's cost structure without sacrificing profitable volume, Alternative A produced a somewhat lower ROE but much higher growth in economic profit over time and, thus, a higher warranted value. After some debate, management implemented the four-plant configuration strategy, which, indeed, improved the business unit's performance within three years, as predicted.

As this case illustrates, when a business develops creative cost and asset options, it can benefit enormously from a detailed understanding of the strategic drivers of economic cost. Combined with accurate product and customer profitability data, these drivers can be used to make fundamental changes in the way a business competes in its product markets and significant improvements in its long-term profitability.

Pricing Strategy

For all those businesses that are not simply "price takers" in a commodity market, the strategy for pricing the unit's products and services can have a profound impact on profitability over time. Yet pricing is often one of the most underexploited opportunities for creating value. Because many companies lack the information and the analytical framework needed to determine the likely impact of pricing options on economic profit over time, they miss opportunities to exploit competitive advantages or cope with disadvantages more effectively. Many advantaged products and services that could command substantial price premiums are discounted in attempts to build market share, thus sacrificing economic profit at best and generating competitive price-cutting at worst. Conversely, some advantaged products may be overpriced, sacrificing valuable market share and encouraging competitive entry.

The goal of pricing strategy is to determine for each product offering the price over time that most effectively exploits a competitive advantage or copes with a disadvantage, producing the highest level of value creation. While this goal is straightforward, the issues surrounding pricing strategy are usually quite complex. In particular, since price changes are so visible for most businesses, the likely customer and competitor response to each pricing option must be thoroughly assessed and integrated into the financial forecasts.

In general, for any product or service that is advantaged, management has two polar pricing options. Price can be set at parity with competing offerings in an attempt to exploit the advantage by building share; or price can be set at the highest premium over competitor offerings that is justified by the perceived differentiation, so the advantage is exploited through higher margins and higher profitability over time. Alternatively, if a competitor has achieved an offering advantage and decided to attack, attempting to exploit its advantage by building market share, management can discount price below the competing offerings to protect market share and sacrifice profitability, or match the price of the advantaged offering to protect profitability and sacrifice share.

The same polar options are available for any product or service that has achieved an economic cost advantage. Management can exploit the advantage by pricing at parity with competitors and boosting profitability over time while holding market share, or it can discount from competitor prices in order to build market share while maintaining its profitability. Alternatively, if a competitor has a substantial economic cost advantage and chooses to reduce price in an attempt to gain share, management can respond by matching the price cut, thereby sacrificing profitability in order to maintain share, or holding price, thereby sacrificing share in order to protect profitability.

There are, of course, many alternatives between these two extremes. For example, a business unit with a substantial advantage in a particular product offering might choose to price at a premium over competitors but not as high as the advantage would justify. Management might then decide to reinvest a portion of the earnings produced by the price premium in additional promotion which, if effective, would add another increment to the offering's advantage. The overall effect of this option might be only a slight increase in profitability but a significant gain in market share, as competitors struggle to match both the offering and promotion advantages.

Given the wide range of options and likely responses from both customers and competitors, we have found the guidelines in Exhibit 8.7 a useful starting point for evaluating alternative pricing strategies. At-

EXHIBIT 8.7

Formulating a Price Strategy: The Starting Point

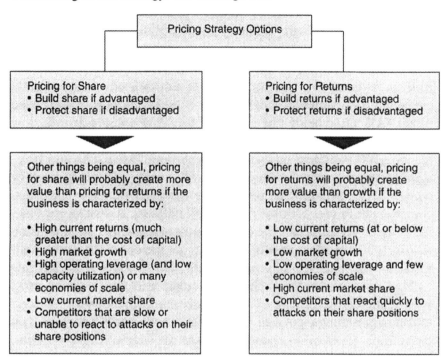

tempting to exploit an advantage by pricing to build market share (or cope with a disadvantage by pricing to protect share) will probably be the most valuable option for businesses characterized by high current profitability, high market growth, high operating leverage, low current share, and competitors that are likely to react slowly, if at all. Taco Bell is a case in point. As noted in Chapter Two, in the early 1990s this U.S. chain of Mexican fast food restaurants gained a large advantage in economic cost by reconfiguring its activity chain. To exploit the advantage, management adopted "value pricing" (a term used to describe price cutting) to attract consumers from the more expensive burger giants, notably McDonald's, Burger King, and Wendy's. Taco Bell offered an entire menu for under $1.00 and heavily promoted the price difference between its fast food and that of its rivals—the Big

Mac, the Whopper, and Wendy's Deluxe—each priced at nearly $2.00 in some regional markets. Since its larger competitors were slow to match Taco Bell's pricing, the strategy contributed significantly to a nine-point increase in the company's share of the profitable fast-food market over the 1988–1992 period.

In contrast, pricing for profitability—that is, pricing to increase ROE if advantaged or protect ROE if disadvantaged—will generally create more value than pricing for share if the business is characterized by an ROE at or below the cost of equity, low market growth, low operating leverage, an already-high market share, and competitors that react quickly to attacks on their share positions. The new Disney management team pursued such a profitability-oriented pricing strategy when it first took over the reins of the company in 1984. For years, even though Disney's theme parks drew millions of visitors per year, they earned ROEs below the cost of equity capital and suffered from relatively low market growth. Management increased the price of admission to the parks by 30 percent in 1985 and was relieved when gate receipts continued to grow. Since customers at Disney's theme parks were relatively insensitive to ticket prices and competitors were eager to follow the company's lead, its price hike had virtually no impact on the millions of families clamoring to see the Magic Kingdom. Thus, the pricing strategy produced a large increase in profitability without much, if any, reduction in the growth of its customer base. In fact, management's pricing strategy was a key factor in boosting Disney's consolidated return on equity from 7 percent to more than 20 percent in less than three years.

As another example of how pricing trade-offs must be evaluated, consider the choices a large pharmaceutical manufacturer faced recently when a rival undertook a price-based attack on its key product line. Like many ethical pharmaceuticals, this business unit's line was extremely profitable, earning an average ROE exceeding 80 percent. (This high level of profitability was due in part to the fact that the company had already expensed the considerable amount of research required to develop the product years earlier; over the product's entire life cycle, its ROE was closer to 20 percent.) While the business held a 60 percent share of the U.S. market, a new entrant had introduced a product with nearly identical chemical properties and had substantially cut its prices to several large hospital buying groups in an attempt to build market share rapidly. While management was most unhappy about this change in the competitive landscape, it was reluctant to respond by matching these cuts for fear of precipitating an all-out price war. On the other hand, management was well aware of the value of each market share point lost to the new entrant. Thus, the question was: "Which defensive strategy would minimize the decrease in the value of the business unit: holding price and losing share, or cutting price and holding share?"

A study of the two options' impact on economic profit over time showed that a strategy of matching price reductions in order to maintain market share was likely to be worth far more than maintaining current prices and sacrificing share to the new entrant, even though it meant a large sacrifice of near-term profitability. On the basis of data gathered from historical contract bids, management concluded that a 3 percent price cut by the competitor would probably cause the loss of as much as 30 percent market share over time if not matched quickly and decisively. When this analysis was combined with a detailed analysis of the new competitor's economics, it became clear that the "match all price cuts" strategy would produce the least damaging outcome. Indeed, as Exhibit 8.8 shows, this option dominated all others except in the unlikely scenario where management would be forced to match ten consecutive price cuts in one year. In short, the high current returns generated by this business suggested that failure to match the competitor's pricing strategy immediately would result in a significant loss of value for the company's shareholders. When the strategy of matching all price cuts was implemented, the competitor cut prices four successive times until, apparently, it decided that the price war had no further economic benefit. Within months, price cutting stopped and the business unit's share stabilized.

The complexity of pricing strategy reinforces the need for good strategic and financial information and an analytical framework capable of assessing the economic trade-offs inherent in the various options. By understanding the likely impact of each option on customers and competitors, management can quantify the economic trade-offs and make the choices necessary to ensure long-term competitiveness and maximum value creation.

EXHIBIT 8.8

Competitive Pricing Alternatives in Pharmaceuticals

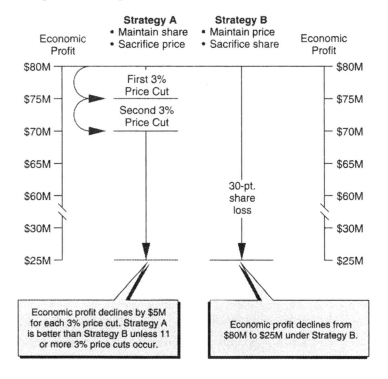

Evaluating Integrated Competitive Strategy Options

Although we have described each of the three elements of competitive strategy separately, in most cases business units must evaluate these elements simultaneously. For example, a strategy that improves a business unit's offering position may well increase economic cost and will always present management with a variety of pricing options. Alternatively, a strategy that lowers economic cost may well reduce product quality and affect perceived differentiation, again requiring an evaluation of pricing options. Given these linkages, the various elements of competitive strategy should be combined into several integrated options so that their likely impact over time on market economics, competitive position, and profitability can be evaluated.

A large U.S. specialty paper company provides a good example of how to develop and evaluate integrated options. Over several decades, the business had aggressively pursued a strategy of international expansion, building a network of seven major plants—one in the United States and six spread around the world. The strategy had been extremely successful, but, as happens frequently, years of success had caused management to become somewhat complacent. This complacency was shattered when a large Japanese rival launched an aggressive campaign to build share in selected markets, focusing particularly on the United States. Over a two-year period, the attack succeeded in taking away share from the business unit and causing a deterioration in its profitability. As a result, management decided to undertake a detailed strategic position assessment as a first step in identifying the best defense against the attack.

The strategic position assessment produced three important insights. The first came from profitability measurement. Since management had traditionally focused most of its attention on operating margins, the shift to measuring economic profit per unit (in thousands of square feet, or KSF) produced a new perspective on where money was being made and lost. More fundamentally, though, the conventional way of matching supply and demand by geographic proximity (e.g., all of Latin America was served by the Brazilian plant) was replaced by "economic matching," in which the highest-priced market was served by the lowest-cost plant (including the modest increment in transportation costs) and the lowest-priced market was served by the highest-cost plant. As illustrated in Exhibit 8.9, this produced a profitability profile that showed only 60 percent of the unit's volume was currently profitable. (Note that economic profit is measured in the graph by the difference between the average selling price in each market and the total economic cost per KSF of each plant, which is represented by the shaded areas between the two lines.)

The second insight came from benchmarking against the Japanese competitor. Even though the U.S. business had a sizable advantage in plant scale, its economic cost was actually much higher than that of its rival, due to poor asset management. In contrast to the unit's own practices, the competitor ran its facilities continuously and adopted a variety of techniques, such as just-in-time delivery, to minimize the amount of capital employed in its business. Furthermore, the competitor exploited its economic cost advantage by pricing aggressively in the most attractive markets to gain as much share as possible.

EXHIBIT 8.9

Profitability Profile of Specialty Paper Business

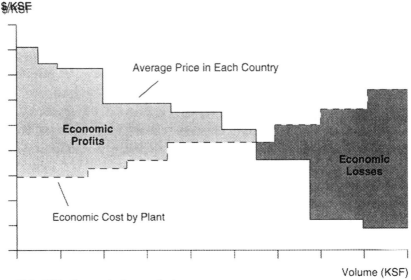

$/KSF

Note: KSF = thousands of square feet.

The third insight came from comparing the unit's differentiation position with that of its main competitor in each market around the world. As the largest supplier with a dominant share, the business had thrived on delivering a standardized product of uniformly high quality. While its competitor's product quality was not quite as high, management was surprised to learn that distributors and other agents in the various distribution channels were increasingly imputing larger benefits to channel support services and local promotion, activities in which the competitor excelled. As a result, the warranted differentiation premium between the two product offerings was much lower than the current price premiums in nearly all markets, so that the U.S. unit was inadvertently pricing to lose share.

The position assessment clearly identified two strategic value drivers: asset management—with a particular emphasis on inventories and fixed capacity—and local marketing and distribution channel management. These drivers and the profitability data stimulated the formulation of a wide range of alternative strategies, consisting of various combinations of modest to radical changes in the unit's product offering, plant configuration, and pricing in local markets. Once the options were converted into financial forecasts and evaluated for their impact on warranted value, one emerged a clear winner. This option involved three related initiatives. First, the two highest-cost plants were removed from the network. One was converted to other uses and "sold" to a business unit within the company; the second was mothballed. In addition, new processes were developed to manage working capital, especially inventories, and increase plant uptime. The net effect of these actions was a decline in economic cost per KSF, which produced a 15 percent advantage for the business unit relative to its Japanese rival. Second, a new organization was developed to create and manage local marketing programs and the business unit's relationships with all agents in the distribution channel. These programs focused on identifying and meeting the needs of both the unit's agents and its end-use customers in ways that the competitor found difficult to match, thus reestablishing most of the warranted differentiation premiums in each

EXHIBIT 8.10

Impact of New Competitive Strategy on Profitability Profile

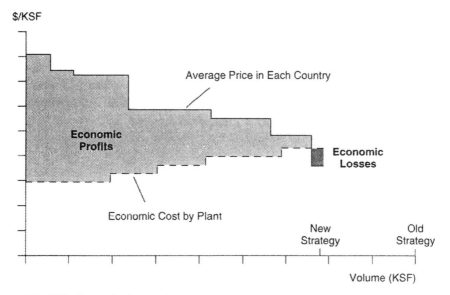

Note: KSF = thousands of square feet.

of the company's major markets. Third, management changed its pricing strategy in each local market, reducing prices in some countries to exploit its advantage by building share and increasing prices in others to enhance profitability. In particular, management intentionally raised prices in a few markets to reduce revenue and minimize the volume sold to the unit's most unprofitable customer segments.

As one might expect, the new strategy produced a substantial change in the unit's profitability profile, as shown in Exhibit 8.10, and a near doubling in its warranted value. In fact, since the strategy was implemented several years ago, the business unit's operating income has increased by more than 50 percent, its capital employed (over and above the plant write-off) has actually declined slightly, and its overall market share has improved by nearly 10 percent. Perhaps just as important, the success of the strategy has had the effect of "taking the wind out of the sails" of its Japanese competitor, forcing it on the defensive in many markets around the world.

Concluding Remarks

Formulating competitive strategy is one of management's most demanding tasks. While strategy development has a very large creative element, we have found that a rigorous strategic position assessment and the guidelines presented in this chapter can stimulate development of many imaginative options. Those managers who become highly skilled in this process will not only improve their ability to find and implement the most valuable competitive strategies, they will also enhance their ability to react quickly to the myriad of unforeseen events and opportunities that impact all businesses.

CHAPTER 9

Participation Strategy

In Chapter Eight we described how a strategic position assessment can be used to make better choices of ways to compete most effectively in a business unit's existing product markets. We also emphasized that making these choices requires the development and evaluation of alternative competitive strategies. In this chapter, we outline how this same approach can be used to make better choices concerning the product markets a business should serve. The process of making these choices illustrates what we call a business unit's *participation strategy.*

The development of a participation strategy involves two tasks. The first is to identify all new markets the business can enter profitably and determine how the entry should take place. The second is to identify any of the currently served markets the business should exit and determine how the exit, or withdrawal, should be accomplished.

In our experience, there are usually many opportunities to create value by developing a better participation strategy. Indeed, because value creation tends to be so highly concentrated, many businesses have the potential to double their warranted value within a two- or three-year period simply by increasing the growth of their most profitable product market units and withdrawing resources from those products and customers that produce large, irreversible economic losses.

In this chapter we describe how the strategic position assessment can be used to help identify entry and exit candidates. We then discuss the formulation and evaluation of entry and exit strategy options. Fi-

155

nally, we show how the development of participation and competitive strategies can be integrated, using a recent case study.

Identifying Candidates for Entry and Exit

Profitability typically varies widely across served markets within a business, due to differences in market economics and competitive position. The position of each product market unit on the matrix in Exhibit 9.1 can guide management's search for entry and exit candidates.

The best entry candidates are usually those product markets that are attractive and closely related to existing markets in which the business has a competitive cost or differentiation advantage. Conversely, most exit candidates will come from those currently served product markets that are unattractive and in which the business is likely to remain competitively disadvantaged over time. In structurally attractive markets where the business is competitively disadvantaged and in unattractive markets where the business is competitively advantaged, the signals are far less clear. However, since economic profit tends to be higher for advantaged businesses even in unattractive markets, there may well be some entry candidates adjacent to these markets. Alterna-

EXHIBIT 9.1

Characteristics of Candidates for Exit From Currently Served Markets and Candidates for Entry in New Markets

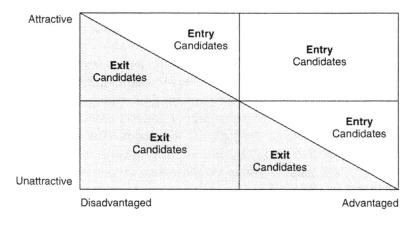

tively, there may well be exit candidates in attractive market segments where the business is highly disadvantaged.

In the next two sections, we discuss some general guidelines that managers can use to formulate effective entry and exit strategies. We note here two different ways to implement any entry strategy: by start-up (often referred to as internal business development), and by acquisition/joint venture (often called external business or corporate development). In this chapter, we focus exclusively on entry by start-up, or internal development initiatives. We deal with external development initiatives as part of corporate strategy in Chapter Ten.

Developing Entry Strategies

Management's search for entry candidates should be guided by three general criteria. First, the market should be economically profitable and likely to remain so over time.[1] Second, the business unit should be confident that it can secure and sustain a competitive advantage in the market. And third, the barriers to entry should be viewed as surmountable.[2] It is important to note that these guidelines say nothing about the size or growth of the market, the two characteristics that dominate most discussions of market entry. As we emphasized in Chapter Six, growth magnifies the attractiveness of economically profitable markets and makes economically unprofitable markets even more unattractive. Thus, growth, in and of itself, should not be used as a criterion for making entry decisions without first determining whether the market is likely to be economically profitable over time.

While it may sometimes be possible to enter unattractive markets and still operate profitably, the effort is analogous to swimming against the tide. Unless the new market is only somewhat unattractive and management is highly confident that it can secure a large advantage, the chances are good that the entry will be unable to overcome the economic forces that are driving the average competitor's ROE below the cost of equity capital. The airline industry is riddled with the remains of firms that did not heed this warning—companies such as America West, Midway, and People's Express.

Even in attractive markets, profitable entry nearly always will depend on the size and duration of the advantage that can be created in the new market. Clearly then, the best candidates will be those markets in which the business unit's strategic value drivers can be leveraged, or extended, to create a sustainable competitive advantage. This may be based on organizational capabilities that enable the business to satisfy customer needs in the new market better than competitors can, or it may be based on the ability to satisfy needs at a much lower economic cost than existing competitors. Typically, the higher the degree of relatedness between a new market and the existing served markets, the higher the odds that a business unit's organizational capabilities can be successfully leveraged to create advantage.

Hillenbrand Industries used this approach in founding the Forethought Group, the company's funeral-planning and insurance subsidiary. In the eyes of funeral directors, Hillenbrand has long had a reputation for service and quality. The Batesville Casket Company, a key Hillenbrand subsidiary, is the leading manufacturer and marketer of caskets in the United States. In 1985, in response to requests by funeral directors for the capability to offer prearranged funeral services, Hillenbrand created Forethought funeral planning—an insurance service that covers the cost of a prearranged funeral. The company's entry into a very attractive segment of the insurance market leveraged its existing relationships with funeral directors and its leadership position in caskets to create a significant differentiation advantage in an entirely new product market.

Finally, most attractive markets have high entry barriers. These barriers can take many forms, but typically they act to drive up the initial investment required to establish a meaningful presence in the new market, drive down the profitability and growth over time, or both. Thus, it is not enough for a business to enter an economically attractive market with a modest competitive advantage. If entry barriers are high, any new entrant must be capable of gaining and holding a *sizable* differentiation or economic cost advantage in order to create value.

The likely size and duration of the advantage is highly dependent on how incumbent competitors respond. Since competition for incremental share is always less intense than for existing share, incumbents in faster-growing markets tend to respond less aggressively than those in mature markets, increasing the odds somewhat that entry into faster-growing markets will be profitable. In slow-growing markets with well-entrenched incumbents, profitable entry can be virtually impossible.

Clorox's ill-fated trek into the detergent business is a particularly instructive example of what can happen if management underestimates the competitive response. In 1989, flush with cash from its success in marketing Clorox Bleach, the company decided to enter the household detergents market.[3] Clorox had long dominated the bleach segment, a relatively small niche of the consumer soap and detergents market. Management at Clorox must have thought the strategy made sense. After all, the markets were closely related, and the advantages necessary for success in the laundry detergent business—existing brand equity, effective brand management (particularly in advertising), and access to distribution channels—seemed similar to those that Clorox had in the bleach segment and could extend to other markets. Regrettably, challenging such a giant as Procter & Gamble in one of its core markets was simply too big a bite for Clorox. Indeed, as one analyst pointed out, "Clorox's $1.48 billion in annual revenue last year doesn't even match the operating earnings Procter reaped from Tide, its flagship detergent."[4] The Cincinnati-based household products giant reacted instantly to the introduction of Clorox Detergent, rolling out its Tide With Bleach brand even before Clorox was up and running with its new product. When unveiling its new detergent to market analysts, Clorox had reported that the company planned to spend $80 million on a national promotion and advertising campaign. In fact, Clorox Detergent never even made it into national distribution. On the eve of the company's exit from the detergent segment, Clorox management lamented: "Since we began the initial expansion of Clorox Detergent, the economics of the detergent business have changed and the long-term outlook for our brand is not promising."[5] The failed entry produced a loss of around $25 million a year for the company between 1989 and 1991.

Many entry strategies obviously produce far better results than this one did. In general, strategies that have followed the guidelines described above have succeeded in creating value. As one example, a large pharmaceuticals manufacturer was able to leverage a proprietary drug delivery technology to successfully enter and gain a significant advantage in several off-patent drug markets. The search for new markets to enter was initiated a few years ago, as growth in the company's primary markets began to slow. After several months the search identified the off-patent ethical pharmaceuticals market as a candidate for entry. This market was structurally attractive—the average incumbent earned an estimated equity spread of 3 to 4 percent—and was growing rapidly. Further, no incumbent in the market at the time was offering a drug delivery system of quality comparable to that of the company's system. By conducting a thorough analysis of each segment in the off-patent market, management ranked the segments by their attractiveness, potential advantage to be gained from their drug delivery system, and barriers to entry. The top segments were then targeted for entry in rapid sequence, utilizing existing facilities to manufacture the new systems. This entry strategy proved quite profitable for the company. Within three years, the business unit had successfully penetrated each of the top-ranked segments, bolstering its equity spread by five percentage points and more than doubling its growth rate.

For those businesses that compete in attractive markets or enjoy sustainable advantages, related entry strategies represent a logical way to increase profitable growth. By successfully entering new markets, managers can often maintain high levels of profitability while simultaneously increasing growth. When successful, this combination of high profitability and above-average growth translates directly into large contributions to warranted value.

Developing Exit Strategies

There are two ways to reduce the scope of participation: Management can exit unprofitable markets or market segments, or it can rationalize unprofitable products. For most businesses, exit options involve some combination of the two.

The case for exiting an unprofitable market or market segment is most compelling when the business is significantly disadvantaged, has been participating in the market for some time, and the odds are high that neither market economics nor the unit's competitive position will improve in the future. In cyclical markets serious consideration of an exit option usually begins in the downturn stage and is thus complicated by the difficulty of determining when market economics will improve as well as the fear of getting out at the bottom. It is crucial in these cases to evaluate both market economics and the business unit's competitive position over at least one entire cycle rather than a shorter time period (such as the company's planning period). By assessing the business unit's strategic position over one or more market cycles, many cyclical markets turn out to be far less profitable, on average, than their managers believed prior to examining the data, while other cyclical markets are surprisingly profitable. In our experience, this process provides a far more objective basis to evaluate an exit option and may lead to a decision to exit closer to the top of the market cycle than the bottom.

In most other markets exit options should be considered as soon as market economics or the business unit's competitive position deteriorate to the point where economic losses begin to mount. Hewlett-Packard pursued such an exit strategy in the hand-held calculator market. Beginning in the early 1980s, HP realized that the capabilities of microprocessor chips would dramatically alter the economics of the calculator market, changing products that were previously highly differentiated (HP's first calculators were priced in excess of $700) into commodities. Instead of participating broadly in the market and competing head-to-head with Texas Instruments and a variety of Asian electronics companies, HP chose to focus solely on the high end of the market. Leveraging its strong R&D capability, HP introduced a continuous stream of innovative calculators with ever-increasing power and functionality at high price points. With each new product introduction, volume surged until competitors were able to duplicate the new features. As prices were cut, HP refused to match them fully and instead harvested its market position, generating large cash flows that it plowed back into R&D to fund the next round of innovation. Thus, HP systematically entered and withdrew from various segments of the calculator market as soon as the market economics deteriorated to a point where earning a return above the cost of capital was no longer possible.

Economic profitability often can be increased not only by withdrawing from unprofitable markets and market segments but also by pruning unprofitable products or product lines. Product rationalization has become a common source of performance improvement in many businesses—profitable and unprofitable alike. However, the economic benefits to be derived from rationalization depend heavily on an accurate analysis of the economic profit produced by individual products and services. When this information is unavailable, the odds go up that the wrong products will be rationalized or the process will be blocked by lack of consensus about where to rationalize.

In one industrial products business, for example, product line proliferation had become a serious threat to profitability. Over the years, the number of products this particular business offered its customers had mushroomed from a single item with a strong competitive position and remarkable financial performance to a complex labyrinth of over 8,000 products. Since the market for the business unit's core product had been extremely profitable, incremental products had been added to the portfolio with little or no evaluation of their potential profitability. Over time, however, market conditions changed. Capable international competitors emerged with more-focused product offerings and extensive customer service networks. When these new entrants began to reduce prices aggressively on the business unit's most profitable core products, the unit's management thus found itself caught in a quagmire—running a cumbersome operation and coming under intense pressure from senior management to improve profitability.

Product line rationalization proved to be the way out of the quagmire. A careful analysis of the profitability of each of the unit's products revealed that over 80 percent of its value was created by a mere 120 products. The remaining 7,900 products in the unit's portfolio were responsible for the lion's share of the support costs, held more than half of the business unit's current assets (primarily unsold inventories), and were not strategically linked to any of the120 strong sellers. By rationalizing the product line and significantly reducing support overhead, management was able to reduce complexity and reverse the slide in profitability in less than two years.

We should point out here that many businesses, including this industrial products company, recognize the need to rationalize products periodically in order to improve performance. Without a thorough grounding in the principles of economic profitability, however, we have found a strong tendency among managers to rationalize based primarily on volume, with the idea that low-volume products are less cost-effective and less profitable than their high-volume counterparts. Once good product profitability data become available, though, it often becomes clear that many low-volume products are highly profitable (because they serve niche markets where premium prices can be charged) and many high-volume products are unprofitable (because the high volumes are the result of heavy discounting). Therefore, managers must be careful to resist the temptation to rationalize products based on volume alone and instead ground their product rationalization decision on a complete understanding of economic profitability.

Since there are extensive interdependencies among the product market units within a business, the decision to downsize is always complex and difficult. The ultimate criterion for making the decision is the comparison of the value of the business before downsizing with the value afterward, taking account of all exit costs and negative side effects. Negative side effects usually occur when the sharing of customers, costs, or assets is extensive, or when the business is part of a vertically integrated activity chain. For example, if distribution channels are linked, shrinking a business unit's product line can cause dealers or distributors to respond by reducing the level of support they give the remaining products. Thus, the benefits of exiting one market or market segment must be weighed against the possibility of reducing the profitability of an entire product line. In another common case, the upstream manufacture of an unprofitable product may be essential to the preservation of a competitive cost advantage in other downstream products that are profitable. Here, too, the benefits of exit from the upstream unit must be weighed against the resulting reduction in the downstream units' cost advantages.

Understanding the linkages between businesses, markets, and product lines is obviously very important. The mere existence of these linkages, however, should not be used as an excuse for inaction. As tends to happen too often in the case of bundled products, the interdependencies between horizontally—or vertically—linked product-market units should not block the analysis of exit options, especially for businesses that are unprofitable or near economic breakeven. Indeed, if too much weight is put on product market linkage, management may overlook consideration of partial exit options and focus only on all-or-nothing exit decisions. Fearful of making radical cuts, the natural response is often to do nothing and suffer the consequences of declining competitiveness and profitability only to later discover that dramatic steps must be taken to save the business.

While the profitability information contained in the strategic position assessment almost always highlights potential exit candidates, in practice, it is often difficult to build a consensus to exit a product market. We find that managers must frequently overcome two obstacles before they can identify and implement the highest-value participation strategy in their business. First, there is a strong tendency in many businesses to evaluate all major entry and exit options by using the analytical technique of "marginal economics." It calculates the net present value of entry and exit alternatives by taking into account only what are perceived to be the "incremental" revenue, costs, and capital requirements rather than analyzing the likely impact of these decisions on the warranted value of the entire business. Since there are almost always some fixed costs and assets in every business, this approach has the effect of making nearly all entry decisions look far more profitable than they really are and making the vast majority of exit decisions look economically unattractive. These errors can be particularly egregious when a business has substantial excess capacity. In these instances, incremental costs are typically so low that entering any new market, or adding any number of new products for existing customers, will look promising. A senior manager of a large manufacturing company made the point effectively this way: "We made all the right incremental decisions, but today we find ourselves in a bunch of businesses we should not be in and holding a bunch of assets we never should have acquired . . . If we're not careful, we'll end up incrementalizing ourselves into oblivion."

Second, in addition to marginal economics, the institutional imperative for growth is so prevalent in large companies that it frequently precludes managers from considering exit alternatives properly. While many aspects of the institutional imperative act to bias decisions toward higher growth, the most familiar of them perhaps is the tendency among most large companies to reward their senior executives in proportion to the number of people working under them or to the absolute size of the business measured in terms of sales, assets, and earnings. Wherever this type of reward system exists, most managers will be highly enthusiastic about entering new markets and developing (or acquiring) new products, and will be loath to part with any piece of their empire. Who can blame them for responding rationally to the rules of the game? Unless these obstacles can be overcome, identifying the highest-value participation options will be most difficult. We will return to this subject in Chapter Eleven.

Evaluating Integrated Participation Strategies

For nearly all businesses, especially those with multiple product lines serving a variety of different customer groups, the development of participation options will focus simultaneously on entry and exit. Thus, while understanding how to evaluate specific entry and exit options is important, the issue most managers face is not whether to participate in one market or another but the degree to which it should participate in each market. In most cases, management must choose between participating broadly and serving all segments of a given market, or participating more narrowly as a niche competitor.

Changes in a business unit's participation strategy usually will necessitate changes in its product offering, cost and asset, and pricing strategies as well. For instance, a narrow participation strategy might involve segmenting the market by customer needs, tailoring the product offering to enhance differentiation in several target segments, and increasing prices to more than offset the increase in economic cost incurred. The choice of which strategy to pursue should be made, of course, by determining which integrated option produces the highest warranted value for the business.

A recent assignment with a large printing materials manufacturer illustrates how integrated participation strategies can be formulated and evaluated in a way that helps managers make better choices concerning the future direction of their business. This business was a major supplier to the printing and publishing industry. With the advent of computer technology and related storage media, the growth of most printing materials markets slowed, putting pressure on profitability. Indeed, in the early 1980s the market was very attractive, earning equity spreads in the range of 15 to 20 percent, but by the end of the decade most competitors were earning equity spreads barely above zero and a reversal in this trend was nowhere in sight. Starting in 1987, the business entered more and more customer markets with the hopes of maintaining its historical sales volumes. Unfortunately, while the strategy was successful at maintaining revenue growth, margins declined and overall profitability suffered.

As Exhibit 9.2 shows, a strategic position assessment for the business uncovered an astounding concentration of value creation—more than 100 percent of the value creation was generated by four major product lines. The remaining 15 product lines were responsible for the majority of the sales and support costs and more than half of the business unit's capital investment. Value creation was also concentrated across customer segments. For example, the product line sold into the high-volume, low-priced Newspaper segment was actually worth less than

EXHIBIT 9.2

Product and Customer Profitability Profile

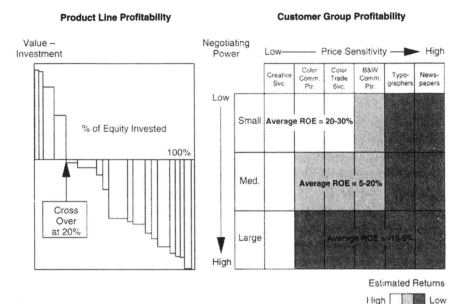

nothing—generating accounting losses for the business and requiring far more capital than any other segment. At the other extreme the Creative Services and Color Commercial Printers markets were enormously profitable, generating returns on equity well above the cost of equity capital.

Most of the business unit's growth over the past few years, however, came from adding high-volume Newspaper accounts. This occurred because the sales force consciously neglected the hard-to-reach, low-volume segments in order to concentrate on getting high-volume orders from newspapers. When management examined sales force call data, it was disturbed by the findings. As it turned out, a sales representative had to make only five calls to convince the average Newspaper customer to purchase the company's product—largely because the customer's buying decision was based almost entirely on price. Landing an average Color Commercial Printer sale, however, could take as many as 30 calls. Nevertheless, the margin on these accounts more than offset the sixfold difference in call intensity. Since the sales organization was compensated entirely on sales volume, it naturally focused on those customers that would generate the largest commissions in the shortest period of time and spent very little time calling on the lower-volume accounts. In effect, the sales force was working diligently to garner more and more unprofitable account volume, effectively ignoring the most valuable customers.

With this information in hand, management developed two alternative participation options. The first was a "selective-growth" strategy, which called for continued participation in each existing customer segment, coupled with a substantially increased investment in the more attractive customer markets. The second was a "refocused-segment-participation" strategy, which called for the business to exit the unprofitable Newspaper segment, prune the product portfolio, and channel the sales effort toward Color Commercial Printers, Creative Services, and other attractive markets. While the first option required a substantial refocusing of the sales and marketing organization, it did not require the elimination of any items from the existing product line. The second option, on the other hand, required a shift in sales focus and elimination of 30 percent of the business unit's product line. Both options required a significant reduction in support overhead and elimination of all nonproductive assets.

As Exhibit 9.3 shows, the evaluation of the participation strategy alternatives indicated that while both alternatives would create more value than the business unit's current strategy, the refocused-segment-participation strategy had the highest value. The valuation results were driven largely by differences in segment mix across the three strategies. Under the current strategy, only 43 percent of the business unit's volume was sold into attractive market segments; the remaining 57 percent represented volume sold in customer segments that were not expected to be economically profitable in the long run. Under the selective-growth strategy, the segment mix was forecast to improve dramatically—to more than 63 percent—but the unprofitable base business was still likely to be a drag on equity spreads. Finally, under the refocused-segment-participation strategy, the percentage of volume sold into profitable market segments was expected to increase to more than 80 percent—dramatically improving profitability. Thus, despite the fact that sales were the lowest under the refocused-segment-participation strategy, profitability was the highest under this alternative and so was the warranted value of the business.

EXHIBIT 9.3

Evaluation of Integrated Participation Strategy Alternatives

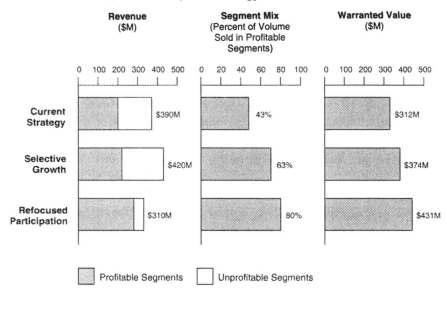

Note: M = millions

Concluding Remarks

In our experience, changing a business unit's participation strategy can have a tremendous impact on its long-term profitability and growth. Indeed, since value tends to be highly concentrated in most businesses, options that focus on entering attractive, related markets and exiting the most unattractive, unprofitable markets should always be carefully evaluated. By combining the competitive strategy options described in Chapter Eight with the participation options described in this chapter, most management teams can significantly improve their ability to formulate imaginative new strategies and create more value over time.

CHAPTER 10

Corporate Strategy

Senior management at the corporate center can create value for shareholders in three ways. First, the corporate center can proactively manage strategic value drivers within the company that two or more business units share. Second, the corporate center can manage the corporate portfolio by acquiring new businesses to enhance profitable growth and divesting existing businesses that are worth more to someone else than they are to the company's shareholders. Third, the corporate center can establish value creation as the company's governing objective and build an organization capable of achieving this objective over time.

This chapter discusses the first two ways for the center to add value. Fostering the organizational capabilities necessary to sustain value creation is the subject of Chapters Eleven through Sixteen. We begin by describing a corporate value assessment, which is essentially a strategic position assessment "writ large"—that is, applied to all business units in the portfolio. Companies that have internalized this technique have found it to be a valuable tool for identifying the most important strategic issues affecting individual business units as well as the entire company. Next we discuss the management of the shared strategic value drivers and the development of effective coordination strategies among business units. Finally, we describe a process to increase the odds that acquiring new businesses for the portfolio and divesting old ones will create value.

The Corporate Value Assessment

One of the earliest applications of value based management was to produce an unbiased appraisal of the value created and destroyed by each business unit in the company's portfolio, a process we refer to as a corporate value assessment. In the first half of the 1980s, for example, corporate value assessments at companies such as Westinghouse, Marriott, the Sun Company, and Walt Disney led to significant changes in resource allocation within each organization's business portfolio. In several instances, these assessments triggered major acquisitions and divestitures. In each case, the information contained in the corporate value assessment led senior management to initiate the process of liberating the value that was being consumed by unprofitable operations, of increasing growth in the most valuable businesses, and managing the shared strategic value drivers with greater effectiveness.

The strategic position assessment of each of the company's business units feeds directly into the corporate value assessment. In other words, the company's position assessment is a consolidation of the business unit assessments, and the company's warranted value is equal to the sum of the business unit values. As long as each business unit develops financial forecasts that are grounded effectively on a thorough analysis of market economics and competitive position, the resulting warranted values can be used as a starting point for devising strategic options for the company as a whole. This "bottom-up" process is the only one we know that can produce an accurate appraisal of each business unit in the portfolio. If the financial forecasts are not well grounded, the valuations can send erroneous signals to management concerning alternative portfolio strategy options.

The results that flow from a rigorous assessment of a company's portfolio are always revealing. As might be expected, the general rule that value creation is highly concentrated nearly always holds true for a corporate portfolio, just as it does within the business units. Indeed less than half of the company's invested capital is usually responsible for all the value created by the company.

EXHIBIT 10.1

Value Concentration in Typical Portfolio

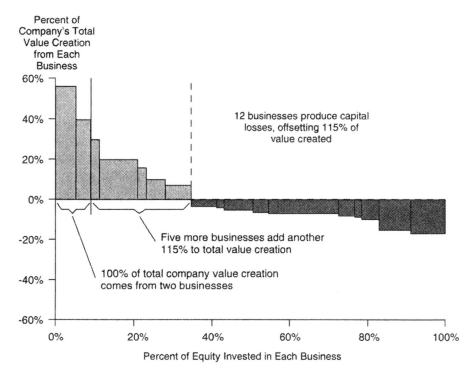

Exhibit 10.1 illustrates the concentration of value creation within a portfolio of business units belonging to a successful European industrial company. In this company, two major business units accounted for 100 percent of the value created by the entire portfolio. In addition, more than 60 percent of the company's capital was invested in businesses that were not creating value, an amazing fact considering that the company as a whole was viewed very favorably by investors—its common stock traded at nearly two times book value and 15 times earnings. Even though the company was widely perceived as a financial success, the assessment revealed that the value of the company would more than double if alternative strategies could be found to lift the performance of each unprofitable business so that each unit would earn an ROE just equal to the cost of equity capital over time.

The assessment also raised important questions about the way management allocated the company's resources. A careful examination of the profitability information led to three important insights. First, value creation was largely unrelated to a business unit's sales growth or market share. Indeed, many businesses that the company had long considered "stars"—because they had high market shares in rapidly growing sectors, actually created very little value for shareholders. On the other hand, many of its mature and niche businesses, which tended to command very little attention, were actually prodigious value creators. This immediately called into question the conventional wisdom around the company that successful businesses had to be number one or number two in their markets in order to be worthy of receiving corporate resources. Second, the level of research and development spending was not correlated at all with value creation. In fact, business units with low R&D intensity—measured in terms of R&D spending as a percentage of sales—were just as likely as highly research-intensive businesses to create value. This information caused management to reassess its process for allocating R&D resources across the business units. Finally, the existing plan for capital appropriations over the next five years was also at odds with the portfolio's value-creation profile. More than two-thirds of the company's planned capital investments for the next five years were targeted at businesses that were not currently earning an economic profit and were not expected to break even within the planning period. To everyone's surprise, more than 20 percent of the planned capital outlays were actually targeted for two business units that were worth less than nothing. These "black holes" in the portfolio had positive operating income but were pursuing strategies that called for reinvestment in excess of income each year, generating a constant stream of economic losses and negative equity cash flow.

With this level of detailed profitability information in hand, senior management developed a long list of critical strategic issues to be resolved, both for individual business units and the corporate center. As these issues were addressed over the next year, new business unit strategies were developed and approved, causing a substantial shift in the allocation of both capital and R&D resources. While the total level of spending changed only slightly, the distribution of capital across the portfolio became more closely aligned with value creation. Further, the new resource allocation process was largely free of the political infighting that had always accompanied the company's previous discussions about resources.

Managing Shared Strategic Value Drivers

In many companies, typically several strategic value drivers are shared among various business units or across all units. These shared value drivers consist of important organizational capabilities that must be centrally managed, or at least coordinated, by the corporate center so that the full impact of their value-creating potential can be realized. These drivers can span as few as two units (as in the case of a shared manufacturing process), they can encompass many business units (as in the case of shared brand management), or they can cover the entire portfolio (as in the case of a superior planning and resource allocation process). We note here that these strategic value drivers must be *primary* sources of competitive advantage, not simply the reflection of shared costs and assets, shared marketing and distribution, or vertical integration within business units.

Identifying these shared strategic value drivers is an important part of a corporate value assessment. As each business unit searches for and identifies the organizational capabilities that are the fundamental sources of competitive advantage in its markets, it will become apparent in the corporate assessment that some business units have common capabilities as well as common strategic assets that must be managed or coordinated. Examples include du Pont's Polymer technology, which is shared by many business units in one of its departments or sectors; Kellogg's brand equity, which is shared across multiple, independent products and geographic regions; and Wal-Mart's capability to restock its stores faster and cheaper than competitors, now shared by each of its retail businesses.

In addition to identifying the strategic value drivers within each of its business units, the corporate center should benchmark its own key management processes, such as strategic planning, resource allocation, and corporate development, with the aim of determining whether one or more of these processes might qualify as a source of competitive advantage. While this can be a difficult task, it is necessary to ensure that widely held views ("We're the best acquirers in the industry") constitute a sustainable competitive advantage. When subjected to this reality test, many of the supposed drivers come up short. For example, a senior executive of a large bank recently claimed that its capability to recruit talented loan officers and train them in the institution's credit analysis process was an important strategic value driver. When put to the benchmark test, however, this capability did not produce a clear competitive advantage. In reality, each of the bank's major competitors recruited from the same pool of people with more or less the same success rates and used similar training techniques.

In general, the list of shared strategic value drivers should be quite short, on the order of a half dozen or so. This, of course, in no way diminishes the importance of managing these drivers aggressively; they are always very important to the value-creating potential of the enterprise. The list is short because it is very difficult to develop organizational capabilities that span many businesses and can produce profitable competitive advantages. Given these qualifications, the traditional corporate center services, such as accounting and tax, treasury, legal, human resources, and information systems will seldom, if ever, make the list. These services must be managed in a highly efficient manner to be sure, but it is unlikely that management will be able to leverage its skills here into an extensible advantage. In essence, management's objective for these services should be twofold. First, it should determine whether the service should be centralized to ensure standardization and reap economies of scale, or decentralized so that it can be tailored to the needs of each business. Second, management should search for the least costly way to provide all centralized services, subject to predetermined quality standards. This search can be guided by an economic assessment of costs and benefits, or management can establish an internal market for these services, in which the service providers become internal businesses that "sell" their services to other units.

Managing shared strategic value drivers involves three important tasks. The first is to ensure an adequate flow of human and financial resources to each capability. This is particularly important for capabilities that are knowledge-intensive, such as management of a common product or process technology. Since the effectiveness of this capability depends on continuing investment in discovery and innovation, the corporate center (or some level of management between the corporate center and the business units) must determine resource requirements and make investment decisions. Without this central intervention, there is a danger that none of the individual businesses would be willing to invest on its own, thus starving the capability to death over time. Indeed, this fear has stimulated an argument against organizing and managing diversified companies around independent business units. For example, in a widely read article published several years ago in the *Harvard Business Review,* two business school professors wrote about "The Tyranny of the SBU," arguing that systematic underinvestment in "core competencies" (another way of describing a type of shared organizational capability) is one of the principal reasons that Western companies are losing the competitive battle with Japanese and Asian rivals.[1] While there may be some truth to their claim with respect to some markets, we believe that a massive reorganization around core competencies is an inappropriate solution to this problem. The business unit form of organizational structure, assuming that unit boundaries are drawn appropriately, offers enormous potential for managing value creation in large companies. With identification of the shared strategic value drivers that exist in the company and development of a strategic plan for managing them aggressively, there need be no fear of underinvestment in shared value drivers.

The second task is the mirror image of the first. It involves ensuring that no individual business unit overexploits a shared capability, thereby reducing its value to the company as a whole. For example, a valuable brand can be "cheapened" by mismanagement, particularly if it is overexposed and placed on the wrong items. In one instance, a business unit attempted to put one of the world's most widely recognized brands on Christmas tree lights in a bid to generate a bit more earnings in the fourth quarter. The sales tactic produced few economic benefits, but ran the risk of tarnishing the business unit's brand image. Another area where the corporate center should intervene involves the question of how best to exploit a valuable technology that is shared by two or more businesses. For example, a large, vertically integrated company developed a proprietary technology in one of its upstream businesses. The general manager of the business wanted to sell products containing the new technology into the merchant wholesaler market, while the general manager of the downstream unit argued vehemently that the value of the new technology should be realized in the pricing of the systems sold exclusively by his business. In this case, the corporate center intervened on behalf of the downstream business, on the basis of a thorough analysis of the economic trade-offs between the two units.

The third task in managing shared strategic value drivers is to ensure that the company leverages them to the fullest extent possible to fuel profitable external growth. This is typically accomplished by effectively capitalizing on opportunities to create value by entering new markets and developing new products, where extending the company's strategic value drivers is a means to create competitive advantage. WMX Technologies (formerly Waste Management) is a classic case of a company that developed a unique capability to acquire and manage local garbage collection. Over two decades, its management exploited this capability to enter new markets throughout the United States, effectively consolidating a fragmented market. In recent years, management realized that it had also acquired a great deal of technical expertise in solving waste disposal problems. This capability is currently the basis for a major investment and acquisition program focused on engineering- and technology-based companies (hence the name change). Together, these shared capabilities have helped build a company with over $9 billion in annual revenue and a market capitalization exceeding $15 billion relative to a book value of less than $5 billion.

Examples such as these should make clear the important role that shared value drivers can and should play in corporate strategy. If these drivers are not included in the corporate planning process and are not proactively and aggressively managed by the corporate center, large opportunities to create value may be missed and individual business units may become unnecessarily vulnerable to competitive threats.

Making Profitable Acquisitions

During the past decade it has been reasonably well established that most acquisitions are not economically profitable, that is, they fail to create value for the acquiring company's stockholders. In fact, after carefully dissecting hundreds of mergers and acquisitions that took place over the course of the 1980s, some academic studies have put the success rate well below 50 percent.[2] Toward the end of the 1980s, we surveyed 400 large transactions and found that only one in five of the acquisitions in the sample clearly created shareholder value, in the sense that the price of the acquirer's stock was bid up relative to that of its peers during the two weeks before and after the announcement.[3]

With millions of dollars and so much internal effort expended on this activity each year, one can't help but wonder why the odds of success are so low. On the basis of our experience in this area, the answer seems relatively clear: the odds are low because, for most companies, a series of secondary objectives interferes with realizing the primary objective of creating shareholder value when they target and make acquisitions. All too often, managers pursue acquisitions in an attempt to utilize their company's excess resources, replace a major declining business, enter new geographic markets, exploit potential competitive advantages, or simply achieve an earnings-per-share growth target. While some of these secondary objectives may be desirable, the historical record suggests that they are frequently achieved only by transfering a portion of the shareholders' wealth to the acquired firms' owners in the form of an excessive price.

There are three prerequisites for beating the odds. First, a creative strategy must be conceived to direct the search for candidates and identify those targets with the greatest potential to create value. Second, to avoid overpaying, management must adopt a disciplined approach to analyzing acquisition economics. And finally, each acquisition must be integrated successfully so that, at a minimum, the premium paid for control can be recaptured quickly. As Exhibit 10.2 conveys, many potential acquisitions might fit well with a company's current business from a strategic standpoint, others have attractive prices, and still others could be integrated successfully. There are, however, relatively few acquisition candidates that meet all three prerequisites.

The purpose of an acquisition strategy is to direct management's search for candidates that are likely to be worth more to its shareholders than to the seller's. In some instances the direction of this search is obvious. For example, if competitors begin acquiring key suppliers, distributors, or other companies with new technology capable of significantly enhancing product quality, the direction of the search is

EXHIBIT 10.2
Targeting Profitable Acquisitions

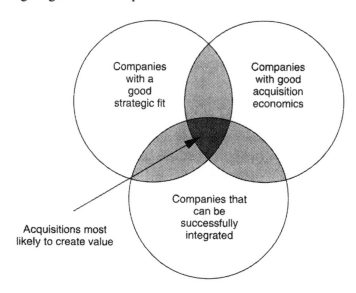

clear from the outset. In the absence of this type of competitive threat, though, the search activity must be directed in a more systematic manner.

Generally speaking, three directional options are open to any company. The first involves looking for direct extension opportunities. These consist of businesses or companies operating in product market segments that are closely related to one or more segments already served by the acquirer. The relationship may come in the form of similar products sold to different customer groups or in different regions, or from products that are either substitutes for or complements to products offered by one of the acquirer's businesses. Typically, these candidates are identified by management within the acquired company's business units. In seeking these direct extensions, the acquiring company's management hopes to leverage its considerable knowledge of its existing products or customer groups to create or enhance a competitive advantage in its own business, or in the acquired company, or possibly both. Chrysler's acquisition of American Motors, which made the popular Jeep vehicle, and California-based BankAmerica's acquisition of SeaFirst Bank, located in Seattle, are good examples of direct market extensions.

The second directional option is to search for candidates in which the acquirer's shared strategic value drivers can be used to create and exploit a competitive advantage in the acquired company's markets. Known as indirect extensions, these acquisitions require a thorough understanding of how the company's organizational capabilities and strategic assets can be profitably extended, or transplanted, into another company.[4] For example, in 1987, Ralston-Purina entered the consumer battery market through acquisition of the Eveready business from Union Carbide. Since consummating the deal, Ralston's strategy has been to leverage its considerable organizational skills in consumer marketing and asset management to produce faster growth and higher returns on capital than Eveready was able to generate when the business was managed by Union Carbide. Investors' confidence in this strategy was reflected in the very favorable impact of the news of the Eveready acquisition on Ralston's stock price. On the day of the announcement, Ralston's stock price climbed more than 10 percent above that of its industry peers, creating nearly $500 million for shareholders.

The third directional option is to search for opportunities in unrelated markets. This is clearly the most risky of the three options and warrants the greatest caution. Two of the more popular current strategies are to target industries in the growth phase of their life cycles (such as biotechnology or software) or industries undergoing structural change (such as financial services, telecommunications, and health care). In general, the odds of creating significant value through unrelated acquisitions are very low. Given such low odds, the most profitable (or least unprofitable) strategy for entering unrelated markets is likely to be through "beachheading." This involves a series of acquisitions, where the first one, usually a small, well-managed company, effectively establishes a beachhead in the new market. After the new products and markets are well understood, the small business forms the base from which subsequent acquisitions, start-ups, and joint ventures are made. The best beachhead opportunities are obviously those rich in possibilities for direct and indirect extensions. A firm called K-III, for example, funded by Kohlberg Kravis Roberts &

Co., has become a major publishing company in just five years by acquiring niche magazines all over the United States.

Once the search effort produces candidates, the companies must be analyzed to determine whether they can be profitably acquired. Nearly every acquisition will involve paying a premium over the preacquisition market value (or standalone value) for the privilege of control. In the 1980s, when the acquisitions drive was at its most-heated peak, premiums averaged around 50 percent of preacquisition values. Between 1985 and 1990, the average premium paid for targets believed to have a reasonable brand image was even higher, averaging around 60 percent. Since a company's stand-alone value already reflects a consensus view of its future performance, the acquirer must be confident of improving the candidate's or its own performance significantly in order to create value for shareholders. In other words, the candidate must exhibit a set of characteristics—we call them *bargain characteristics*—that will enable the acquirer to more than recapture the control premium. These bargain characteristics can be classified in five categories:

(1) *Synergy Bargains*   Although many sins have been committed in the name of synergy over the years, there are two types of synergy that actually exist and can be exploited: synergy in demand and synergy in cost. Demand synergies can be created by combining complementary products or services (e.g., software and hardware) or marketing and distribution skills and assets in a way that the combination produces more revenue than the units would if they were operated separately. The acquisition of Stokely Van Kamp by Quaker Oats is a good example of demand-related synergies. Stokely produced a regional beverage, Gatorade, which Quaker was able to roll out nationally and build into a powerhouse niche brand in the highly profitable beverage market. Synergy in cost comes from eliminating overlap in activities, such as procurement, assembly, marketing, R&D, and administration. Of the two types of potential synergy, cost synergies are more likely to be a source of significant value creation. Wells Fargo's acquisition of Crocker Bank is one of the most stunning examples of cost-based synergy. Wells Fargo paid more than $1 billion to acquire its neighbor and, we estimate, has created more than $500

million of additional value for its shareholders by rationalizing overhead and consolidating the branch networks and back offices of the two banks.

(2) *Undermanagement Bargains* This type of bargain exists when one or more businesses of an acquisition candidate are underperforming its competitors in terms of growth and/or profitability, and the acquirer is confident that the mistakes can be corrected. We believe that undermanagement bargains have the greatest potential for significant premium recapture, especially for businesses that are closely related. The management buyout of Duracell, the battery company, from Kraft Foods which we described in Chapter Two, is a good example of an undermanagement bargain. By significantly expanding the capital committed to the business, the new management upgraded facilities, improved the company's cost position and boosted marketing outlays, resulting in a large increase in economic profit and a huge return for the investors in the management buyout.

(3) *Restructuring Bargains* A restructuring bargain exists when the acquirer is confident that the divestment value of one or more of the candidate's businesses exceeds its operating value. This disparity in values may occur because of poor operating performance or because one or more of the candidate's businesses may simply be worth more to someone else due to synergy. During the 1980s, several spectacular restructuring bargains energized the market for large company takeovers. One of the first was Hanson Trust's acquisition of SCM Corporation. After paying $925 million for SCM in 1986, Hanson sold off businesses that were, for the most part, worth more to someone else and recouped virtually the entire purchase price within several years. The remaining businesses, including the highly profitable Titanium Dioxide unit and the old Smith Corona typewriter company, were, in essence, acquired for nothing, suggesting that the acquisition may have created between $500 million and $1 billion for Hanson.

(4) *Finance/Tax Bargains* Finance and tax bargains exist primarily when the candidate company has excess cash or underutilized borrowing capacity. In the U.S., this allows the acquirer to borrow against the candidate's assets and cash flow, generating tax-deductible interest expense that is typically worth 30 to 40 cents

in equity value per dollar borrowed. Nearly all the leveraged buyouts prior to the 1986 Tax Reform Act took advantage of these characteristics to generate a high proportion of their windfall gains for the buyout group's shareholders.

(5) *Valuation Bargains*   Although the stock market is usually efficient, investors occasionally make pricing errors. Thus, valuation, or forecast, bargains exist when the acquirer can spot and exploit a valuation error before it is corrected. Warren Buffett has built a fortune by acquiring such undervalued companies, although even he admits that it is extraordinarily difficult to find a company with a valuation error that exceeds the required control premium. Valuation bargains may also occur when a big corporation whose shares are publicly traded acquires a closely held company whose stock is discounted due to lack of liquidity, and when a domestic company acquires a foreign business that has difficulty gaining access to capital markets.

Once the bargain characteristics of any acquisition candidate have been identified, the next task is to carry out a premium recapture analysis to determine whether the candidate can be profitably acquired. A good example of premium recapture analysis appeared several years ago when IC Industries, the successor company to the Illinois-Central Railroad, acquired Ogden Foods for $320 million to expand its food group, which at the time consisted of Pet Foods. Ogden Foods was a hodgepodge of underperforming consumer foods businesses—ranging from Progresso soups and sauces to Las Palmas Mexican ingredients—that had been placed on the auction block by Ogden Corporation as a result of a massive portfolio restructuring. Although we estimated at the time that the stand-alone value of Ogden Foods was only $125 million prior to the acquisition, IC Industries' acquisition created value for its shareholders because of the number and size of the company's bargain characteristics.

As shown in Exhibit 10.3, the combination of the two food-processing businesses was forecast to yield cost and demand synergies exceeding $70 million. These synergies were driven primarily by the elimination of redundant overhead, updating of Ogden's packaging designs, consolidation of corrugated box plants, and new product extensions.

EXHIBIT 10.3

Acquisition Bargain Determination—Ogden Foods

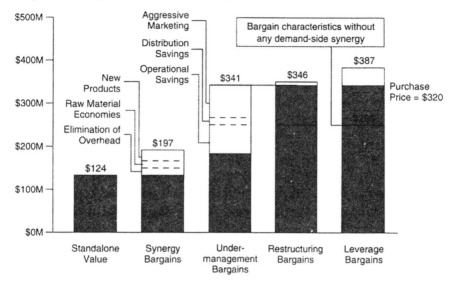

In addition to the synergy characteristics, IC Industries management identified a range of undermanagement characteristics. These consisted of improvements in operation, distribution, and marketing, which had an expected value contribution exceeding $140 million, or 115 percent of Ogden Food's estimated stand-alone value. Examples of these improvements included shutting down one production facility, upgrading the remaining plants, slashing working capital, consolidating Ogden's highly fragmented distribution system, replacing nearly two-thirds of the company's brokers with Pet's sales force, and increasing advertising to reposition Progresso soups. On top of the synergy and undermanagement characteristics, Ogden offered the prospect of additional value creation through restructuring and financing, which we estimated to be worth as much as $40 million.

In bidding $320 million for Ogden, IC's management believed that it could realize more than $60 million worth of value improvements once the two companies were combined. The loud applause heard on Wall Street the day of the announcement suggested that investors agreed. The price of IC Industries stock shot up by more than 15 percent during the two weeks following the company's announcement of its intention to acquire Ogden Foods.

Once the thrill of negotiating an acquisition subsides, management faces the often daunting task of actually putting the two companies together. Two challenges must be met if the integration is to succeed. First, management must develop and execute a detailed premium recapture plan. Without such a plan, odds are high that many of the pro forma bargain characteristics described earlier will never be realized. The plan must specify the actions to be taken once the deal has been closed, who has accountability, the desired results, and a target completion date. The plan should also reflect the nature of the acquisition economics and should be directed by the bargain analysis that took place prior to negotiation. Using this approach, the acquisition premium should be systematically recaptured within a relatively short time (often within twenty-four months).

The second challenge is to integrate the two management teams in such a way that the talent needed to execute the premium recapture plan remains in the company. In any business combination, there will be conflict between the two cultures and management systems. If cultures are widely divergent, as was clearly the case with General Motors' acquisition of E.D.S. under H. Ross Perot, the economics must be very positive to justify the transaction. In all cases, management should be prepared to amend and integrate the acquired company's budgeting, planning, and compensation systems so that the new people will be motivated to produce the results necessary to make the acquisition a success.

Creating Value Through Divestment

In addition to creating value by profitably acquiring new businesses, the corporate center is responsible for formulating and evaluating all opportunities to create value by divesting *existing* businesses. As noted earlier, the fact that value creation in most large, diversified companies is so concentrated means that there will always be opportunities to create value through divestment. This does not mean that unprofitable business units should immediately be put on the block to fetch the best price available. As we emphasized in Chapters Eight and Nine, many unprofitable businesses can be turned around through changes in both competitive and participation strategy, a process that should, if at all possible, run its full course before divestment is considered. It does suggest, however, that most companies, no matter how profitable, can benefit from a continual refocusing of energy and resources into those products and markets that can create value and away from those that destroy it. This is particularly important for management teams that push hard for profitable growth, since usually only a minority of the growth initiatives can be expected to create substantial value while the mistakes must be dealt with early and often. Management should also be aware that even some profitable business units may be candidates for divestment, especially if they are not central to the company's strategic direction and might be worth far more to another firm.

Identifying candidates and making the divestment decision involves a three-step process. It begins with a corporate value assessment, which we described earlier and which yields a "waterfall" chart similar to the one depicted in Exhibit 10.1. Given that the forecasts of cash flow and economic profit for each business unit are thoroughly grounded strategically, the obvious candidates for divestment are the units on the far right of the graph—those whose warranted values fall far short of the amount of capital invested. These are most often business units that exhibit one of two characteristics. They are unprofitable because the market economics are unattractive and unlikely to improve, or they are unprofitable because they are competitively disadvantaged and likely to remain so. (While we instinctively believe that there is always a way to improve competitive position, there are many cases where the cost is too high or where organizational barriers prevent the required changes from being implemented.) Those unfortunate businesses that exhibit both characteristics are literally trapped in the southwest quadrant of the "market economics—competitive position" matrix, doomed to a future of struggling just to generate positive accounting earnings. In short, for any business that cannot improve its competitive advantage and whose prospects for improved market economics are poor, divestment may well be the highest-value strategic option.

The valuation floor for evaluating divestment options is established by the liquidation value of the business. Unless the assets of a particular business are primarily fixed and highly specialized, or unless the unit faces high exit costs (say, for environmental cleanup), the option of liquidating the working capital, selling the fixed assets for a small percentage of their book value and taking the tax loss typically produces a liquidation value in the range of 35 to 65 percent of book equity invested. For example, after nearly a decade of operating losses financed largely by selling off all other assets, Pan American Airlines found itself still trapped in a highly unattractive market with a huge competitive disadvantage. Although the managers and employees of Pan Am fought long and hard to become as competitive as possible, a strategic blunder (the acquisition of National Airlines) and the deteriorating economics of the world airline market finally forced them to throw in the towel and liquidate in 1991, salvaging only a small fraction of the capital invested over the years.

Once divestment candidates have been identified, and management has estimated each candidate's liquidation value, the process moves to step number two—determining the highest possible operating value for each business. Ideally, this should be accomplished through the in-depth process described in Chapters Seven through Nine. A thorough strategic position assessment is conducted, which facilitates a valuation of the business unit under its current strategy. Detailed profitability measurement and identification of strategic value drivers are used to develop strategic options, which are converted to grounded financial forecasts and valued. The highest value option is, by definition, the highest possible operating value for the business.

The final step is to determine the "net divestment value," or NDV, of each candidate. This is the present value of after-tax proceeds from selling the business, liquidating it, or spinning it off. The decision to divest should be made by comparing NDV with the highest operating value—whenever NDV substantially exceeds the business unit's highest operating value, the unit should be divested. Thus, the divestment of a business unit must be not only a value-creating transaction, it must be worth more to shareholders than holding onto the business and harvesting it or conducting an orderly liquidation. Note that this criterion does not require consideration of any accounting effects, such as write-offs, that seem to stall so many divestment decisions. Note also that when an unprofitable business unit's NDV is very low (possibly negative due to exit costs), the value-maximizing strategy may be to continue operating the business, even though it may never earn a return on book capital close to its cost of capital.

Along with the highly unprofitable units, other businesses might have NDVs substantially greater than their operating values. This might occur for four reasons that are essentially the mirror image of the bargain characteristics described in our discussion of acquisition economics. The first is the existence of significant synergy with another company, which would allow the acquirer to pay a significant premium over warranted value. The second occurs when a business is being undermanaged, and management perceives turnaround to be too difficult. This is especially relevant to unprofitable businesses but may also be true of profitable units that are simply underexploiting their potential. This was the case with the Lily-Tulip business, a manufacturer of styrofoam cups, which Owens-Illinois sold to a leveraged buyout firm in the late 1980s. In order to improve its cost position, the management of OI knew that it would have to drastically cut corporate overhead, relocate the plants to the southern part of the United States, and hire nonunion labor. Since management was convinced that none of the three options could be carried out effectively while Lily-Tulip was part of OI, the business was sold to Kohlberg Kravis Roberts, which brought in new management and carried out the cost reduction strategy quite effectively. Owens-Illinois received a price that was substantially greater than the unit's operating value and Kohlberg Kravis Roberts reaped a windfall profit when it took the company public three years after the buyout.

The third reason that a business unit's net divestment value might exceed its operating value is the possibility that the acquirer might simply pay too much for the acquisition. This is frequently caused by either overly optimistic financial forecasts or application of an incorrect criterion, such as minimizing the impact of the acquisition on accounting earnings per share. Finally, the prospective buyer may simply be advantaged from a finance/tax perspective. For example, it may make sense for a parent company with a large tax loss to divest a business that is currently losing money to a profitable company, which can immediately offset the loss with other income. Alternatively, the acquirer of a real-estate-oriented business, or a cable television business may be willing to incur far more debt than the seller, so that a portion of the value created through the interest tax savings is transferred to the seller in the purchase price.

Up to this point, we have couched the discussion of divestment value in terms of an outright sale of either the entire business or its assets. It is also possible simply to spin off a business to existing shareholders, creating two publicly traded companies. The economics of spin-offs are, for the most part, quite simple. Value is created primarily through the elimination of negative synergy between the two units and the increase in management focus that results from separation of the two businesses. The negative synergy is nearly always caused by one unit cross-subsidizing the other, as was the case when TWA spun off its services and hotel businesses to keep them from being forced to finance the high wage rates that were producing losses in the airline. In this case, the spin-off forced the airline to renegotiate its labor contracts because it would not have survived without wage concessions.

Although there is always a lively debate about the merits of spinning off businesses whose competitors are trading at a much higher price/earnings multiple than the parent, we are skeptical that value can be created with this tactic unless there is reason to believe that economic profits and cash flow will actually be greater after the separation than before. The idea that a parent company with a P/E of 10 can spin off a business that would command a P/E of 15, thereby creating value, is based on the notion that investors would pay more for two separate streams of equity cash flow than for one. Unless there is a fundamental shift in profitability and growth in one or both of the streams, odds are high that the values of the separated businesses will be equal to the value of the combined businesses.

Concluding Remarks

As long as there are companies that are organized around independent business units, the value added by the corporate center will be a subject of some debate. The intensity of the debate will depend, of course, on the magnitude of corporate expense allocated to the businesses and each general manager's perception of the benefits received from corporate services relative to the cost. Of the many activities that occur in the center, we believe four have the potential to make a substantial contribution to the company's ability to create value for shareholders.

The first of these activities is the management of the company's shared strategic value drivers, which consist of those organizational capabilities that are significant sources of competitive advantage and also span two or more businesses. The corporate center must ensure that these drivers are adequately funded, protected from overexploitation, and leveraged to the fullest extent possible.

The second activity consists of increasing the odds that all acquisitions will create value rather than transfer the shareholders' wealth to the selling company's stockholders. This requires a disciplined approach that focuses primarily on identifying attractive candidates, evaluating the sources of premium recapture, and developing an integration plan that converts the individual premium recapture elements into a series of concrete actions.

The third activity involves divesting those business units in the company's portfolio whose operating values are far less than their net divestment values. These units will typically have one of two profiles. They will be permanently disadvantaged businesses participating in unprofitable markets with little, if any, hope for a significant turnaround; or they will be business units that are not central to the company's overall strategic direction and can be sold at a premium over their operating values.

The fourth activity is in many ways the most difficult and challenging. This consists of establishing value creation as a governing objective and building an organization that can consistently develop and implement value-maximizing strategies over time. More than anything else, this involves identification and management of the company's institutional value drivers, the subject of Chapter Eleven.

PART 4

Creating a Higher-Value Organization

CHAPTER 11

Institutional Value Drivers

We use the term value drivers to identify the key processes and capabilities that enable a company to generate and sustain high-value strategies over time. In Chapters Seven to Ten, we discussed strategic value drivers, the processes that enable business units to achieve a more valuable customer offer and operating configuration than competitors. In this chapter we shift our focus from developing superior strategies (overcoming the forces of competition) to developing superior organizational capabilities (overcoming the internal barriers to value creation), beginning with an overview of institutional value drivers. If we think of strategic value drivers as equivalent to the systems and capabilities a battlefield commander needs to develop and execute a winning strategy, institutional drivers might be thought of as equivalent to the systems and capabilities the entire military organization needs to have the right forces with the right skills, equipment, and supplies on multiple battlefields simultaneously. Both sets of systems and capabilities are necessary to win the war.

Like the organizational systems in the military analogy, institutional value drivers determine the company's potential for creating value in all its business units all the time. This propensity to create wealth can be influenced by many institutional factors, most important of which are the ability, drive, and determination of the chief executive to lead the company toward that objective. But even if the chief executive is totally dedicated to creating shareholder value, he or she must have the support of an organization that can deliver the required performance, and for most companies this means that a number of key management processes must change significantly. Our particular focus will be on the five key processes that constitute the institutional value drivers: *governance, strategic planning, resource allocation, performance management,* and *top management compensation.*

To support the governing objective, these key processes must enable the institution to accomplish two critical tasks. First, the processes must give managers the knowledge and tools they need to generate better options. Second, they must help managers select and implement only the best options. By generating better options, we mean generating those strategic alternatives with the highest potential for creating new wealth. By making better decisions, we mean decisions to actually implement the highest-value strategies and eliminate any strategies or activities that destroy wealth. If the first task is achieved, better decisions might seem to follow naturally. But this is not always the case. The force of the institutional imperative is such that managers often tell us they know how to achieve better strategic and financial performance—for example, by restructuring certain parts of their businesses and putting more resources into growing other parts—but they are prevented or at least discouraged from doing so by institutional goals and constraints. And they are usually right.

If key management processes are redesigned to achieve these two tasks, the company will gain a tremendous organizational advantage over its rivals. The company will work smarter by focusing more efficiently and effectively on increasing good growth and will eliminate time- and resource-wasting investments in bad growth strategies. This results in a highly confident management team with a winning attitude; a superior work force, because the company's success allows it to better attract and hold top talent at all levels; an extremely strong balance sheet that allows for the funding of all good growth opportunities; and an institutional capacity for continually improving performance and meeting new challenges better than the competition does. Of course, good performance for shareholders can sometimes be achieved without good processes, just as a battle can sometimes be won without a numerical or material advantage. But in neither case can the victory be sustained.

This chapter provides an overview of the institutional value drivers, emphasizing principles for developing the processes needed to achieve the company's governing objective. Each key process will be detailed in Chapters Twelve to Sixteen.

Principles

The institutional processes we call key value drivers exist in some form at nearly all companies, but they are largely underutilized and ineffective in helping the company achieve superior performance. Rarely do the chief executive and top management view these processes as a potential source of competitive advantage. Often they have no expressed linkage to the company's objectives, are poorly designed to support those objectives, and are virtually never integrated into a common overall process for dealing with the most important organizational and strategic decisions the company faces. Consequently, managers view the company's processes for governance, strategic planning, resource allocation, budgeting, and top management compensation as basically separate and unrelated activities rather than as carefully coordinated elements of a single integrated approach for managing the company to reach its objectives. The poor design and inefficiency of these processes often leads to contradictory decisions (e.g., strategy targets embody one objective, the budget targets something else, and pay may not be related to either one) and frustration of managers who try to do what they think is best in spite of, rather than with the help of, these processes. Even worse, such processes produce little learning. Very few managers would say that these key management processes actually help them achieve better performance over time.

Why are these processes so underutilized and ineffective? There are many reasons, but in our experience several general factors characterize a majority of companies. First, managers simply do not think of these processes as true performance drivers. While compensation and budgeting are commonly employed as the carrot and the stick for achieving annual profit goals, neither process contributes to the generation of any good ideas for meeting the goals. In fact, the conventional compensation and budgeting processes, with their single-year focus on reported earnings, usually do more to undermine the achievement of superior performance than to enhance it. Second, it must be said that frequently chief executives are not especially interested in process. Many view it as time-consuming, constraining, staff- driven, and not all that helpful in solving hard problems. Considering their years of coping with the ineffective processes chief executives are used to, this opinion is not so surprising. However, one very unfortunate consequence of this attitude is that chief executives sometimes conclude that process is important—but only for other people. Once the organization perceives this attitude in a chief executive, any hope of creating and utilizing effective processes for making important decisions might as well be abandoned. Another frequent and equally unfortunate consequence is that the chief executive simply adheres to the processes as they exist, which usually means that budgeting rather than strategy dominates decision making. A final observation to help explain the poor state of management process is that changing existing processes and creating good new ones is an immense task. The prospect of adding considerable work and disruption to people's lives, combined with the common underestimation of the benefits, is unlikely to stimulate a strong commitment to change. However, we find that once the potential benefits are better understood, the commitment for change will come.

Regardless of their attitudes toward existing processes, managers make important decisions every day, and they use some kind of process, formal or informal, to make these decisions. However romantic and appealing the vision of a strong leader proceeding on "gut feeling" may be, few large companies today would consider someone's intestinal sensitivities to be sufficient justification for the commitment of vast resources. And anyway, we would argue that even "gut feel" is a process—perhaps not one we would want to examine all that closely, but a process nevertheless. Thus, the question companies must address is not whether to use processes for decision making but whether to use good or bad processes.

Improving or reengineering the company's institutional value drivers requires adoption of four straightforward principles. (1) The processes must share a common objective, and top management must be able to express clearly how each process supports that objective. (2) The processes must share a common philosophy, or design framework, linking them to top management's expressed objective—it is not helpful to have, as many companies, figuratively speaking, do, a

Victorian governance process, a Jimmy Carter strategic planning process, a Marxist resource allocation process, an Attila the Hun budgeting process, and a Bill Clinton executive pay plan. (3) The processes must be fully integrated, sharing not only a common goal and framework but with all elements actually fitting together as parts of a unified system for managing the corporation. (4) The processes must be implemented at the corporate level and within each business unit.

The goal of each key process must be to support as effectively as possible management's efforts to achieve the company's governing objective. For example, the goal of senior managers' incentive compensation plans should be to reward them for creating wealth, and this in turn will imply an entirely different way of setting targets and payouts from what we find typically in incentive plans. Similarly, the business units should be given only one financial objective, namely, to maximize their warranted value, with the implication that specific performance targets will follow from the strategic plan instead of being set before planning even begins, as is commonly done. We will elaborate on these and other process goals in subsequent chapters, but we want to emphasize here that clear, specific linkage to the company's governing objective is the essential first principle of good process design. In our experience this is rarely done, and consequently, the institutional value drivers are likely to be dysfunctional from the start.

Very few companies design their management processes through application of a common philosophy or framework. Differing philosophies and heritage behind each process produce a veritable Tower of Babel inside the company. Governance theories about global matrix management compete with the need to know precisely who *is* responsible for meeting performance objectives for every product in every market. A "visionary" long-term, no-numbers strategic planning process conflicts with a short-term budgeting process that is full of constraints and consists of little but numbers. Internal financial information systems are designed to help with auditing and financial reporting but tell managers practically nothing useful for creating a good business strategy. Financial tests for evaluating capital investments often give precisely the wrong answer about the economic merits of a project. Incentive programs prompt managers to pursue objectives that do not lead to competitive advantage or value for shareholders. And the list goes on. These key management processes have been created at different times by different people to serve different needs. While they are necessarily patched together in some sort of Rube Goldberg configuration to allow a company to function at some level, they are still unable to deliver anything like the consistent, effective support that managers need to achieve and sustain great performance over time.

The principles of value based management provide a common framework for the design and operation of these management processes. Companies adopting these principles and incorporating them into their management processes often refer to them as "value based" planning, or "value based" resource allocation, "value based" performance management, and "value based" compensation. While they are value based, these processes are not off-the-shelf or one-size-fits-all solutions by any means. Companies must tailor the processes to suit their particular industry, their culture, and their capabilities over time, but the common principles enable managers to employ the processes constructively to reach the governing objective instead of climbing over them like old tires on an obstacle course. One of our clients put it best when he said, "What value based management has given us is a common language for managing the company."

Management processes are most powerful when they are integrated into what is, in effect, a single large process for making the company's key strategic and organizational decisions. By integrated, we mean not only that they share a common goal and reflect in their design a common framework, but they work together in an almost seamless fashion. Taking them together, managers regard these processes as a source of competitive advantage. There are usually very sharp edges between strategic planning, resource allocation, budgeting and pay programs. But with value based management, ideally there are no sharp edges— managers understand exactly how strategic planning will influence resource allocation and performance objectives, how these in turn will influence top management compensation, and how all of these processes will function within an organizational structure designed to keep the clearest possible focus on individual responsibilities for value creation. Exhibit 11.1 illustrates how we think these processes should work together.

As Exhibit 11.1 shows, there is a hierarchy among the processes. The process for governance serves as an essential foundation for supe-

EXHIBIT 11.1

Institutional Value Drivers

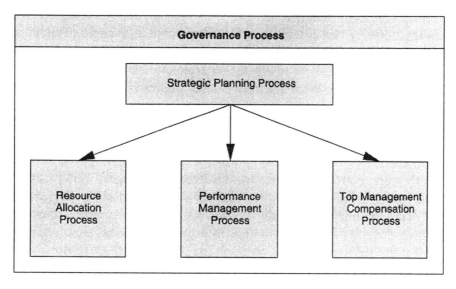

Note: *These key management processes that we identify as the institutional value drivers are all* **decision** *processes. There are other important processes that we think of as* **enabling** *processes, such as management education and information resources management (specification, distribution, and systemization of information necessary to manage for value creation) that are also potential sources of organizational advantage and extremely important to the successful implementation of value based management.*

rior performance. If organizational structure or managerial account-abilities are inconsistent with wealth creation, the effectiveness of other processes (even if they are notionally "value based") will suffer tremendously. Strategic planning is the driver of drivers, the primary process for helping management "do the right things." If all the business unit strategies and the strategies of the corporate center are not value creating, the processes for resource allocation, performance management (including budgeting), and top management compensation in themselves will not suffice to fix the company's problems. The choice of resources (both human and capital) to commit, performance goals to set, and incentives to provide are, or should be, determined by the specific requirements of the business unit and corporate center strategies that maximize value. Therefore, these three processes are *dependent* on the strategic planning process. They serve strategy *but should play no role in determining strategy.* This approach represents a dramatic departure for most companies, where inappropriate resource constraints, budgeting targets, and pay practices usually do impinge, directly and forcefully, on management's strategic decisions. However, as we will argue in Chapters Twelve through Sixteen, allowing these dependent processes to affect strategic decisions is yet another manifestation of the institutional imperative undermining the company's capacity to create wealth.

The fourth and final principle for managing the institutional value drivers as effectively as possible is to embed these processes in the operations of every business unit in the portfolio. The goals, design framework, and basic features will be determined largely by the corporate center, ensuring that all business units follow the same basic practices in their interactions with "headquarters." But the specific ways in which different businesses define their product market units, or develop the best strategic alternatives, or determine their resource requirements and performance objectives will necessarily vary. Therefore, these processes will never be really effective if they are used only by the corporate staff and more or less imposed on the business units. The business unit general managers and their direct reports must adopt these processes as the institutional value drivers of not only the company but the business units themselves. Managed properly by the business units, these processes are as much a source of competitive advantage as any brand, any proprietary product, or any leading-edge technology.

Concluding Remarks

Creating value on an episodic basis, through one-time restructurings, successful new product introductions, or effective marketing campaigns to revitalize older brands is all to the good. But building the institutional capabilities necessary for creating shareholder value consistently—day in and day out—is a much greater undertaking. Sustainable excellence at value creation requires excellent management processes—the institutional value drivers. In Chapters Twelve through Sixteen we will elaborate on how companies can reengineer their current processes to create lasting competitive advantage and value.

CHAPTER 12

Governance

Corporate governance applies most commonly to the roles and responsibilities of the shareholders, the board of directors, and the chief executive officer in managing the legal and economic relationships between the company and its owners or other stakeholders. We expand this meaning somewhat to include the roles and responsibilities of business unit general managers and top managers in the corporate center, including the chief financial officer and the heads of the human resources, corporate planning, and legal functions. We think this is important because these executives can play a significant part in achieving the company's *governing objective,* and their responsibilities should certainly be defined in the context of how best to govern the company for the purpose of creating maximum wealth.

The corporate governance process involves determination of two related elements: the best organization *structure* and the right *roles and responsibilities* for managing value. Determining the best organization structure enables managers to achieve the greatest *clarity* in deciding where, how, and how much value is being or could be created within each business unit and within the company's total portfolio. Determining the right roles and responsibilities enables managers to achieve the highest degree of *accountability* for creation or destruction of value. In our experience good clarity and accountability are essential for achieving consistently superior returns for shareholders. Companies with a poor definition of business units or an aversion to holding managers strictly accountable for specific aspects of performance will find it nearly impossible to maximize (or even create) wealth. Conversely, companies with a clear economically based business unit structure and an unambiguous accountability of managers for performance will find it much easier to achieve the organization's highest potential.

The principal structure issue facing management is how to align strategy and organizational boundaries—specifically, how to segment the portfolio into the appropriate economic and organizational units for managing value. We begin, however, by assuming that the organizational boundaries are in order and addressing first the major accountability questions: "What are the roles and responsibilities of the chief executive and the corporate center, the business units, and finally, the board of directors?"

Establishing Accountability for Performance

Top management and the board of directors share accountability for the rate of return earned by the shareholders over time. If the rate of return is consistently above that of comparable companies, top management and the board can be said to be doing an outstanding job. If the rate of return is about the same as for comparable companies, top management and the board are certainly doing an adequate, although perhaps not exceptional, job. However, when rates of return fall consistently below those generated by comparable firms, there is seldom, if ever, any place to hide: For whatever reason, top management and the board are not choosing the right strategies for the business units or the company as a whole.

The Chief Executive and Corporate Center

The primary responsibility for making sure that the company performs well for its owners rests, of course, with the chief executive and, by extension, with his or her direct reports in the corporate center. While few chief executives would argue with the principle that they must accept responsibility for the company's performance, there is little agreement about what that great responsibility implies for the chief executive's specifically defined day-to-day role in managing the company. Some chief executives, like John Sculley when he was CEO of Apple Computer, see their role as "envisioning the future" and marshalling the company's resources to achieve that vision. Others spend an enormous amount of time on the operating details of the businesses, "helping" the business unit general managers improve short-term performance. Harold Geneen at ITT in the 1970s was a celebrated example of this type of chief executive. Some are able to blend exceptional strategic, financial, and organizational capabilities with strong leadership to drive companies toward superior performance: Jack Welch of General Electric, Percy Barnevik of Asea Brown Boveri, Roberto Goizueta of The Coca-Cola Company, Brian Pitman of Lloyds Bank, and Michael Eisner of Disney are among the more prominent examples of this too-uncommon type of individual.

While the specific roles and responsibilities of any chief executive will always reflect the culture and needs of the company as well as his or her personal characteristics, we believe that some important generalizations can be made about the roles and responsibilities of the CEO and the corporate center at any firm. The three main tasks, illustrated in Exhibit 12.1 are as follows:

- Making the *rules,* including the governing objective, by which the company will be managed.
- Creating the *organization* needed to achieve the company's governing objective.
- Ensuring that all corporate and business unit *strategies* support the achievement of the governing objective.

This list is short but formidable. It does not fit readily with prevailing ideas about centralization at headquarters versus decentralization into the business units or directive management versus "empowered" employees. In some ways, the role of the chief executive and center that we propose calls for a very high degree of responsibility and authority for creating value to be vested in the business units. For instance, once the chief executive and the business unit have agreed on the best strategy, the business unit general manager and his team must be left alone to get on with the job. As long as they are achieving the agreed-upon goals, they must be left alone regardless of performance shortfalls in other business units or any other unrelated events. Yet in

EXHIBIT 12.1

The Role of the Chief Executive and the Corporate Center

To establish the rules or principles by which the company will be managed

- Specify and communicate the governing objective of the company
- Specify and communicate the policies and standards of the company
- Specify and communicate the cultural norms/values of the company

▼

To create an organization capable of achieving the company's goals, consistently and over time (maximize organizational effectiveness)

- **Structure:** Set the corporate center and business unit boundaries, and managers' roles and responsibilities
- **Process:** Design and support the key management processes necessary to achieve the governing objective

- **People:** Select, develop, and deploy managers to ensure that the company is capable at all levels of achieving the governing objective
- **Information:** Ensure that all necessary information necessary to achieve the governing objective is generated and shared throughout the company

▼

To ensure that all strategies at the business unit and corporate level are conducive to achieving the company's goals (maximize strategic effectiveness)

- **Corporate Level:** Develop and implement strategies for managing company's strategic value drivers and the portfolio

- **Business Unit Level:** Ensure that the business units have in place only those strategies that achieve the governing objective, and those strategies are being implemented effectively

---

some ways, this approach also calls for a much more intrusive role for the chief executive and center than some company cultures currently allow. For instance, in a value based company, business units do not "own" or have exclusive control of the information needed to determine the highest-value strategy for the business. We will develop these and other trade-offs more fully in the next several chapters.

Making the Rules

By far the most important "rule" for the chief executive (and the board) to establish and enforce is the specification of the governing objective itself. This should not be confused with vision and mission statements, which, when unrelated to concrete economic objectives, have little, if anything, to do with the company's performance over time. Although he was widely criticized at the time and the results are still to be seen, we like what Louis Gerstner said about vision early in his heroic attempt to lead the turnaround at IBM:

> There has been a lot of speculation that I'm going to deliver a "vision" of IBM. The last thing IBM needs right now is a vision. What IBM needs right now is a series of very tough-minded, market-driven [and] highly selective strategies that deliver performance in the marketplace and shareholder value.[1]

A chief executive committed to the governing objective is more likely to ask, "If we implement the strategies that will create value for our shareholders each and every year, what might the company look like in ten years?" rather than "What is our vision of the future and, therefore, what should the company look like in ten years?" This is an extremely important difference in perspective. The shareholders are not interested in what the company per se will look like in ten years. They do not care how big its sales or assets will be, they do not care what businesses it will be in, whether it will be global or local, or even whether it will be an independent entity. Shareholders really want to know, or be able to forecast, only one thing: How much wealth will the company create in the future? And that very simple, unadorned question must be the chief executive's focus as well.

Along with specifying and enforcing the governing objective, the chief executive and center must also determine another set of rules, namely, the policies that will constrain the drive for that objective. These are the broad, important policies concerning the values and behavior of the organization, not detailed regulations of such matters as executive auto leases. For instance, we assume that all companies want every employee to pursue value creation only within the limitations of the law. Yet even this seemingly self-evident policy is sometimes open to question. For years, many retailers in the United Kingdom have engaged in a form of civil disobedience by remaining open on Sundays in defiance of the law against trading on that day. There has been more than tacit approval from at least some of the authorities (who probably like to shop on Sundays, like the rest of us), with the companies simply paying fines that are deemed an acceptable cost of doing business. Even companies that would much prefer to remain closed on Sundays are faced with an unattractive dilemma when competitors are open for business, taking away customers and market share.

Given the complexities that bedevil even supposedly simple policies and given, too, the propensity for policy proliferation, there are some guidelines we find useful. First, corporate-level policies should be *important*, meaning they should have a significant impact on the company's potential value, such as policies to protect invaluable brands, or negatively, as in policies to prevent harm to customers, employees, and the environment. Second, and largely a consequence of the first guideline, there should be as *few* corporate policies as possible, to ensure that they are well known and fully understood in the organization. One company we know conducted a full audit of corporate-mandated policies and found that some 125 had been established over the years. Of course, most had little effect on the company's value. Consequently, most (such as the permissible level of spending for Christmas parties) were either dropped or passed down to the business units. The company has issued a very manageable list of 25 corporate policies, which are recognized as very important to its value and not within the purview of any individual business unit to define entirely for itself. All other policies, including quite a few previously sacrosanct corporate personnel policies, are the responsibility of the individual business units. Finally, it is certainly very important that the corporate policies are clearly *enforced* by the chief executive and all of top management— otherwise they have no meaning, or worse, breed cynicism in the organization.

In addition to setting the governing objective and critical policies, the chief executive and corporate center can influence the culture of the company in important ways. The impact of culture on wealth creation is clearly important. A company, undoubtedly has a set of cultural characteristics—such as being outward looking, imaginative, open, objective, demanding, energetic, focused—that are consistent with, but do not necessarily guarantee, value creation. Conversely, a company with a culture that is primarily inward-looking, risk-averse, unrealistic, defensive, unfocused, undisciplined, and lacking in real energy is obviously a poor candidate for value creation. Yet it is extremely difficult to answer the fundamental question of how a chief executive can help build the right culture for future wealth creation. Chief executives who have had notable success in this area in recent years include Robert Allen at AT&T and Percy Barnevik at Asea Brown Boveri. As *Business Week* noted, Allen took "one of the world's most entrenched corporate cultures and turned it around, shattering the old icons, clearing out the deadwood, luring in outsiders, and infusing a sprawling empire with a simple, overarching vision of the future."[2] At ABB, Barnevik managed to combine two large, and complex companies from different cultures—Swedish and Swiss—into a global firm competing successfully in industries as varied as power plants, power transmission, maritime telecommunications, and financial services. On the other side of the ledger was General Motors, which, before Jack Smith became chief executive, stood as perhaps the most profoundly dysfunctional organization for wealth creation in the United States. The challenge facing Smith and his management team, similar to the challenge facing Gerstner at IBM, cannot be overestimated. Changing the culture of these corporate behemoths from one of institutional complacency and self-absorption into fully competitive and wealth-creating enterprise represents the most monumental of management tasks. The first step, as Gerstner noted, is to refresh people's memories in no uncertain terms about what the organization's primary purpose is—and must be—to survive in the long term. But that is only the first step, and cultural changes must follow that will take many years to achieve, if they can be achieved at all.

Creating the Organization

As shown in Exhibit 12.1, the chief executive and corporate center have to play a pivotal role in designing and building a company with the propensity to create wealth. In other words, they must determine how the company is going to manage its key institutional value drivers. Designing and maintaining the right structure, processes, information, and management capabilities to induce the organization to produce superior returns for shareholders over time is an extraordinarily demanding responsibility. It is not made easier by these twin realities. On one hand, many chief executives are less enamored of these subjects than they are of pursuing more "strategic" goals, while on the other hand, other corporate executives often respond to this partial vacuum by implementing their own ideas for addressing the company's needs without necessarily linking them to the governing objective. As a result, too many companies have organizations that, at best, cannot cope with the institutional imperative that works incessantly to erode value. At worst, these companies are so dysfunctional that, like General Motors and Champion International in the 1980s, they become persistent wealth destroyers in spite of strategies they believe will have the opposite effect.

The reasons for underestimating the importance of management process vary, but they tend to include such factors as lack of experience (many tasks associated with building an exceptional institution seem like "staff" rather than "line" activities, and most chief executives have come up through the line), and the perception that the tasks are not as inherently gratifying as, say, forging a new strategic alliance (who wants to worry about the process for setting business unit performance objectives when there are deals to be done?). Frequently, an effective chief operating officer or chief financial officer with more of a process orientation can serve as the chief executive's principal ally in changing the way the company is managed. However it is accomplished, the fact remains that bringing the organization to and keeping it at a point where there is a strong institutional propensity to create rather than to waste value is a critical responsibility. Too often in recent years the intervention of the board, and sometimes the appointment of a new chief executive, was required before these fundamental issues of governance were properly addressed even in the short term.

We address the importance of structure and its management in this chapter. The key management processes we discuss here include strategic planning, resource allocation, control, and top management compensation. We consider these processes so important to the performance of the company that we explore them separately in Chapters Thirteen through Sixteen.

Ensuring the Right Strategies

The chief executive, and the executives who support him or her in the corporate center, must ensure that all strategies support the goal of maximizing shareholder value. At the corporate level, this is a direct responsibility. It includes developing and implementing strategies for adding new businesses; divesting businesses, products, and customers when appropriate; and managing the company's shared strategic value drivers. At the business unit level, it is an affirmative responsibility to ensure that all good growth strategies are properly and fully resourced and no resources are invested in bad growth strategies. As subsequent chapters on strategic planning, resource allocation, and performance management will detail, these responsibilities of the center can, if necessary, be quite intrusive, particularly when it comes to information required from the businesses. However, the chief executive must be able to act at all times as the representative of the shareholders to ensure that their money is properly invested. This role cannot be performed without a good deal of intervention at times to ensure that the best decisions are made and company performance is living up to expectations.

Business Unit General Managers

The primary responsibilities of a business unit general manager and his or her direct reports are, first, to determine the highest-value strategy for the business, and second, to implement that strategy successfully, realizing the full economic potential of the business in the process. Obviously, it is essential for the top management of every business unit in the portfolio to fulfill this immense responsibility if the company is to achieve its overall objective. The specific tasks required of business unit management mirror those of the corporate center—specifically, setting the right goals, building an organization capable of achieving those goals, and ensuring that all product market strategies within the unit support the creation of higher wealth.

For most general managers, to be held formally accountable for achieving the highest possible value of a business unit would represent a dramatic change from conventional management practice. Typically, the primary financial objective of a business unit is to increase pretax earnings by some double-digit amount each year. Some companies may set return or cash flow targets, typically on an annual basis. But very few companies task the business to demonstrate in a rigorous way that its recommended strategy will generate more value than any alternative and then set appropriate multiyear strategic and financial targets to ensure that the promised performance goal is met. Such a responsibility requires the general manager to devote far more time to the major strategic and organizational issues affecting the value of the business and far less time to budgets and other matters that have little impact on the unit's capacity to generate value. This may mean that many day-to-day operating aspects of the general manager's role, important as they are, should be delegated to other senior managers. The general manager should be, first and foremost, the leader of the continuous strategic and organizational improvements needed to achieve superior performance over time.

To illustrate this point in concrete terms, we estimate from our experience that the typical business unit general manager spends as much as half of his or her time on matters that, from a value creation perspective, deserve no more than a 10 percent commitment. Exhibit

EXHIBIT 12.2

Business Unit General Manager's Use of Time

Activity	Typical Time Commitment	Recommended Time Commitment
Trying to improve operating performance in parts of the business where the strategy is inherently value consuming	25–40%	5% (should not have more than 5% of BU portfolio in this situation at any point in time)
Budgeting and related activities	15–20%	5%
Strategic planning and performance management, i.e., managing the strategic value drivers of the business	10–15%	30–40%
Improving organization structure, management process, information, and management capabilities, i.e., managing the institutional value drivers of the business	5–10%	25–35%
Other, including normal administrative duties, customer visits, community activities, etc.	Approximately 25%	Approximately 25%

12.2 shows what we consider a fairly typical use of time and compares it with a recommended allocation.

Wealth creation requires the full-time leadership of a general manager, much as it does of a chief executive. Typically, at least 85 percent of a company's value is determined by business unit strategies. Thus, it is not asking too much for the general manager to spend between 55 and 75 percent of his or her time on managing the value drivers, ensuring that the business is constantly assessing high-potential options and pursuing those that create the most wealth.

Holding business unit general managers accountable for this standard of performance might also require companies to rethink their career development tracks. It is not uncommon, particularly in U.S. companies, for general managers to be rotated every two to three years. While this has the virtue of providing breadth of experience, it comes at the cost of depth of knowledge of any particular business. And depth of knowledge is absolutely essential to doing a good job of managing for value. We believe it can take two to three years just to learn the business well enough to hit full stride with effective strategies for quantum performance improvements. In addition, longer tenure in the job enables the chief executive to see which general managers can perform well consistently, through good times and bad.

The Board of Directors

The board of directors has two responsibilities that dominate all others. The first is to ensure that the company has the right governing objective. The second is to ensure that the company has the right chief executive. Other board activities, such as audit, compensation, decisions on the dividend or acquisitions, are important and must be carried out well. However, these activities matter little if the company is being managed to achieve the wrong objective, or the chief executive cannot achieve consistently at least average, if not superior, shareholder returns over time.

It is interesting to note that few boards take direct responsibility for ensuring that the company's governing objective is to put its resources to their highest and best economic use, that is, to create as much as possible value. This seeming lack of interest in the shareholders' welfare may be due in part to the discomfort most boards feel about appearing to place shareholders ahead of other stakeholders. However, as noted in Chapter One, we do not believe there is an inherent conflict between shareholders and other stakeholders, least of all in companies that are good producers of wealth. Boards should not be confused or uncomfortable about their role in asserting that the purpose of a business enterprise is to create wealth, the benefits of which accrue to everyone. This is not simply a matter of principle. The long-term competitive health and prosperity of the company, which most boards would agree *is* their responsibility, depends critically on the capacity of the enterprise to maximize the value of its resources.

In most of the exemplar companies with which we are familiar, the chief executive (who has often been chairman of the board as well) has been the champion of managing for shareholder value. This is, of course, as it should be, but the irony in some cases has been the initial reluctance of other board members, usually those still adhering to the earnings-per-share school, to embrace the new governing objective as wholeheartedly as the chief executive does. In any event, the board should not leave it to the chief executive alone to determine how much weight should be given to the shareholders' interests. When, as in the exemplar companies, the chief executive takes the lead in pursuing the governing objective, the board should give its full support to that goal. But in the absence of such management leadership, the board should assert itself. The choice of achieving the company's governing objective should not be optional. Nor should the board allow that objective to be obscured by a cloud of visions, missions or statements of "strategic intent" unrelated to the achievement of exemplary financial performance.

Given the governing objective, the board must also do its utmost to ensure that the chief executive is able to lead the company to the achievement of that objective. Here, boards of directors have become much more active in recent years, at least when a company's fortunes have fallen so low that a change in leadership has been seen as essential. The list of companies with board-led changes of chief executive is long. In the United States, IBM, General Motors, Eastman Kodak, American Express, Westinghouse, and Digital Equipment are among the blue-chip organizations that have replaced chief executives on grounds that a new approach was needed to improve company performance in both the product markets and the capital markets.

In each of these cases, the changes were precipitated by unfavorable events. In more normal succession decisions, the board needs the best possible information on each candidate's track record as a wealth creator. Since it is very desirable to select a chief executive from the company's own management ranks, the board should be able to determine which managers score highest on this most difficult test by evaluating critically the performance of the businesses and functions they have managed over time. Of course, this will be much easier to do if the company has a history of successfully employing value based management principles. If the board feels that there are no qualified internal candidates (most unlikely in a company where every general manager is held accountable for maximizing the value of his or her business unit over time), the primary qualification for an outside candidate should be a demonstrated record as a wealth creator at another company of comparable size and complexity. Charming personality, a visionary mind, good political connections, attractive appearance, and related business experience are all pluses but no substitute for the real thing.

In our review of the roles and responsibilities of the key players who manage the company's value drivers, we have assumed that the company's organizational structure is already aligned with the governing objective. But often this is not the case, and we need to address this major issue.

Aligning Strategy and Structure

Throughout this book we have assumed that business units are essentially independent economic entities that constitute the basic organizational building blocks of the company. As we work with many companies, however, we find little agreement in practice—either within or across companies—about what a business unit is, how its boundaries are drawn, or what powers and responsibilities it has. In some companies, such as General Electric, business units are fairly discrete economic and organizational entities that are responsible for their own strategy development and implementation. Not only are the jet engine business, the consumer appliance business, and the financial services business unlikely to be confused with each other, each has its own distinct strategy and the organizational resources to achieve that strategy. At the other extreme, prior to 1990, IBM did not segment itself in terms of business units at all. Upstream organizations controlled vertically integrated manufacturing and most of R&D, while downstream organizations were responsible for sales and distribution throughout the world. In the United States, for example, the marketing and sales organization was a separate entity that sold all IBM products to all large customers. Of course, sales and marketing interacted with both manufacturing and development, but they did not report to the same executives. Worldwide product pricing was set at corporate headquarters in Armonk, New York. These functions did not come together into an integrated "business unit" below the level of the chief executive and the corporate center. In effect, there was only one global strategy, covering R&D, manufacturing, customer service, and pricing across all products for the entire company. Between the GE and IBM "extremes," other companies adopt many variations, including "business units" that contain several easily separable economic entities and "business units" that are really planning organizations with no resources or capacity to actually implement the strategies they are supposed to develop.

Since we seek to align organization structure and strategy, and since the purpose of strategy is to create value, we also seek the maximum clarity between management's decisions and the future strategic and financial performance of the business unit. This means a business unit must be defined so that its warranted value and the value of its strategic options can be measured independently of all other units. Further, it must be possible for the general manager to control or strongly influence the strategic and institutional value drivers of his or her business. If these two conditions are not met, insight and accountability become so weakened that the company's capacity to develop and implement value-maximizing strategies is seriously compromised. To illustrate this critical point, we ask our clients to consider the following questions: "At what level within the company should the chief executive pursue the governing objective? In other words, at what level within the company is there enough clarity for the chief executive to be comfortable that he or she has all the information and the control necessary for approving strategies, commiting resources, and setting performance targets?"

We begin to answer these questions by drawing what we call an economic map of the company. The economic map has two primary types of units: value centers and cost centers. A value center can be thought of as the smallest economic unit in the company with essentially independent equity cash flows and economic profits. The management of a value center can generally develop and implement strategies to maximize warranted value without reference to other value or cost centers in the portfolio. At the same time, the activities within the value center are so linked that its strategy alternatives cannot be evaluated independently or implemented at any lower level. However, many value centers can be subdivided further into product market units.

These product market units are somewhat, but not totally, strategically independent of one another. For example, a company may manufacture a product line, such as fax machines, with both consumer and commercial applications. These products may have closely shared R&D and production costs but very different marketing and distribution needs. Thus, all the assets in the fax machine business may be grouped into a single value center, but the consumer and commercial product market units each have their own marketing strategies. Each of these product market units generates some controllable equity cash flow or economic profit, and each makes a measurable value contribution to the company, but neither can function entirely independently of the other.

Cost centers are basically production or service units supporting two or more value centers. They can best be thought of as utilities with no material external sales but with a "captive" downstream market. Cost centers can sometimes be very large, as in the case of facilities making intermediate chemical products, for which there is little or no merchant market. Their objective is to minimize the economic costs of production subject to the volume and quality requirements of the value centers they serve. They have no independent strategy of their own, as their investment requirements should be determined entirely by the strategies of the downstream units.

In our experience, drawing the economic map of a company can be quite challenging, but it is almost always very insightful. To do it properly, managers must start by defining the company's value centers on the basis of a thorough examination of the economic linkages within the company. For instance, the availability of external merchant markets plays a big role in determining whether two vertically linked businesses are potentially separate value centers. Similarly, the nature and extent of shared costs and assets between horizontally linked units will dictate whether the units are single or separate value centers supported by a cost center. In determining value center boundaries, it is important to avoid considerations that commonly define organization units but are irrelevant to the definition of economic units. For instance, value centers have no predetermined size constraints, so they can be very small or very large. Also, there is no limit to the number of value centers a company can have as long as each can be managed for value largely independently of other units.

Of course, defining value centers in this way often leads to an economic map that is quite different from the existing organization structure. In some cases, several existing business units will become part of a larger value center. In other cases, several value centers will fall within an existing business unit. And in some cases, the value center will be the same as the existing business unit. This often leads to alternatives to the existing organization structure that improve its alignment with the economic map and the governing objective. For example, Exhibit 12.3 shows the economic map of a client company and compares it with the existing organization structure.

In this somewhat simplified example, the company was previously organized into 15 businesses and had no cost centers, apart from the corporate center (not shown). Three of the business units served industrial markets and 12 served consumer markets. Each of these groups reported to a group executive, who in turn reported to the chief executive. As part of its ongoing efforts to improve performance for shareholders, the company decided to review its organization structure to determine how well it aligned with the objective of value creation. The result was the economic map shown here, with six value centers and one cost center oriented primarily toward industrial markets, and five value centers and one cost center oriented primarily toward consumer markets.

Briefly, on the industrial side, what are actually four value centers and a cost center had been structured previously as a single business unit, with the company's chief executive seeing only a single business unit "strategy" and a long-range forecast. Under these circumstances, he simply did not have the information and insight necessary to evaluate the strategic or economic merits of the business plans or make value based resource allocation decisions. Further, accountability for performance within the previous business unit was weakened by the

EXHIBIT 12.3

Economic Map of a Multi-Business Company

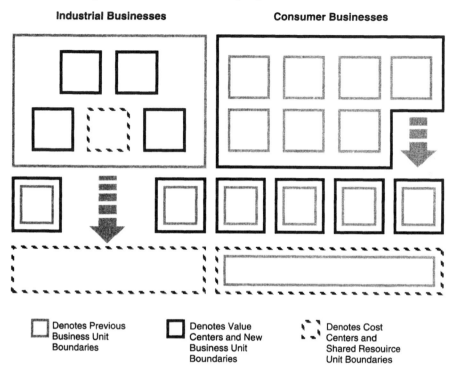

Industrial Businesses   **Consumer Businesses**

| | Denotes Previous Business Unit Boundaries | | Denotes Value Centers and New Business Unit Boundaries | | Denotes Cost Centers and Shared Resouirce Unit Boundaries |

fact that its components had reported along functional lines rather than to separate general managers.

On the consumer side, the company concluded that eight business units previously within a division really constituted one large value center, containing seven product market units and one small value center that could seek its best strategy independently of the others. Each product market unit had a distinctly different customer "offer," but all shared brands and production facilities and targeted largely the same customers. Even more important, however, all faced a complex array of competitive threats that no individual unit could deal with alone. Thus, their separate strategies were beginning to put at risk the considerable competitive advantages of these businesses and making it impossible for them to find the best alternatives for maximizing value. Organizing as a single value center was essential to their strategic coordination and cooperation. After changing to the new organization structure based on the economic map, units representing 80 percent of the company's value reported directly to the chief executive for approval of strategies, resources, and performance targets.

As this case illustrates, there is a direct linkage between the economic map and the organizational, or "political," map of the company. In the terminology we generally use, value centers translate into business units, and cost centers translate into shared resource units. We find that analyzing the company from a purely economic perspective and using different terms such as "value center" helps managers take a fresh look at the company's fundamental economic structure without the burden of some political baggage that usually causes confusion in discussions of business unit boundaries. Note, too, that neither the economic map nor the new political map that follows should be influenced at all by the current "legal" or financial maps of the company. These legal entities may or may not be true managerial units.

Developing the economic map and translating it into a new organization structure that enables the company to measure and manage value effectively usually raises many issues. Among the most common and difficult are the following:

- *Matrix management.* We have worked with a number of large, complex companies with "matrixed" organizations, where it was literally impossible to determine who was responsible for performance because business unit boundaries were not tightly drawn and accountability for economic profit at all levels was shared by several managers. Complex companies unquestionably need a matrix of management input and information to make informed decisions. However, we do not believe that this very legitimate need to provide essential information to decision makers should lead to uncertainty about decision-making responsibilities. Every company can be segmented into value centers and cost centers, and each of these units should have a general manager who is clearly accountable to the chief executive for its performance. Some of these units may be very large and complex—some may even be global in scope—but they must be defined in such a way that they are measurable and manageable to ensure good alignment between strategy and structure as well as between performance and accountability.
- *Transfer pricing.* Few topics generate more heat and less light than

transfer pricing of goods and services within the company. This is not only because the subject can be difficult, which it sometimes is at large, vertically integrated companies, but because managers usually worry about it for the wrong reasons. Internal transfer prices should not be set to permit "fair sharing" of profits between units or even to minimize taxes for the company.[3] The primary objective of a company's transfer-pricing policy should be to ensure the clearest possible economic "signaling" between units. When boundaries have been drawn correctly, transfer pricing should be based on two straightforward rules: (1) all transfers between value centers are at open market prices (if this cannot be achieved, the boundaries need to be redrawn); and (2) all goods and services are transferred from cost centers to other units at their full economic cost (cost of production plus cost of capital). These rules preserve the integrity of economic profit and cash flow measures for all units, so that the full value creation implications of alternative strategies can be captured in the value centers (where they belong), and signals affecting profitable capacity expansion or reduction are captured in the cost centers (where *they* belong).

- *Materiality.* Value centers and cost centers do not come in convenient sizes or numbers. Some value centers/business units may be very large. Others may be a mere dot on the corporate landscape. Should they all report directly to the chief executive for purposes of strategy approval, resource allocation, and target setting? Ideally, we would answer "Yes," in the sense that making these decisions is the chief executive's most important role in leading the company to achievement of its governing objective. As a rough guideline, we would say that the strategies of units comprising 80 percent of the company's value certainly should be reviewed directly by the chief executive, with the review of others delegated if necessary. But the responsibility for allocating the shareholders' equity to the best business unit strategies cannot be delegated—ultimately it is the chief executive's alone, whether he or she chooses to delegate a small part of it on grounds that it has less materiality for value creation. Of course, oversight of strategy implementation can and must be delegated to others. But if the chief executive does not deem a business unit strategy and its impact on the company's value really material, why is the business in the portfolio anyway?

Concluding Remarks

Explicit consideration of the company's governing objective is vital in determining the most effective organizational roles and responsibilities for performance as well as the most effective structure for aligning strategy and organizational boundaries. We have tried to show that the objective of maximizing shareholder value has very significant implications for how companies can best deal with these questions, which are among the most complicated that managers face.

The theme we have stressed above all others is the need for clarity—clarity of purpose, clarity of accountability, clarity of performance measurement, and clarity of organization structure. It is extraordinarily complicated to manage modern corporations under the best of circumstances, but it quickly becomes impossible to manage them in any accepted meaning of the word if there is a lack of consensus about what the company is in business to do, or how it is organized to do it, or who is responsible for the results. We believe a value based governance process is essential for dealing with these vital issues.

CHAPTER 13

Strategic Planning

Strategic planning is the most recently developed of the major management processes. Companies have long had formal budgeting and single-year operating planning processes; indeed, these have been and continue to be the primary processes that drive key business decisions in most companies. Also long formalized (although changing continuously) have been processes for evaluating individual investment projects, developing multiyear financial forecasts, and management incentive compensation. By comparison, formal strategic planning is a relative newcomer whose history began only in the mid-1960s with the advent of new business strategy tools such as those developed by the Boston Consulting Group and McKinsey & Company. The first formal corporate strategic planning process to receive wide attention and be emulated by other companies was introduced at the General Electric Company in the 1960s. Even after 30 years, however, strategic planning is still far behind its older cousins in terms of its impact on investment decisions (regrettably, investment decisions are too often labeled "strategic" only when they clearly make no economic sense; on setting of performance targets; and on the design of incentive compensation programs. The only characteristic of the strategic planning process that we find common among most companies is that, whatever form it takes, it involves a lot of work and has almost no everyday consequences.

We believe that strategic planning deserves not only a more important role than it has thus far enjoyed, but it should be the dominant process for managing the company—not only for the long term but even on a day-to-day basis. Strategic planning, unlike budgeting, requires both a short- and long-term view. It must also be based on a thorough, objective understanding of customers, competitors, and the fundamental economics of the business. In other words, *a good strategic planning process is the foundation for managing for shareholder value.* A company's strategic planning process should be viewed as both a key value driver and a source of competitive advantage—development of consistently superior strategies will almost always require a distinctly advantaged process for doing so.

As the primary decision-making process of the company, we believe that strategic planning should have certain characteristics. First, of course, it should be *value based.* Second, it should be *consequential,* driving the major business unit and corporate decisions that will determine both the short- and long-term performance of the company. Third, it should be *continuous,* with important issues under constant assessment and discussion. We discuss the importance of these characteristics and address their application to both business unit and corporate center strategic planning.

Value Based Strategic Planning

The strategic planning processes of most companies exist and function without management consensus concerning their purpose. To the extent that any rationale is offered, it generally includes vague references to the need to manage for "the long term," to build "competitive advantage," to serve "customer needs," or perhaps to the need to build a "global business." However, even while "seeking to build a long-term competitive advantage by serving customer needs better on a global basis," the underlying reality is that company strategy is driven by the objectives and constraints imposed by the annual budgeting process. In the absence of a true consensus within the top management group concerning the purpose of strategic planning, there cannot be agreement on the desired content, quality, or structure of the process. People go through the motions of preparing plan documents according to management instruction, but they have a hard time explaining why they follow this procedure.

We believe that the purpose of the strategic planning process should be stated explicitly: It is to *identify, develop, and select the highest-value strategies for each business unit in the portfolio and for the corporate center.* To achieve this objective, the process must be value based, designed to support the governing objective through application of the principles discussed in earlier Chapters Seven through Ten. Strategic planning must be rigorous and objective. This means, among other things, that it will require managers to generate high-potential strategic options for comparison on the basis of their value creation potential for the company. It also means that good strategic planning cannot be done without numbers. We understand managers' frustration with so-called strategic planning processes that amount to little more than exercises in generating ungrounded financial forecasts for three to five years. The problem with these forecasts is not that there are numbers, it is that no one believes (or should believe), those numbers. As described in Chapter Seven, forecasting based on a detailed understanding of the linkages between strategic options and probable financial outcomes is an essential discipline of good strategic planning.

Value based strategic planning upholds no particular orthodoxy of business strategy. For instance, if more market share, more customer service, more quality, or reengineering the manufacturing process to increase efficiency will create more value for the business, it is a good thing. If the effort does not create higher value, further investment in share, service, quality, or efficiency is unjustified. There is no *a priori* view on whether markets should be served globally or locally, large scale is better than small scale, a full product line is better than a focused product line, vertical integration is better than outsourcing, cost or differentiation should be the basis of competitive advantage, growth should be sacrificed for higher ROEs, or vice versa. The right answers to these questions will depend on a detailed understanding of the financial and strategic determinants of value for the business, and the options afforded by the strategic value drivers for a particular business.

Strategic Planning with Consequences

For all the thousands and tens of thousands of hours that go into strategic planning at the typical company, the remarkable fact is that so little of this effort has a noticeable impact on day-to-day decision making or business performance. For instance, one client, a global consumer products company, has calculated that 40,000 man-hours are devoted annually to producing a four-year plan that is seldom, if ever, referred to by the line managers who are required to prepare it. While this may be a bit extreme, it is not all that far from the reality at a majority of companies. It is by now a tiresome cliché that strategic plans, once documented according to the required script and presented to top management, are simply filed away to gather dust. Sadly, the cliché holds true more often than not. It's hard to know whether there is more managerial cynicism about the annual budgeting process, which is often viewed as wrongheaded and politicized, or about the strategic planning process, which is viewed as promising much but delivering little.

For a company's strategic planning process to have real consequences, especially for value creation, it must first be assigned higher importance than the company's traditional budgeting and project approval processes. Despite all efforts to convince managers to think longer-term and more strategically, they know the real action is in getting their budgets and projects approved because "that's where the money is." But budgets and project approvals are heavily influenced by top-down, short-term accounting targets as well as the widely-held belief that capital is limited and must be rationed. Both of these concepts conflict directly with the principles of value based management presented in Chapters Fourteen and Fifteen. Budgeting and project approvals are essential elements of a company's performance management process. But they are suitable primarily for controlling financial performance, not for making or even influencing strategic investment decisions. In fact, we feel that subordinating budgets and projects to strategies is the single most important step in transforming ordinary management processes into true value drivers.

When the chief executive "approves" a business unit or corporate center strategy, it should mean more than a general agreement that the strategy is directionally correct or can be pursued, provided it ultimately fits with the financial targets and constraints imposed by the top-down company budgeting process. This type of strategy approval is common and almost meaningless. It carries no explicit promise of resources for implementation, no rewards for success, or sanctions for failure. In fact, no one would notice or mind particularly if the strategy were not implemented at all, as long as the short-term earnings growth goals of the company were met. On the other hand, a business unit could do its utmost to implement a strategy successfully, only to be told that the resources it requires are being diverted because of the company's need to reach this year's earnings-per-share target or redirect capital to subsidize some underperforming business unit.

Chief executive approval of a strategy should mean at least three things:

- The chief executive is convinced by seeing and discussing the strategic alternatives that the option he or she is approving is value maximizing—that no other options appear to have higher value for the owners—and therefore the approved strategy (and no other) *must* be implemented.
- The chief executive is approving the *resources* required to implement the strategy for at least the next two to three years provided the promised performance is being delivered. This means that, except under the direst financial circumstances, the company will deliver the promised resources regardless of performance problems elsewhere in the portfolio or the short-term fluctuations of the company's reported earnings. This idea is nowhere near as alarming as it might first appear and is discussed more extensively in Chapter Fourteen.
- The chief executive is approving key *performance targets and milestones* as the basis for monitoring the success of the strategy and linking managers' rewards directly to that success. These targets and milestones emerge from the approved strategy itself and are therefore entirely consistent with maximizing value and motivating managers to do what is best for the company. These ideas are expanded in Chapters Fifteen and Sixteen.

These are the primary consequences of an effective strategic planning process—they form the basic "contract" between the managers responsible for the strategies and the chief executive who approves them. In effect, the chief executive is requiring that the approved strategy become the formal, or contractual, basis on which the business units and corporate initiatives are managed.

The prospect of giving strategic planning such a vital role in the management of the company makes many executives uneasy at first. This reflects their justifiable concern, based on the quality of strategic plans and forecasts they normally see, that it would be too risky to pin major decisions on information of such uncertain integrity. However, the alternative is to fall back on the budgeting process for planning, which is much worse. It may seem more reliable and less risky because companies have been doing it for so long, but holding business and corporate strategies hostage to the budget process will not produce consistently superior shareholder returns. The solution is to create a strategic planning process that is value based and has real consequences for the way the company is managed, giving the firm a competitive advantage in both the product and capital markets. No budgeting process can do this.

Continuous Planning

There are always significant strategic (and organizational) issues impacting value that need to be resolved in the business units and at the center. These issues do not appear at the beginning of the scheduled planning cycle and conveniently disappear again until next year's cycle starts. Thus, documented *plans* or forecasts may be produced on a periodic schedule, but the process of strategic *planning* needs to be continuous to ensure that all important issues are systematically and effectively addressed.

This distinction between planning and plans is not merely a matter of semantics. If the strategic planning process is to be the primary vehicle for corporate management decision making, it must be used as a day-to-day management tool, not reserved for an annual spasm of analysis and chart making. The top issues affecting the value of the company and business units should be clearly identified and form the basis of the agenda every time top management meets. As old issues are resolved, new ones should be added to the list, keeping management focused always on the things that matter most. Plans can be filed away and forgotten. An effective planning process cannot be ignored so conveniently.

Companies need two separate but related planning processes—one for the business units and one for the corporate center. Since the business units normally generate 85 percent or more of the company's value, the business unit strategic planning process is by far the more resource-intensive and important of the two. We look first at the business unit process and, more briefly, at the corporate center process.

The Business Unit Strategic Planning Process

We think of the business unit strategic planning process as having four major sequential activities: the strategic position assessment, an "issues and alternatives" meeting, strategy development, and one or more "review and approval" meetings.

The Strategic Position Assessment

As discussed in Chapter Seven, the business unit's purpose in this activity is to generate the basic high-quality information that management will need to undertake the development of strategic options. The most important output of the position assessment is the general manager's list of high-priority issues that the business unit faces in its efforts to increase its warranted value, along with the proposed alternatives for dealing with these issues. This list provides the basis for the agenda at the issues and alternatives meeting.

When a business unit undertakes a position assessment for the first time, the required effort can be substantial. For a typical business, the initial effort might involve three to six months of hard work, although future updates should be less time-consuming. But the benefits are also substantial. First, the general manager and his or her direct reports will reach a consensus on the fundamental strategic and economic factors critical to their business, the value of the current strategy to the company and its owners, the key value drivers, and the major issues facing the business. Second, the assessment output will enable the chief executive to develop a fairly quick and accurate understanding of the business unit well before he or she is asked to approve any strategies. Finally, this information will provide a sound basis as well as a catalyst for generating and evaluating strategic options later in the planning process.

Issues and Alternatives Meeting

The purpose of this meeting is for the chief executive and general manager of the business unit to agree on the specific issues to be addressed and alternatives to be considered when the business develops its strategy. Such a meeting and agreement are important for several reasons.

The first reason is to increase knowledge and understanding of the business. It is not uncommon for the chief executive to become formally involved in a business unit strategy only when it is presented for his or her approval, generally without serious alternatives to consider, in a meeting lasting one to three hours. This is too little, too late. The psychology and time pressures of these meetings make it extremely difficult for the chief executive to do anything more than ask due diligence questions and approve the strategy more or less as presented. Thus, the opportunity for the chief executive to really understand the business and provide quality input to the strategic thinking of the management team is extremely limited. The issues and alternatives meeting is designed to provide the chief executive with all the salient output of the position assessment. It allows the chief executive and the general manager to debate and reach agreement on the basic economics of the business, its key value drivers, and the major strategic and organizational issues it faces. This meeting also provides a forum for airing any disagreement. For instance, if the chief executive is uncomfortable with the assumptions about future market economics, the sources of competitive advantage, or the key value drivers, that input can be given without threatening to undo a carefully prepared strategic plan because the plan has not yet been developed.

A second reason is to provide a focus for planning. Once the chief executive is comfortable with the strategic position assessment, the foundation exists for a discussion of the key issues and alternatives facing the business unit. The issues, needless to say, can be key only if they are judged to have significant consequences for the value of the business. Generally, there will be no more than three or four issues of this magnitude that the business should be asked to resolve at any one time. They could include concerns about a major new competitive threat (e.g., the invasion of "category killers" in retailing); concerns about an increasingly disadvantaged cost position (e.g., competition from lower-cost imports); or concerns about changes in market economics (e.g., a shift toward greater customer bargaining power). For each issue identified, there also has to be discussion and agreement about the alternatives to be considered as part of the strategy development effort. Typically, only two or three alternatives are presented, but it is important that the business unit be prepared to deal with those that the chief executive considers important. For instance, faced with competition from lower-cost imports, the business unit may wish to examine the benefits of moving its manufacturing to a lower-cost country. The chief executive may agree that this option needs to be considered but asks that another option—outsourcing—be considered as well (if the business unit has a strong manufacturing culture, outsourcing might not have been considered otherwise).

A third reason is to reach consensus. The output of this meeting is a short document, often in the form of a letter from the chief executive to the general manager, detailing the issues and alternatives the business unit will be required to examine and evaluate in its strategy development effort. This gives sharp focus to the work and ensures that when the strategic options are next presented, they will cover the most important questions on the chief executive's mind and provide a high degree of understanding of the business before approval of any particular option is sought or given.

Following the issues and alternatives meeting, the business unit management team has a clear mandate from the chief executive to proceed with the strategy development phase of the planning process.

Strategy Development

As the tasks involved in this element of the strategic planning process have been discussed previously in Chapters Eight, Nine and Ten, we emphasize that at the end of the strategy development effort, the business unit general manager must "own" every detail of the recommendations he or she takes to the chief executive. In fact, the general manager should always lead the plan development process, to ensure that the best alternatives are surfaced and evaluated and the final strategy recommendation is the one he or she is fully prepared to defend and live by.

Review and Approval Meeting

The purpose of this meeting is to enable the chief executive and business unit general manager to agree on the highest-value strategic alternatives for the business (usually, but not always, these will be the strategic alternatives recommended by the general manager). Most important, a key outcome of this meeting is a consensus concerning the concrete actions to be taken to implement the approved strategy successfully. To reach his or her decision, the chief executive will look at the evaluations of the options presented as well as at the underlying assumptions and data critical to understanding those evaluations. Thus, the chief executive would seldom be in the position of having to say "No" to an entire strategy. Instead, if the chief executive and general manager differ in their views of the best alternative for dealing with a particular issue, further work may be needed to resolve the difference. Of course, if the chief executive is entirely unpersuaded by the quality or integrity of the analysis, which unfortunately happens sometimes, the recommended strategy should not be approved. It is also obvious that any strategic option or overall strategy unlikely to create value must be totally rejected.

When the chief executive and general manager reach agreement on the recommended options and strategy, the chief executive will approve the resources required to implement the strategy over the next several years as well as the performance targets, both strategic and financial, that will signal whether the expected value creation benefits are being realized. The general manager's contract with the company will be to deliver the projected performance or, if that should prove impossible, to reopen the issues and alternatives discussion to determine whether a different strategy or better implementation of the present plan is needed. The full agreement between the chief executive and general manager should be confirmed again in a letter from the CEO that authorizes the strategy, the resources, and the targets for the business over the next two to three years.

The Business Unit Planning "Cycle"

Up to this point, we have focused on the strategic planning process for a single business unit, without reference to the linkage to planning activities of other business units or to the company's annual operating plan or budget. At almost all companies we know, however, the strategic planning cycle is linked directly to the budget cycle, with strategic plans due from all business units just prior to commencement of the annual corporate budgeting process. Typically, the chief executive is expected to review and approve a large number of strategic plans during a brief period each year, say, a month or two, then turn around and do the same for the business budgets a few months later. This linkage is, in our view, not only unnecessary but counterproductive. There is no reason for strategic planning needs to be tied to the budget at all; in fact, there are good reasons for making sure that the two processes are largely decoupled.

Strategic planning is, or should be, a decision-making process. As we have said earlier, it should be *the* decision process for resolving all major strategic and operating issues of the firm. As such, it should take up most of the time of the chief executive and general managers. Budgeting is important, to be sure, but the budget numbers must reflect the most current update of approved strategic plans—nothing more, nothing less. Consequently, the chief executive needs to spend very little time on budgeting because the budget should not yield any new information that is material to top management decision making.

We can extend this proposition further to suggest that there is no reason to have all business units submit strategic plans at the same time each year. If the business units are properly defined, their strategies are largely independent (allowing for the possibility that shared strategic value drivers may be considered with respect to particular units). Consequently, *approval of a particular business unit strategy should generally have no bearing on the approval of any other business unit strategy.* Once this liberating idea is accepted, it becomes possible not only for the chief executive to be personally involved in reviewing more business unit strategies but to contribute more to the quality of strategic thinking throughout the company. For instance, a large company has 72 business units, and it seems to make sense to have formal strategic reviews about every two years on average (although key issues are *always* on the table regardless of the calendar). Thus in any one month, the chief executive would participate in about three issues and alternatives meetings and about three review and approval meetings: a total of six meetings and, allowing for some depth of discussion and consensus building taking perhaps four to five working days per month. Considering that this process is the primary means of achieving the company's governing objective, the time involved does not seem excessive.

One objection to decoupling strategic planning from the budget is that the company needs to know the total capital required for all strategies before they can be approved, i.e., the strategies are contingent on approval of the capital budget. In our view, this turns the process backwards. The company should fund all value maximizing business unit strategies and expand or contract the capital budget accordingly. The budget should not be a constraint on wealth maximization but an aid to implementation of the best strategies to achieve that goal, a subject we will explore in more detail in Chapter Fourteen.

Corporate Center Planning

The purpose of this process is to identify, develop, and select the highest-value options for managing the company's strategic value drivers, managing the portfolio by adding or divesting businesses, and managing the organization—most especially the institutional value drivers. Each of these tasks should be considered in the formal planning done by the corporate center each year. The general activities required for planning at the center are the same as for business units. For each task a fundamental analysis has to be conducted ahead of an issues and alternatives meeting, to be followed by the actual development of the strategy, and a review and approval meeting with the chief executive. For most companies, especially those that are not too acquisitive and have fairly "clean" portfolios, there may not be a need for much work on some of these tasks in any one year. But doing nothing is a decision that should be made only after the chief executive and the top management from the center have discussed that option as part of the issues and alternatives meeting.

In Chapter Ten we discussed the principles of strategy development for the corporate center. Here, we suggest how companies might organize the planning effort itself.

Planning for Shared Strategic Value Drivers

The corporate center has primary responsibility for shared strategic value drivers. The planning process should be designed to address three questions: Is the current list of shared value drivers complete and valid? What is the best strategy for achieving the highest value from these sources of advantage, both in existing businesses and potentially from new businesses? Are the strategies being implemented as effectively as possible? Simply to review these questions in the annual plan will provide an early warning system for any opportunities or problems.

Planning for the Portfolio

Planning for Expansion

For most companies, acquisitions of new businesses, even joint ventures and "strategic alliances," are episodic and often opportunistic rather than planned. Nevertheless, planning can help improve the odds that when these deals are done, they make good strategic and economic sense. Most companies would want to review periodically the following issues:

- *Related New Businesses.* Does the company have valuable and proprietary sources of competitive advantage that are transferable to other indirectly-related businesses, and could such businesses be developed or acquired profitably? If the answer is "Yes," portfolio growth should be a major activity for planning at the center—perhaps with dedicated specialists to evaluate and negotiate with prospective candidates.
- *New Markets.* Entering a completely new market is sometimes managed initially as a corporate rather than business unit initiative. This is particularly true when new market economics are so unique, as in China or Russia, that market entry might entail risks and investments similar to adding an entirely new business unit to the portfolio. For instance, consumer product companies like Coca-Cola, McDonald's, and Kellogg's in the United States and Unilever in the United Kingdom have generated enormous growth in new markets, where the center has often taken the lead to evaluate the opportunities and make the initial investments to set up the new business unit. For these kinds of companies, a continuous effort to find, evaluate, and gain early advantage in profitable new markets is a high priority and should be

fully supported by a planning process designed to identify and invest in these opportunities.

- *Unrelated New Businesses.* The opportunities for large companies to create value via the start-up or acquisition of businesses unrelated to their existing businesses are very rare, and it is certainly difficult to plan for them. Few companies have hurt themselves by avoiding this temptation, and many that took the plunge have suffered large value losses. Unless acquisition economics are extremely favorable, this means of growth should be avoided.

Planning for Divestiture

Companies that employ value based management principles always have good information about the operating values of their business units. As discussed in Chapter Ten, from time to time the gap between the operating value of a business unit's best strategy and the proceeds available from its sale to a third party becomes wide enough to make divestiture the highest-value option. The center should have a routine process to identify these gaps if they open and act on them. To the extent that the company has a portfolio of businesses that enjoy good competitive advantages and are managed to maximize value, there will be few buyers willing to pay a premium high enough to make the divestment of these businesses worthwhile. But, of course, there may well be situations where for various reasons the company feels it cannot achieve the highest-value strategy for a business and chooses instead to sell it for a price that creates value for the shareholders. As the business unit itself will seldom make such a proposal, the corporate center must take the initiative in this matter.

Planning for the Organization

The company's annual plan should include plans to improve the management of the major institutional value drivers: the governance process, the strategic planning processes for business units and the corporate center, the resource allocation process, the performance management process, and the top management compensation process. Each of these processes can be an important source of competitive advantage. Taken together, they comprise a very formidable arsenal of weapons to minimize the negative effects of the institutional imperative and give the organization an enormous advantage in wealth creation.

Creating value on a sustained basis requires continuous improvement of all management processes. There are always issues and alternatives to be evaluated to improve these processes. Because they are so critical to the company's short- and long-term strategic and financial health, these processes should be considered as important as any business unit strategy. Looking after them, asking critical questions about their condition, and always seeking to improve them, are key responsibilities of the corporate center as well as the business units. But the corporate center must take the lead in making sure that these institutional value drivers are in excellent condition at all times.

The Company's Strategic Plan

We regard strategic planning as a bottom-up process. Cash flow and economic profits come from only one place, the product markets, and value creation requires a business to succeed in particular ways in those markets. Value creation is about details, thousands of them, that must be addressed successfully for product market performance to translate into superior returns for shareholders. These details are found largely at the levels of the product market unit, business unit, and shared resource unit. It is at these levels that the great majority of important strategic decisions must be made.

"Corporate strategy" is a term that gives us some difficulty because it seems to imply that the corporate center can lead the business units and cause their strategies to improve by expressing an appropriate vision or by following some general guidelines, such as "being number one in our markets" or "achieving 15 percent earnings growth." Large multibusiness, multinational companies really cannot have a corporate strategy apart from the collective business unit and corporate center strategies that constitute the corporate plan. Companies can usefully express their blocking criteria, or rules for what they will *not* do. For instance, it is important to say that "we are a focused mousetrap company" because it tells employees that we will not do anything else besides make and sell mousetraps. But it certainly does not tell anyone how to compete in the mousetrap business or how to generate great returns for shareholders. This is a matter of the most important details that cannot be captured at the corporate level by any vision statement, mission statement, or strategic intent statement.

To be the company's blueprint for wealth creation, the corporate plan cannot be a top-down plan. Certainly, as we have noted, the chief executive should be fully engaged in approving all the business unit and corporate center strategies to ensure that the company's resources are put to their very best economic use. So the chief executive, and by implication, the corporation, have very demanding responsibilities in generating the corporate plan. But the plan is the sum of the many strategic options selected to maximize the value of the business units and the contribution of the center. It is not an overarching strategy for the entire multi-business company.

Concluding Remarks

For large, complex companies, an effective strategic planning process is an essential prerequisite for consistently maximizing good growth and eliminating bad growth. This cannot be accomplished through reliance on dependent processes like budgeting or resource allocation, because these processes do not and cannot deal with the fundamental issues of business economics: how best to serve customers and configure operations to generate the highest economic profits and cash flow over time. To address these issues effectively, in our view, strategic planning must be a value based, consequential, and continuous process. Creating such a process is potentially one of the most profitable investments a company can make.

Excellent strategic planning requires more than a well-designed planning process. It also requires processes that help to improve management's strategic planning capabilities and provide managers with the very high-quality information they need to generate good strategic alternatives for increasing the value of their businesses. These "enabling processes," which should be designed specifically to support the strategic planning process, have two primary goals. The first is to ensure that top corporate and business unit managers have good knowledge of the principles of value based management and are capable of applying these principles to the wide range of strategic and organizational decisions they are required to make. The second is to ensure that management at all levels either has, or knows how to generate, excellent information on current and future customer needs and product market economics, current and future competitors' capabilities and costs, and the company's own current and future capabilities and costs. Combining this quality of information and knowledge with an effective strategic planning process gives a company an extremely powerful competitive advantage for creating value over time.

CHAPTER 14

Resource Allocation

If strategic planning is the company's primary process for generating wealth-creating ideas, resource allocation is the primary process for making those ideas reality. Determining the right quantity of resources, both human and capital, to invest in a business should be the most important operational consequence of strategic planning. By the "right" quantity, we mean the quantity of resources needed to implement the value-maximizing strategy—no more and no less. The strategic planning and resource allocation processes are key institutional value drivers and, taken together, constitute the heart of value based management. Their alignment requires resource allocation to be strategy driven, not budget driven, and designed to support fully the governing objective of maximizing shareholder value.

Coupled with the responsibility to approve strategies, the approval of the resources to implement those strategies is the principal means by which the chief executive can ensure achievement of the governing objective. In our view, the proper exercise of the "power of the purse," by which we mean the power to fund or not fund recommended strategies, is so critical that it should never be delegated. It is the chief executive's primary responsibility to be sure that all the company's resources are put to their highest and best use. This responsibility is difficult or impossible to fulfill if the strategic investment decisions themselves, or the processes for making those investment decisions, are determined by other executives. The buck starts and stops with the chief executive.

A most important principle of value based management is that capital resources are allocated *to* business units, not between them. The investment issue in a value-managed company is not whether one particular business unit or project is more deserving than another. The issue is how much capital is needed by all the business units and the corporate center to achieve the highest warranted value of the company. Each and every business unit in the portfolio should receive exactly as much capital as its value-maximizing strategy requires. That is what investors expect. If the immediately available funds are insufficient for the needs of the businesses and the corporate center, the capital markets stand ready to provide the required funds in the form of new debt or new equity to support value creation.

Key Principles of Value Based Resource Allocation

The resource allocation process at many companies can defy description. When we try to figure out how resourcing decisions are made at client companies, it is not uncommon to find that no executive, including the CEO, is able to describe to his or her own satisfaction the set of principles or processes that the company actually uses (as opposed to what it says it uses) to determine how and where to allocate resources. And sometimes the more formalized the process is, the less agreement there is on its merits. For instance, in companies that generate large cash flows in relation to their internal growth needs, it is not uncommon for capital to be viewed as plentiful but investment ideas to be viewed as scarce. In these companies, business units often find it very easy to obtain approval for additional capital, and the "tests" for approval are fairly relaxed. On the other hand, companies that view themselves as capital constrained and unable to fund all the business units' requests tend to have more formal and elaborate tests, usually including a discounted cash flow test of some kind, in order to prioritize investments in some way. This climate of capital scarcity breeds a surplus of cleverness among managers seeking ways to beat the tests and get the capital they feel they need. The whole process becomes something of an elaborate game, which no one finds very satisfactory over time.

A value based resource allocation process concerns itself with the quality of the investment opportunity first and the availability of funding as only a distant second, if considered at all. To ensure that the process fully supports the governing objective, we have found that these four principles of resource allocation work well at all companies, regardless of their profitability, their growth rates, or their current cash-flow-generation profile: resource allocation decisions should be zero-based; management should fund strategies, not projects; management should assume that no capital rationing is necessary; and management should enforce a zero tolerance rule for the unproductive use of resources.

The Principle of Zero-Based Resource Allocation

Except for major restructuring decisions, virtually all resource allocation decisions at large companies are focused on *incremental,* new capital investment and addition of people. Capital investment decisions in particular tend to focus mostly on growth projects, such as building a new manufacturing facility, entry into a new market, or expanding R&D spending. Far less attention is paid to the capital and human resources already committed to, or "sunk" in a business unit, particularly if the overall business is doing well. Certainly in recent years there has been a commendable drive toward using assets more efficiently, for instance, by reducing inventories through the use of just-in-time management techniques. But few companies routinely evaluate the use of all resources, sunk as well as incremental, all the time. Once resources have been committed, they are generally not subjected to routine testing to be sure that the investment is still warranted.

The evidence of this neglect of sunk investments is clear when we see in virtually every company we know, including companies that are very well managed in most respects, 100 percent of the value created is concentrated in less than 50 percent of the capital employed. This means that, year in and year out, resources are committed to activities that consume value. Exhibit 14.1 shows the case of a large United States company that earns well above its cost of capital overall and is valued at nearly two times book value.

As this very typical case shows, despite the fact that the company's

EXHIBIT 14.1

Sources of Value Creation

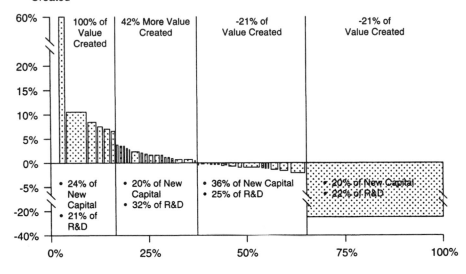

- 6 BUs contribute 100% of value created
- 16 more BUs contribute another 42% of value created
- Those 22 BUs are worth $15.5 billion, on an equity investment of only $4.2 billion
- 44% of new capital investment and 53% of R&D spending over the next three years is going to BUs earning economic profits
- **56% of new capital investment and 47% of R&D spending are going to BUs that will be generating economic losses**

projected ROE is over 20 percent, about 50 percent of new investment in capital and R&D is committed to business units that are not even projected to earn their own cost of capital. The cash flows from the very profitable "left-hand tail" business units are largely squandered on "right-hand tail" businesses that create no wealth. Thus, about half of *both old and new* investment is committed to undermining the company's long-term competitive position and financial performance. But the old, or sunk, investment is seven times as large as the new, or incremental, investment. So from the shareholders' perspective, while both kinds of investments are economically unprofitable, the old investment is most damaging because there is so much more of it.

The question most managers want to address is this: "How much capital investment should we add (or take away) to make the business more profitable at the margin?" The question we think they should be asking is: "What is the right amount of capital (and the right number of people) to have in this business in order to support the strategy that will create the most wealth?" This second question is zero-based. It does not refer to or need to refer to how much human and financial capital is already invested in the business—it refers to the future product market strategies that will determine how much human and financial capital is required to meet the governing objective. For example, one industrial company business unit with $800 million in assets recently proposed an investment of $150 million over three years to increase capacity for its most profitable product line and improve manufacturing efficiency around the world. The investment passed the parent company's 20 percent required "hurdle rate" of return and was approved, meaning that in three years' time the business would have assets of over $1 billion.[1] However, from a value based perspective, the investment profile looked quite different. Of the $800 million of sunk investment, almost half was supporting value-consuming products and customers. Some of these products and customer groups could have been restored to positive economic profits through significant strategy changes, but others could not and should have been eliminated. On balance, the business had excess investment of about $250 million—that is, by making the right strategic changes, the business could see its value increase while its existing assets could be reduced from $800 million to $550 million. Thus, the proposed new investment of $150 million, which was value creating, could be financed entirely from the proper restructuring of existing assets. Initially then, the business did not need $150 million of *additional* investment. It actually required a net $100 million *less* investment. And in three years' time, the business would have assets of only $750 million instead of over $1 billion, but it would have a far higher value to shareholders.

Incremental resource allocation serves the institutional imperative well because of its strong bias toward constantly growing rather than "rightsizing" the commitment of people and capital to a business. While this tendency is understandable, it is not the basis of good resource allocation. But even if a company accepts the principle of zero-based resource allocation, it cannot be implemented until some other conventional allocation processes change. Most important, companies need to shift the focus of resource allocation from individual projects to total business strategies.

The Principle of Funding Strategies, Not Projects

Since this concept was first introduced, it has been increasingly noted and accepted in principle.[2] In practice, however, the great majority of companies are still encumbered with archaic and often useless project-based capital appropriations processes. There is no doubt that when discounted cash flow analysis of projects was introduced and widely adopted in the 1960s, it represented a step forward from length of payback period and other less-rigorous tests that new investments were required to pass. But what seemed initially a useful innovation soon became part of an elaborate control process designed more to limit or prioritize capital expenditures than to support value-creating growth. In addition to the discounted cash flow test, companies also imposed additional controls in the form of capital spending limits on different levels of management. These controls serve to reinforce the project mentality. For example, a plant manager can approve projects (that are documented to pass the right discounted cash flow test) of up to $100,000, business unit managers can approve projects of up to $250,000, a chief executive can approve projects of up to $3 million, and all other projects go to the board of directors for approval. It all seems fairly rational, even a bit scientific, but managers know instinctively that something is seriously wrong with this approach: The capital budgeting process, together with discounted cash flow tests and project spending limits, are really control rather than decision-making processes. They have weakened or broken the necessary linkage between strategy and resource allocation to the point where managers often feel there is no longer any meaningful connection between the two.

We see three major problems with the typical project-based capital appropriations process. The first problem is that the measurement of project returns (net present value or internal rate of return) is often irrelevant in making the right investment decisions. For instance, in one case, the internal rate of return from a project to improve plant efficiency may be an impressive 30 percent, but the plant itself is contributing to chronic industry overcapacity and probably should be decommissioned to improve market economics and increase the total rate of return of the business. In another case, the installation of pollution control equipment has a negative internal rate of return in a highly advantaged and profitable business unit earning ROEs exceeding 25 percent. Obviously, this investment should be made despite failing the internal rate of return test. Managers know that in cases like these and many others, traditional discounted cash flow or payback analysis tells them virtually nothing about whether the investment is a good idea. Still, the old processes are slow to change, and mostly they are just ignored or bypassed in haphazard fashion.

The second problem is that companies often employ project analysis primarily for the purpose of comparing and prioritizing unrelated investment proposals. This is the problem of trying to decide whether an investment recommended by one business unit to expand capacity is more or less valuable than an investment requested by another business unit to develop a new product line. These are false choices, imposed by a capital rationing mentality we will address next. But unfortunately, the mere existence of project-based appropriations processes lends a legitimacy to these choices that they do not deserve. If both investments help to maximize the warranted value of the business units, they should be approved and funded. If neither business unit would be worth more after the investments are made, neither proposal should be approved. In other words, there is nothing to prioritize. The virtues of one proposal have nothing to do with the virtues of the other, and the respective investment decisions should be made entirely independently.

The third major problem with project-based capital appropriations is that the process is easily and frequently circumvented by skillful managers. Project-based discounted cash flow analysis is very easily manipulated to produce an acceptable answer. Indeed, it is characteristic of smart managers that they are able to create a seemingly reasonable financial case for even the most unpromising investments. Further, projects are usually presented as the only choice versus doing nothing, rather than as one alternative versus a number of others for achieving the business unit's highest value. Even when alternatives are presented, they are often "straw men" designed to ensure that the preferred project appears to have the best returns. Given the very real problems with project-based appropriations, this gaming is understandable and even justified in many cases. However, gaming to evade a deficient allocation process does not mean that the resulting investments are, on balance, any better than they would have been if the formal procedures had been followed. After all, what is needed is not to waste more management time circumventing the existing process but a new process altogether.

A business strategy is, in effect, a bundle of projects. In making the best resource allocation decisions, it is the value of the entire bundle that matters. In particular, we look for the bundle of projects, or strategy, that produces the highest value for the total business, and this cannot be determined by looking at individual projects in isolation. Thus, the chief executive must be concerned with the entire bundle, or alternative bundles, of proposed projects and make the investment decision on that basis. At the business unit level, gaming the answer is much harder than at the project level. With the benefit of a good position assessment, the chief executive has the advantage of knowing how market economics, competitive position, and alternative strategies are likely to interact to produce a credible forecast of financial performance. Obviously, every future project cannot be known or forecast, but a close approximation of the total cash, accounts receivable, inventories, and fixed assets necessary to support a particular strategy can be projected with some confidence. Thus, the chief executive can make an informed decision about the best strategic alternatives for the business unit, including an approval for overall levels of resources over the next several years, and leave the details of implementation, including specific project approvals, to the general manager. As we will discuss later, this does not mean approval without controls, but it does mean that the control process will help guide the strategy to success rather than impede its development and implementation.

The Principle of No Capital Rationing

It is surprising how many companies operate as though capital must be rationed. The general practices we observe seem to be based on a belief that capital is scarce but free. It is apportioned, although not usually charged, to the business units as though it is a rare good—the proper uses of which can be understood by only a few corporate wise men and women. We argue that the opposite is true—capital is plentiful but expensive. This principle is absolutely essential to an understanding of value based management.

The great majority of companies employ some form of the scarce-but-free model and are run somewhat like the old Soviet Union. When the allocation of an allegedly scarce resource—in this case, investment capital—is at stake, central planning is substituted for a market pricing mechanism. As in Communist countries and their governments, this approach is very inefficient and ineffective for companies and their managers. It leads to the following problems: micromanagement by the center; much management time spent battling for supposedly scarce funds instead of battling competitors; distorted (i.e., political rather than economic) decision making; and worst of all, substantial underperformance throughout the portfolio because of the extensive cross-subsidies within and between business units that accumulate over time.

The scarce-but-free model arises for two reasons. First, managers often view the company's immediately available cash—after payment of the dividend—as the limit of available capital, at least in the short term. But this is not the case. More funds are readily available from two sources, one internal and the other external. Internally, liberating capital from chronically unprofitable uses would increase its availability by a factor of *at least two* for most companies. Externally, the capital markets stand ready to fund, via new debt or new equity infusions, all value-creating growth. Even the U.S. airline industry, one of the great value consumers of our time, can still raise fresh funds from internal restructuring and external loans and equity investments. *For large investment-grade companies, there are almost no circumstances—short of outright bankruptcy— where insufficient capital is available to fund value-creating strategies.* If management believes it is capital constrained under any other circumstances, this is a sure sign of a lot of underperforming sunk capital or an unimaginative use of the capital markets, or both.

A second reason that many managers perceive capital to be scarce but free is that they are not charged directly for it. This is why adoption of an economic profit measure is so important. It tells managers that capital is available but at a price. With the mind-set that capital is plentiful but expensive, business units are free to seek their highest-value strategies independently of one another or of any preset, top-down limits on capital availability. The company does not want to limit available capital. Rather it wants—or should want—to maximize good growth by investing as much capital as possible wherever and whenever value can be increased. As long as all product market units, and therefore all business units, are pursuing strategies that increase wealth, there will be no shortage of capital for the growth of existing businesses. For entirely new businesses requiring very large initial investment, such as Iridium, the $3.8 billion satellite-based global cellular phone service envisioned and sponsored by Motorola, raising the necessary funds can certainly be challenging.[3] Yet even these huge amounts are available in today's global capital markets if prospective investors are convinced that there is some reasonable possibility of a good return. One of our favorite examples, the funding of the Channel Tunnel between Great Britain and France, offers evidence that huge sums are available—in this case £1.2 billion was raised in the initial public offering—even when it seems (to us at least) that the basic business economics are somewhat unpromising.[4]

A final note on the company's capital budget. We recommend that the capital budget be prepared simply by adding up the capital required by all the strategies approved by the chief executive. Period. This consolidated capital budget can be used by the chief financial officer to forecast external financing needs, if any, and to monitor total capital spending over time. Otherwise, it is of little use. It should never be used for investment decision making or to limit investment, except perhaps in a company that is in bankruptcy.

We would not want to disappoint the reader by failing to note that we believe there *is* a limiting resource facing all companies: that resource is management talent, not capital. In particular, there is and always will be a scarcity of managers who are naturally good wealth creators. The chief executive may find that good growth is limited because the company has too few managers who can reliably develop and implement high-value strategies for all business units in the portfolio. This we accept as a real limitation. But this is an issue of high qualifications standards, effective recruitment, and management development—not limited funding. The solution has to come from building the depth and capabilities of the management team or from reducing the number or complexity of businesses, but not from throttling investment in ways that reduce shareholder value.

The Principle of Zero Tolerance for Bad Growth

In sports, a well-understood technique for winning is to make fewer mistakes than any competitor. It is a sound technique that applies equally well to resource allocation. Two types of mistakes have to be minimized: first, though less important, is the failure to evaluate the initial investment decisions properly; and second is keeping expensive capital tied up in strategies that are clearly value consuming. No matter how skilled and disciplined management is, some mistakes of the first type will always be made—it is an unavoidable part of trying to create wealth. But the second type of mistake is entirely curable by management. It requires adopting an attitude of zero tolerance for resources committed to unprofitable, or bad, growth. Proper redeployment of such resources alone will increase the value of most companies by at least 25 percent, and often much more.

Even within a generally successful and wealth-creating strategy, a large percentage of investments in new product ideas will fail to earn an adequate return for shareholders. One recent study finds that almost 50 percent of new product development costs are consumed by products that fail to survive.[5] Other studies suggest that only 56 to 65 percent of new products survive on the market as long as five years.[6] The failure rate of new businesses is similar.[7] While no reliable figures are available, we estimate that probably no more than 20 percent, and perhaps as little as 10 percent, of the total start-up investment in new products, new markets, and new businesses ever earns a sustained return above the cost of capital. Of course, the great companies of today are the inheritors of some of the best investment decisions ever made, and this tends to be confirmed by the very high concentration of value creation in their portfolios that still stems from the original products, services, or technologies and their related extensions. Disney's theme parks and animated movies, Ford's trucks, Kodak's photographic films, du Pont's fibers, Coke Classic®—all developed by investments made long ago—have been engines of value for many years.

Many companies today are wisely trying to improve their records of new product and new business investment. In effect, they are working to create a more effective "customer model" to increase the yield of new good growth ideas and make more of the good growth ideas they already have. Applying value based analysis can certainly help companies achieve better results when pursuing good growth opportunities. Simply requiring much more rigorous assessments of market economics and the competitive advantage needed to generate good returns would greatly improve the odds of success. However, while an improvement in the economic success rate of 10–20% is possible, we think it is unlikely that even a majority of new products or new businesses will ultimately earn their cost of capital. Successful wealth creation seems to require a lot of trial and error, with high risks and high but infrequent rewards. There are no data, and nothing in our experience, to suggest that large companies, as a group, are in any way advantaged over small companies in picking winners. Thus, a lot of risk taking is absolutely necessary to create wealth from new ideas, including new ideas for old products and long-served markets. Many failures have to be expected, even in the best-managed companies. But it is not necessarily the number of failures as much as the company's response to those failures, that should concern managers and shareholders most.

While incurring failures is an essential part of creating wealth, perpetuating them is not. This second type of resource allocation mistake, permitting human and financial capital to be chronically committed to bad growth activities, is extremely costly and entirely avoidable. As we have noted, a significant amount of virtually every large company's resources, sometimes over half, is invested in value-consuming products, customers, and markets. This is an inevitable consequence of leaving the institutional imperative unchecked. Business unit strategies that may have created value in the past but no longer do so may be maintained for years, sometimes decades, with management claiming (long after the fundamental economics of the business have deteriorated) that if only the company had more capital, all would be well again. New strategies may fail to meet their promised objectives, but rather than change the strategy or perhaps the management of the business unit, the company wrongly concludes that the answer is still more investment to try to save the day. For every time this is the right thing to do, there are at least ten times when it is precisely the wrong thing to do. It is possible for any business to have too much capital— every bad growth business does—and adding more is simply fueling the fire. One of our clients noted wisely that so many new business development efforts failed at his company because they were over-funded from the start. He was convinced that with less funding and more frequent reviews, the success rate would go up.

For a company committed to maximizing wealth, liberating all resources employed in value-consuming activities has to be a continuing priority. We call this the zero tolerance rule—any business unit (or the corporate center) with resources making a negative contribution to value must either fix the problem very quickly or see the resources redeployed. For any particular business, we think that on average somewhere between 5 to 20 percent of its resources likely need to be redeployed from value-consuming products, customers, markets, and functions *each year.* Of course, the business may well be adding prof-itable activities at an even faster rate, so that overall, its assets may be growing. But good performance in some product markets should not be permitted to mask the inevitable effects of the forces of competition in others with no credible strategic alternatives able to generate ade-quate rates of return. As its name implies, there should be no excep-tions to the zero tolerance rule. With the relentless force of the institu-tional imperative at work, one exception will quickly breed others (after all, it will be perceived as unfair if poor performance is tolerated in one business but not in others). Before long, the company's portfo-lio will once again have the shape characteristic of the waterfall, with a large percentage of investments earning substandard returns and fail-ing to create value.

The zero tolerance rule is important not only to help minimize bad growth but also to maximize good growth. Since most companies op-erate as though capital is constrained, and since a high percentage of their resources may be tied up in the wrong places, truly wealth creat-ing products, customers, markets, and activities are frequently under-resourced. This cross-subsidization occurs in virtually all companies, and the damage to value resulting from the failure to provide the right resources to support good growth can be far greater than the damage caused by subsidizing bad growth. Even a modest improvement in a business unit with large economic profits will have an enormously positive impact on the company's value. So adopting the zero tolerance rule has a doubly beneficial effect—it eliminates bad growth and frees up resources to help maximize good growth. The impact on value can be dramatic, not only from a one-time restructuring to redeploy resources to more productive uses, but from the ongoing discipline of continuous microrestructuring at all levels of the company. The competitive strength of companies such as Wal-Mart, Microsoft, Merck, Coke, Hewlett-Packard, and Lloyds Bank, which minimize bad growth, is, of course, extraordinary.

Features of the Resource Allocation Process

A resource allocation process incorporating the four key principles we have been discussing can be relatively simple in design. The two major elements of the process are approval and control.

Approval

The prerequisite for resource approval is strategy approval, as discussed in Chapter Thirteen. Once the chief executive is satisfied that a proposed business unit strategy is the highest value alternative, a close review of the resource requirements can occur. The chief executive and business unit general manager need to agree on whether the resources requested to support the strategy over the next two to three years will be adequate but not excessive under foreseeable circumstances. Scientific precision is not required here. With good information and experience, it is usually enough to answer two questions. First: "Do the basic assumptions that drive forecasts of required head count, R&D, working capital, and fixed assets make sense, given the historical performance of the business and its best competitors and given the expected future capacity required to implement the strategy?" Second: "Are any resources tied up in chronically value-consuming products, customers, markets, or functions, and if so, how quickly can these resources be withdrawn?" Once these two questions are answered to the satisfaction of the chief executive, he or she can formally approve the resources to implement the strategy.

The precise terms of the approval will vary, but certain guidelines are useful. First, the approval should be for several years, typically two or three. For some businesses, such as jet aircraft or petrochemical manufacturing, resources must be committed over much longer periods because of the very long time frames required for strategy implementation. In other cases, like specialty retailing, business conditions change so rapidly that strategies, and therefore resource commitments, may need to be reviewed more frequently. Second, the approval should be irrevocable as long as the business unit meets its agreed-upon performance objectives. Under no other circumstances, short of the severe financial distress of the company, should committed resources be withheld or withdrawn from the business. Doing so would reduce the value of the company and violate the governing objective. This means that whenever overall company performance falls short of plan, the consequences must be felt only by the business units that are falling short of their plans, never those that are achieving their strategies. Of all of the changes to the resource allocation process that we recommend, this is often the most difficult to accept. But it is a direct consequence of managing to maximize wealth—cross-subsidies from better-performing businesses to poorer-performing businesses will not create value, they will destroy it. If the company is performing below plan, the best response is to fix the performance or the strategy of the business unit where the problem is occurring, not to tax other business units and the shareholders by misallocating resources.

Control

Details of the company's overall control, or performance management, process will be discussed in Chapter Fifteen. However, we do not want to give the impression that we suggest a chief executive simply approve strategies and resources, then sit back to see in two to three years' time whether he or she did the right thing. But it is also critically important that the company's control processes not be allowed, in effect, to hijack effective strategic planning.

As long as strategy is driving the resourcing decisions, three questions have to be answered in approving specific appropriations: Is the expenditure necessary for the strategy to succeed? Is the expenditure within the overall amounts allocated for the approved strategy? Is the expenditure the most efficient way to implement the strategy? The first question is to protect against the possibility that the business unit or center will make investments that are really not related to the approved strategy—this happens quite often, especially when strategic plans are not translated into concrete business plans for implementation. The second question is designed to protect against carelessness in forecasting capital requirements or managing the shareholders' money—the business unit may not overspend without a formal change in its approved strategy or an amended approval from the chief executive to cover some specific unforeseen opportunity, such as a profitable acquisition. The third question is designed to ensure that even required investments are not "gold-plated" unless they need to be, e.g., that new plants are built in low-cost locations with advantageous tax environments. Note that the question of whether to build new capacity is not reopened or subjected to new hurdles; this decision is made in the strategic planning process, including some estimate of its likely cost. But when the capacity is actually to be built, the chief executive and chief financial officer may reasonably require some assurance that it is being done in the most cost-effective way.

These approval and control design features are quite straightforward. They ensure good linkage between strategies and resource commitments and also between resource commitments and the company's governing objective. Often, this type of process simplifies considerably the amalgamation of budgets, discounted cash flow tests, and informal politicking that characterizes resource allocation at many companies. It is more open and more focused on the true economics of the product markets in which the company participates. And it calls for more responsibility on the part of business unit and corporate center managers to develop and implement the best strategies. In exchange, these managers are given much more responsibility for deciding how and when the resources with which they are entrusted will be employed. They have assurance that if they perform as promised, they will always have readily available the resources they need.

Concluding Remarks

If the strategic planning process determines the direction in which a business will travel, the resource allocation process is where "the rubber meets the road" on strategy implementation. It is the first line of support for giving good growth strategies all the resources they require and the first line of defense against allowing bad growth strategies to consume any resources at all. The ability to make this distinction the basis of its strategic investment decisions is a hallmark of a value based company.

Shareholders are generally not in a position to know what the best strategies for a business of a company are—that is why they hire professional managers. But the capital markets are extremely astute at detecting which companies are good at resource allocation and which are not, and this is the primary measure investors use to judge the capabilities of a company's management over time. It may not be easy for shareholders to see what the true wealth creation potential of a company is, but it is usually very easy for them to see when significant resources are being underutilized or simply squandered. Thus, managers should not be surprised when investors come forward to demand that their funds be put to better use. They are usually right to do so.

CHAPTER 15

Performance Management

Performance management is the term we use to describe the company's high-level strategic and financial control process. The primary purpose of performance management is to align business unit and corporate performance targets, both short-term and long-term, with the objective of maximizing shareholder value. The principal activities of performance management include setting targets, monitoring performance, and responding to differences between expected and actual results. While we will comment on all three of these activities, in this chapter we focus on the first—setting the right performance targets.

Broadly speaking, there are two schools of thought about the best way to set targets and control performance. The first (and more popular) school believes that business plans or strategies should be target driven. By this we mean that in the great majority of companies today, it is normal practice for top management to set overall strategic and financial goals and targets for the corporation and then task the business units to achieve them. The primary means of assuring compliance with the corporate directives is the budgeting process, an annual ceremony of great seriousness in which a complex iteration of business unit proposals and corporate counterproposals produces a consolidated financial forecast that embodies top management's desired targets. The second school takes the view that performance targets should be plan driven, meaning that, *except for the governing objec-*

tive itself, the company's performance targets should be products of, rather than determinants of, the business unit and corporate center strategies.

There is a world of difference between these two approaches to performance management. Value based management falls squarely in the second school, and we will elaborate on this theme of plan driven targets throughout Chapters Fifteen and Sixteen.

Key Principles of Performance Management

Two principles of performance management are critical to maximizing shareholder value, particularly in complex multibusiness companies. The first is that performance targets should be plan driven, and the second is that the process must have integrity, meaning that a performance contract should be crafted between the chief executive and the business unit and honored by both sides.

Plan Driven Targets

What is wrong with the traditional top-down approach to setting overall corporate performance targets in the chief executive's office? The problem we see is that these "macro" targets are usually counterproductive. They are not particularly useful to managers seeking to maximize the warranted value of their business units, and they often result in reducing rather than increasing profitable growth. All of this is quite unintentional, of course, but these negative outcomes are an almost inevitable consequence of a top-down target-setting process.

The first problem with the corporate targets is that they are hardly ever useful to the business units. A typical set of macro targets, as set forth in the company's mission statement, might read something like this: "We are seeking to have a leading share in all of our markets and earn a return on equity of 20 percent while growing earnings per share at least 15 percent per year." This sounds eminently sensible and would no doubt create value, if achieved. So what's wrong with it? To begin with, there is an extremely important but unstated qualification to the mission statement *"We want to do this without having to eliminate most of the bad growth in our portfolio."* Virtually any large company in the world could easily achieve the strategic and financial targets in that mission statement within a year or two. All that is required is to shrink the company to only those product market units in the portfolio that already achieve these targets and those that are close to doing so, probably leaving the company at approximately half its initial size. Should the general managers infer from the corporate goals that they are to submit strategies calling for the wholesale restructuring of their own business units, thereby reducing the company to half its size? Very few general managers would read the goals that way and, of course, they probably would not be expected to submit such strategies.

If business units are seeking to maximize their warranted equity value and, therefore the warranted equity value of the company, no universal set of financial or strategic goals or targets will be appropriate for each of them. Today the typical large company has many dozens of business units, each with its unique path to value creation. There is no information in the corporate goals or targets that illuminates that path. Some units may not be market leaders, but they still have a competitive advantage in markets with attractive economics— so they meet the financial tests of high returns and growth but not the strategic requirement for a leading market position. Are they supposed to expand into related markets where they are less advantaged and, if so, will that increase their warranted value? Other units may meet neither the 20 percent ROE nor the 15 percent growth targets but still create a lot of value. Should these units change their strategies to try to hit at least one of the corporate targets and, if so, which one?

These examples illustrate the first problem with typical top-down corporate goals and targets: They do not, and cannot, motivate value-maximizing behavior at the business unit level. The second problem is really a direct result of the first. If the company actually attempts to impose "one-size-fits-all" targets on the business units, it is almost certain that wealth will be destroyed by the resulting massive cross-subsidies. We observed a particularly dramatic case of this in a well-known U.S. industrial equipment company.

Overall, the company, with over 30 business units, had experienced relatively poor ROEs and low growth. The company was trying hard to achieve its corporate target ROE of 15 percent. It also had a truly wonderful business unit that, owing to a highly advantaged position in a specialized type of transportation equipment, had a worldwide market share of over 50 percent and earned ROEs in excess of 45 percent. Despite these advantages, however, the business was challenged aggressively by established European and capable new Japanese competitors. The business unit management felt that it should invest heavily in R&D and marketing in order to defend its advantages and stop or slow the erosion of its market share. In selected situations, it also needed to use lower prices to prevent competitor entry into markets it dominated.

Of course, this business probably should have been doing all these things and more to protect its extraordinarily valuable position. But doing so would also have lowered the ROEs for both the business unit *and the company.* In fact, the value-maximizing strategy for this business would probably have reduced the company's already-low ROE by two to three percentage points over several years. Thus, driven by an overriding determination to see the company's ROEs improve, the chief executive rejected the business unit's proposed strategy and instead required it to keep returns as high as possible for the foreseeable future. This was not the right decision for at least two reasons. First, it was not value based and therefore threatened to weaken the competitive position of a great business. Second, it diverted attention from making harder decisions about accelerating the curtailment of bad growth strategies in other business units. So the company's shareholders, and ultimately its customers and employees, lost out twice because of the same decision—all in the pursuit of an otherwise innocent and sensible-looking corporate financial target.

Unfortunately, decisions like this are made every day in large companies, and always with the best intentions. But to paraphrase a well-known expression, the road to value destruction is paved with good intentions. In this case, the good intentions are top-down corporate goals, which are intended to motivate better performance but which, at best, leave the business units confused about how to interpret them and, at worst, reduce good growth to subsidize more bad growth.

The only top-down objective the chief executive needs to impose is the governing objective itself—the goal of every business unit in the company is to maximize its warranted equity value. This means that the chief executive is also imposing a *minimum* standard of performance, namely, that all investment is expected to earn at least the cost of capital or be redeployed. But this top-down admonition to manage bad growth out of the company, whether by finding better strategies, improving operating performance, or restructuring, sets an achievable goal and creates wealth. It is a common objective for all business units, tells the managers exactly what is expected of them, is achievable by nearly every business unit, and will not lead to unprofitable cross-subsidies of any kind. On the other hand, the governing objective provides no equally straightforward and universal prescription for the business units' other great task—maximizing good growth. Each business will have to search for its unique solution to achieve that, and the imposition of overall corporate performance targets will not help the unit or the company in that search.

If target-driven plans will not maximize shareholder value, does this mean the company and business units will have no performance targets and there are no controls? On the contrary, we believe the business units and the company should have clear and demanding performance targets. In fact, they should have the most demanding performance targets: those that are commensurate with the governing objective. For business unit managers, this means accountability for the financial and strategic targets rising directly from their approved strategies. And for the chief executive, it means accountability for achieving the corporate financial targets rising from a bottom-up consolidation of the business unit and corporate center strategic plans, as well as accountability for achieving superior returns for shareholders over time.

Abiding by the Rules

The second overall principle of performance management we emphasize is that the contract between each business unit and the chief executive must be honored by both sides. This contract ensures that strategic plans have consequences, both for the company as the supplier of resources and for the business unit as the producer of value.

When the business unit's strategic plan is approved by the chief executive, the business unit commits to implementing it successfully, as evidenced by management's commitment to the financial and strategic targets contained in the plan. A critical condition of value based performance management is that as long as the business unit is operating at or close to its approved targets, it will not be asked, directly or indirectly, to alter its implementation program because of events occurring in other business units or at the corporate center. It will receive the funding committed by the chief executive. It will not be asked, for example, to "help out" with more earnings if the third quarter is looking a little weak, or to defer marketing investments if the company's full-year ROE target is not being met. Value based management requires that these problems be fixed in the business units where they arise, not transferred to business units that are achieving their objectives.

This deviation from the contract is a constant temptation presented by the institutional imperative ("We are all one family here and need to help each other"). It may seem harmless enough in small doses, but it has two bad consequences: It destroys the credibility of the management processes in the minds of the best general managers, and worse, it can significantly reduce the company's warranted value. The company should never risk a successful business plan to achieve some reported financial result—the stock market will see through this shortsighted behavior, and the shareholders will not benefit from it.

But the contract is a two-way agreement, and the business unit must hold up its end of the bargain as well. When the business is off plan because the strategy itself is not proving successful, the contract is canceled by the chief executive and a new strategic plan must be developed. However, when the business is off target because of implementation problems, the performance commitments should remain in force even though it is clear that the targets will not be reached as planned. The immediate consequence will be seen in the compensation of business unit management, a subject we address in Chapter Sixteen.

With the two major principles of value based performance management in mind, we look at the target setting process, first at the business unit level and then at the company level.

Setting Business Unit Performance Targets

General managers are concerned with establishing performance targets at two levels: first, the targets for the business unit that are part of the contract with the chief executive, and second, the targets to be set within the business unit for each product market unit and the key functional activities. While we emphasize setting targets for the business unit, we also discuss setting them within the unit.

Every business unit will have a unique set of financial and strategic targets rising directly from its approved strategy. Since no two business units will have the same strategy, no two units would be expected to have the same targets. However, all the units and the company itself should use the same general financial measures for targets that are set and monitored. These measures should be simple but fairly comprehensive, internally consistent, and generate signals that reinforce the objective of maximizing value. One set of business unit financial performance measures meets these criteria as well as any we know. It is the combination of *revenue growth, economic profit, and equity (or total capital) cash flow*. These measures capture virtually all the high-level financial information that is important for a business unit, and, in combination, it is very difficult for managers to manipulate or "game" them. As long as internal management accounting processes are designed to report these measures accurately, they provide excellent feedback on whether the value creation expectations of the strategy are being met. Moreover, they are good indicators of which questions to ask and where to look for answers when performance is off track.

When the business unit submits its proposed strategy for approval, the financial projections that form the basis for determining the warranted value of the strategy will necessarily include specific projections for revenue growth, economic profit, and equity cash flow during the plan period. These projections will be discussed, possibly even debated, by the general manager and the chief executive. The chief executive will want to be sure that the financial projections are well grounded so that they are credible, and the required performance levels are as demanding as one would expect of a value-maximizing strategy. Once the chief executive is satisfied that the targets are the right ones for the strategy, they become a part of the approval contract and will be monitored regularly to track performance. These are the only financial measures the chief executive needs to be informed of routinely—the business unit budget is a mass of largely unimportant (to the CEO) details that are, in any event, the general manager's responsibility. Of course, if the business unit's results wander too far from performance targets, the chief executive can request additional information from the unit to understand why the variances have occurred.

The business unit should also be held accountable for achieving a limited number of high-level nonfinancial, or strategic, targets. Unfortunately, it is much more difficult to generalize about these kinds of targets because they are unique to the business. Despite this difficulty, however, there will usually be some critical developments in the strategy that top management will want to track. Examples of these would include a successful entry into a major new market, the on-time and on-budget completion of an important capacity addition, or rollout of a major new product, the recruitment of a key new executive, and the profitable acquisition of a related business. These critical developments must meet two criteria: (1) they are expected to have a substantial impact on warranted value, and (2) they are measurable in a reasonably objective and timely way. In all, a business unit would seldom have more than two or three nonfinancial targets in its high-level contract.

For purposes of monitoring the performance of a business unit, the general manager will want to look at progress against targets combined with a review of the strategic position assessment to determine whether there have been important changes in market economics or competitive position. Exhibit 15.1 provides an illustration of the conditions the general manager will want to monitor and the possible implications of different situations that the business unit may face.

While this is a very high-level look at the performance of the business unit, it is typically the appropriate level that top management should monitor regularly. When there are signals of potential problems, managers can begin to "peel the onion" to understand the source of problems and how to address them. Pushing this idea to its limits, we know one general manager who is so confident of his strategic planning process that he monitors regularly only changes in the business unit's market economics and competitive position. He is confident that if these have not changed, the business unit will meet its strategic and financial targets. While we would not necessarily go this far, at least he is not allowing a myriad of budget details to cloud his judgment about what is really important to the business unit's long-term strategic and financial success.

For the business unit to implement its strategy successfully, the product market units and major functional departments must align their own targets with the business unit's contract targets. Much of the

EXHIBIT 15.1

Monitoring Business Unit Performance

	On Track or Better	Off Track
As Good or Better than Estimated	**Ideal Situation**	**Common Situation** Probably an implementation problem — hold to performance targets and make changes needed to meet them
Less Favorable than Estimated	**Unusual Situation** Despite on-track performance, still requires immediate review to determine if new strategy is needed	**Urgent Situation** Almost certainly requires a new strategy and, aggravated by poor implementation, may require a review of management as well

Strategic Position (Market Economics and Competitive Position)

Performance Targets

groundwork for setting these internal targets is laid during the strategic planning process. For example, the business unit strategy must already reflect financial projections made at the product market level, and its operating performance assumptions must already reflect benchmarking against the best practices in activities critical to the success of the business. Thus, the process of setting targets at these levels should be largely one of transforming those assumptions into concrete measures and goals.

As illustrated in Exhibit 15.2, there are two useful financial measures that can be tracked at the product-market unit level and integrated with the overall business unit measures and targets: revenue growth and economic profit contribution (often there are no full allocations to the product market units, so full economic profits may not be captured there). These measures, of course, track directly with the business unit strategy and targets. Some key strategic targets may also be tracked at

EXHIBIT 15.2

Business Performance Objectives and Measures (Example)

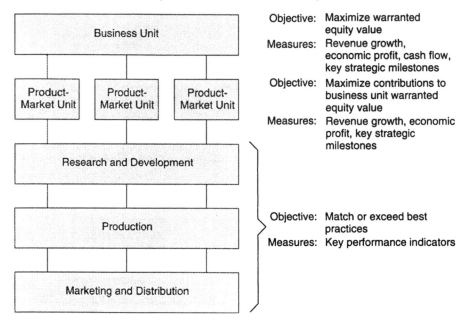

the product market level, as these can be included in the monitoring process. At the functional activity or departmental level, the measures we recommend are *key performance indicators.* These are measures of critical revenue and economic cost drivers, such as customer retention ratios, customer response time, new product development time, and factory yield ratios. Naturally, these key performance indicators will differ for different kinds of business, but they should be included in the business unit's own performance management process to the extent that they have a significant impact on warranted value. They are the link between value creation and "the shop floor."

Setting Corporate Performance Targets

At the corporate level, top management needs both internal and external performance measures—the first to monitor how effectively the company's strategies are implemented and the second to monitor how well they succeed in creating shareholder value. The internal financial measures for the company should be the same as for the business units: revenue growth, economic profit, and equity cash flow. The corporate financial targets should be derived from a consolidation of the business unit and corporate center strategic plans. There is no danger that these derivative targets will strike top management as too modest—in fact, they are likely to be much more demanding than the top-down financial targets that would have been proposed otherwise. In addition, there will be some nonfinancial targets from the corporate center plan, such as a planned entry into a major new market, which should also be monitored for effective implementation.

The corporate financial targets established through this process will be commensurate with maximizing the warranted value of the company, and top management should certainly work very aggressively to achieve them. But this should be a controlled aggression. If the corporate targets are not being met, the chief executive will be able to see exactly why, starting with the knowledge of which business units are off plan and, with some additional information, why the variances have occurred. The chief executive and the general managers of each of these underperforming businesses would have to determine whether the problem is with the strategy, the implementation of the strategy, or with "uncontrollable" factors, and then decide the best course of action for each business unit. When corporate targets are not being met, the chief executive should not issue a general call to arms to every business unit, with special emphasis on the better-performing ones, ordering them to depart from their plans in order to close the company's performance gap. This "win-one-for-the-Gipper" approach to performance management, however appealing, will undermine the achievement of the governing objective.

External Performance Measures

While there are many ways to measure the performance of the company's common stock, no individual measure is entirely suitable for all situations. As mentioned in Chapter Two, we think that, on balance, the best single measure is the company's total return to shareholders relative to the returns of similar, or peer, companies. In effect, management is constructing the portfolio of companies that investors would choose to most closely resemble an investment in the company itself. Over time, if the company's shareholders earn a higher return than they would from owning the peer group's portfolio, it is likely that management has indeed developed and implemented superior value-creating strategies.

To set performance targets that use this measure, a simple approach such as achievement by quartiles usually works well. Achieving shareholder returns high enough to rank in the first quartile of peers would be superlative, or top-tier performance, particularly if it is sustained over many years. Recall that Berkshire Hathaway has maintained this incredible standard for nearly 30 years! If the company's relative shareholder returns place it in the second quartile of peers, that, too, is excellent if sustained. Sustained performance in either the third or fourth quartiles should be considered unacceptable by top management and the board of directors. Generating shareholder returns consistently below the peer average is a certain sign that new strategies are urgently needed.

When we examine returns in the U.S. banking industry, for example, the data suggest that top-quartile performance between 1983 and 1993 would have required average annual total shareholder returns in excess of 25 percent (see Exhibit 15.3). Bottom-tier performance started at 14 percent for First Chicago and went down as low as −8.6 percent for Continental Bank Corp. This wide distribution of realized returns is common. We find that even in relatively homogeneous industries—such as electrical utilities and basic chemicals—the distribution of returns is typically quite broad in comparison with the average realized returns in these sectors.

It is interesting to note that only four banks managed to maintain top-tier performance in both the 1983–1988 and 1988–1993 periods: Fifth Third Bancorp, Old Kent Financial Corp., Southtrust Corp., and State Street Boston Corp. Over the past ten years, these four regional banks have managed to generate an average return of about 30 percent per year for their shareholders, about twice the expected average return for all U.S. banks during this period. At the other end of the distribution, Citicorp and First Interstate Bancorp. were consistently in the bottom quartile, followed closely by Chase Manhattan Corp. and Shawmut National Corp. These institutions averaged well under 10 percent returns for their shareholders, just slightly above the average

EXHIBIT 15.3

Average Annual Shareholder Returns in the U.S. Banking Industry

		1/83 - 1/88		1/88 - 1/93		1/83 - 1/93	
		Company	ASR	Company	ASR	Company	ASR
First Quartile	1	Meridian Bancorp	43.0%	BankAmerica	47.3%	State Street Boston	32.3%
	2	Wells Fargo	37.4	State Street Boston	33.5	Fifth Third Bancorp	31.6
	3	Synovus Financial	35.3	Norwest	31.2	Meridian Bancorp	30.0
	4	Fifth Third Bancorp	35.1	Northern Trust	31.2	Firstar	29.4
	5	NBD Bancorp	34.1	Firstar	28.7	KeyCorp	28.4
	6	National City	32.7	Fifth Third Bancorp	28.1	Northern Trust	28.1
	7	First of America Bank	32.4	KeyCorp	27.6	Old Kent Financial	27.5
	8	Old Kent Financial	31.7	Nations Bank	25.2	SouthTrust	27.4
	9	MNC Financial	31.5	U.S. Bancorp	24.4	Wells Fargo	27.3
	10	Core States Financial	31.3	Banc One	24.2	NBD Bancorp	26.8
	11	SouthTrust	31.2	First Alabama Bancshares	24.1	Synovus Financial	26.7
	12	Comerica	31.2	SouthTrust	23.7	First of America Bank	25.6
	13	State Street Boston	31.1	Old Kent Financial	23.5	Comerica	25.4
Second Quartile	14	Society	30.5	Mellon Bank	22.9	National City	24.5
	15	Firstar	30.2	Bancorp Hawaii	22.7	Society	24.5
	16	Key Corp	29.2	First Virginia Banks	22.6	Norwest	24.3
	17	Fleet Financial Group	27.9	Chemical Banking	22.5	Huntington Bancshares	23.9
	18	Northern Trust	27.4	Huntington Bancshares	22.1	First Alabama Bancshares	23.8
	19	UJB Financial	26.8	Marshall & Ilsley	21.0	Nations Bank	23.0
	20	PNC Bank	26.8	Bank of New York	20.5	Bancorp Hawaii	22.7
	21	Huntington Bancshares	25.7	First Union	20.2	Marshall & Ilsley	22.3
	22	Barnett Banks	25.4	NBD Bancorp	20.0	First Union	22.2
	23	First Fidelity Bancorp	25.0	Comerica	19.9	Core States Financial	21.9
	24	First Union	24.3	Signet Banking	19.4	U.S. Bancorp	21.6
	25	Star Banc	24.1	First of America Bank	19.1	Signet Banking	21.5
	26	Signet Banking	23.7	Society	18.8	Star Banc	21.3
Third Quartile	27	Marshall & Ilsley	23.7	Synovus Financial	18.6	First Virginia Banks	21.2
	28	First Alabama Bancshares	23.5	Star Banc	18.5	Banc One	20.9
	29	First Bank System	23.2	Crestar Financial	18.4	AmSouth Bancorp	20.4
	30	J.P. Morgan & Company	22.7	First Chicago	18.2	Bank of New York	19.9
	31	Bancorp Hawaii	22.7	Meridian Bancorp	18.2	PNC Bank	19.6
	32	AmSouth Bancorp	22.6	AmSouth Bancorp	18.1	Crestar Financial	19.3
	33	Nations Bank	20.8	Wells Fargo	17.9	First Fidelity Bancorp	19.0
	34	Bank of Boston	20.4	National City	16.9	J.P. Morgan & Company	18.6
	35	Boatmen's Bancshares	20.3	Continental Bank	15.9	Boatmen's Bancshares	18.0
	36	Crestar Financial	20.1	Boatmen's Bancshares	15.7	Fleet Financial Group	17.9
	37	First Virginia Banks	19.7	J.P. Morgan & Company	14.6	First Bank System	17.4
	38	Bank of New York	19.2	Republic New York	13.5	UJB Financial	16.8
	39	Shawmut National	19.0	Chase Manhattan	13.4	Barnett Banks	16.4
Fourth Quartile	40	U.S. Bancorp	18.9	First Fidelity Bancorp	13.2	First Chicago	14.1
	41	Banc One	17.7	Core States Financial	13.1	BankAmerica	14.0
	42	Norwest	17.7	PNC Bank	12.8	Republic New York	13.0
	43	Republic New York	12.5	First Bank System	11.8	Bank of Boston	12.4
	44	First Interstate Bancorp	10.9	First Interstate Bancorp	9.9	MNC Financial	11.3
	45	First Chicago	10.2	Citicorp	9.4	Chemical Banking	11.2
	46	Citicorp	9.0	Fleet Financial Group	8.7	First Interstate Bancorp	10.4
	47	Chase Manhattan	4.9	Barnett Banks	8.0	Shawmut National	9.7
	48	Chemical Banking	1.0	UJB Financial	7.5	Citicorp	9.2
	49	Mellon Bank	4.1	Bank of Boston	4.9	Chase Manhattan	9.1
	50	BankAmerica	11.8	Shawmut National	1.1	Mellon Bank	8.5
	51	Continental Bank	27.9	MNC Financial	5.8	Continental Bank	8.6

Note: ASR = annual shareholder returns.

return for long-term U.S. Government bonds over the period. To put this difference into perspective, $100 invested at 30 percent over ten years would be worth about $1380 today, whereas the same $100 invested at 10 percent would be worth about $260, a difference of more than $1100 in value for shareholders. Clearly, the top quartile is a worthwhile target for management to aim.

Attesting to the ever-present possibilities for upward mobility, four banks managed to climb from the bottom to the top tier between the 1983–1988 and 1988–1993 periods: BankAmerica Corp. (which actually rose from number 50 to number 1 after new management implemented an aggressive and very much value based new strategy), Norwest Corp., US Bancorp Oregon and Banc One Corp. Unfortunately, Corestates Financial Corp. and MNC Financial Corp. managed to make the reverse journey, descending from the first tier to the last.

Performance relative to general market averages and to peers are used more frequently by many companies as benchmarks, as can be seen by even a cursory review of annual reports (particularly of companies that have performed well). Less clear from the annual reports, however, are the consequences that flow from achieving particular levels of performance. A small number of companies we know have started to include top-tier performance relative to peers as a driver of top management compensation, but they are still a distinct minority. For the most part, there seem to be no formal consequences of either good or poor performance judged by this measure. Rather, it seems to be used as only one of several indicators of company and management performance over time. However, we believe that total return to shareholders relative to peers is an extremely important indicator of strategic success, particularly over a period of several years or more. Companies would be well served to create appropriate peer portfolios and track performance over time as a rigorous test of how well management's strategies are really working. When performance is below par, current strategies should be rigorously challenged and probably changed.

Concluding Remarks

One implication of setting strategy driven performance targets is that their achievement will be a very demanding task. In a way, these performance targets represent the ultimate in "stretch" goals. They should not be viewed as standards that are normally surpassable, because if they are, the strategic plans are probably not value maximizing in the first place. Taken together, these targets can be thought of as the "edge of the envelope"—the limits that describe the very best performance the business units and the company are currently capable of achieving.

One consequence of setting targets at the limits of performance can be a high "failure" rate, at least until managers become accustomed to the new standards and learn more about eliminating bad growth and maximizing good growth. Managing to the high standard of maximizing value requires exceptionally good managers. Over time, these high standards should attract and challenge the company's very best managers. In our experience, the best managers are the first to support the higher-performance standards required by value based management, provided that the same high standards are evenly applied to all business units so that value-consuming cross-subsidies are eliminated.

A second implication of setting plan-driven targets is that the business unit and corporate budgets are an important tool to help managers implement the approved strategies. At its best, the budgeting process should help managers develop the detailed business plans and programs they will need to make the strategy work. And it should certainly contribute to achieving the key performance targets by instilling a strong sense of discipline in the strategy-implementation effort. But the budgeting process should not involve target setting at the business unit and company levels. Nor should it be used in any way to ration resources or otherwise constrain or prevent the company from achieving the governing objective.

Finally, like strategic planning, performance management must have consequences to be effective. If designed along the lines we propose here, we hope that the first consequence of the performance management process would be the stimulation of far more constructive responses to variances from plans. It is, of course, important to understand "what's wrong" when there are variances from the strategic plan and to be as objective as possible in analyzing the problems facing a business unit and its managers. On the other hand, when performance targets at all levels of the company are linked directly to the governing objective, it should also be possible to identify more quickly, and perhaps more objectively, the best course of action for getting back on track. And when difficult decisions have to be made, it should be easier to make them because managers will understand much more clearly the economic costs of the failure to act.

A second consequence of the performance management process is the closer alignment of managers' advancement and compensation with the interests of the shareholders. For the most part, the measures and targets the company uses to manage its businesses should also be used to manage its compensation programs. If the company has well-defined business units and clear accountability for performance at all levels, it should be possible to link rewards to performance consistent with value creation. We discuss one aspect of the reward system, top management compensation, in Chapter Sixteen.

CHAPTER 16

Top Management Compensation

The purpose of top management compensation should be to reward the achievement of the governing objective.

By top management, we mean specifically the chief executive and his or her direct reports, the general managers of the business units and the major shared resource units, and their direct reports. These are the executives who have the primary responsibility for identifying, developing, selecting, and implementing the strategies that determine the returns shareholders will earn over time. By focusing here on top management, we do not mean to suggest that the prosperity of the rest of the organization should not be linked to that of the shareholders. We focus on top management because we think compensation at this level must first be aligned with the governing objective before changes deeper in the organization can be effective.

By compensation, we mean total compensation, not just "incentive" compensation. We believe a guiding principle of the compensation process should be that, to the greatest degree possible, the average total compensation of top management should be more than, less than, or equal to the average total compensation of top managers at peer companies, depending on whether the company generates shareholder returns that are higher than, less than, or equal to those of peer companies. Put another way, the well-known maxim, "pay for performance," should be changed to *"relative pay for relative performance."* It is very difficult to apply this principle in comparisons of only the variable, or incentive, portion of compensation at various companies. At the end of the day, both managers and shareholders understand that total pay is what matters.

As the principle of relative pay for relative performance implies, we do not see top management compensation primarily as an incentive *to* achieve a particular level of performance so much as a *reward for* having achieved it. Of course, there must be elements of both, but the distinction is not merely one of semantics. A question (often rhetorical) we hear frequently from managers goes something like this: "Why don't we just change the incentive plan and start linking our pay to value creation—isn't that really about all we need to do to get better performance?" In other words, these managers assume that instituting a value based incentive compensation program will cause two things to happen: professional managers will begin to make decisions that closely resemble those of owner-managers and, as a result, shareholder value will increase. These expectations have some logical appeal and are occasionally fulfilled, particularly in highly focused single-business companies with a top management that knows every aspect of the business inside out. But for the typical large multibusiness corporation, we think for several reasons that simply changing incentives to be more value based without also changing the other institutional value drivers will have limited impact.

To begin with, it is really not possible within a large public company to duplicate the extreme incentives, especially those against failing, that owner-managers face. We know of no public company with a pay plan that offers its top managers retirement at age 35 for success and also threatens them with personal ruin if their business units "fail" (the institutional imperative makes recognition of this type of business failure almost impossible anyway). Further, it should be noted that many owners are far from gifted managers—just because they have the right incentives to create value does not mean that they have the right leadership and organizational skills to manage large or complex companies. For every Warren Buffett or Bill Gates of Microsoft, there are probably hundreds of successful entrepreneurs who cannot make the transition from the start-up or early success stages of a business to the building and managing of a large enterprise. Yet no one suggests that paying owners like managers will cause them to suddenly develop these capabilities!

This leads to our final caution against overreliance on incentive compensation alone, however value based it might be. The "let's change the pay and managers will start doing the right things" argument assumes that managers have known all along what "the right things" are but have been holding back while waiting for a better deal from the company, rather like a professional baseball team with several players capable of batting .400 but limiting themselves to .250 until their talents are more fully appreciated by the team owner. We are not so sure that knowledge of how to create wealth is lying dormant in the executive suite, just waiting to be aroused by the right pay package.

The determination of the right things for the business units and the corporate center to do can be made only through the rigorous analysis and tough questioning of alternatives in the strategic planning process, not through the compensation process. It will always be hard for even the best managers to achieve the strategic and financial targets that emerge from a value based strategic planning process—they will not need any further "stretch" from an incentive plan. To the extent that these ambitious targets are met and the company outperforms its peers in the capital markets, managers should certainly be rewarded with above-average pay—they are obviously above-average managers. Conversely, if performance for shareholders is below par, total compensation should be as well.

We will now look briefly at ways to design compensation programs that provide relative pay for relative performance. Once eligibility (in this case, top management) has been determined, three issues in designing the compensation plans remain to be resolved: What is the basic *structure* (measures, targets, time frames) linking total compensation to the governing objective; what is the appropriate *scaling* (mix and magnitude) of total compensation for different levels of performance; and what *form* (cash, stock, stock options, etc.) should the compensation take? While the answers to many of these questions will be similar at both the business unit and corporate levels, a few important differences usually require two separate although closely related plans. Since the corporate plan will depend to some degree on the business unit plan, we begin at the business unit level.

Compensating Business Unit Management

Top management of a business unit should be compensated primarily on the basis of how well the business performs relative to its approved strategy. This means that each business unit will necessarily have a different set of financial and nonfinancial targets. While this tailoring makes administration of compensation programs more complicated in some ways, it is necessary if compensation is to be determined by value creation over time. Thus, while the underlying design of the business unit compensation programs will be the same across the port-folio, each unit will have its unique plan.

Since the approved strategy is expected to maximize the warranted value of the business unit, it will be as difficult to achieve fully as any feasible business plan. Therefore, as noted earlier, the structure and scaling features of the compensation plan should not necessarily be designed to reward managers for business performance that goes well beyond the strategic plan targets, because that would exceed reason-able expectations. Rather, the compensation plan should be designed to reward managers with above-average pay simply for achieving the objectives of the strategy.

Business Unit Compensation: Structure

The structure of the compensation plan will determine how closely it is linked to the business unit strategy. The three major factors that de-termine this linkage are the measures, targets, and time frame selected for establishing the variable portion of total compensation. Direct link-age to the strategic plan requires that the measures and targets forming the business unit performance contract with the chief executive also be used as the basis for evaluating the performance of the business unit general manager and his or her direct reports. Thus, if the business unit's approved financial targets are for specified levels of revenue growth, cash flow, and economic profit in each of the next several years, these targets should also be used in the compensation plan. In this way, strategy, resource allocation, performance management, and pay are fully aligned with the governing objective.

Frequently, this objection is raised: Because business performance can be influenced by so many factors beyond management's control, the measures and targets used as the basis for awarding variable compensation should be limited to those that are "controllable" by managers. There is a good deal of merit to this argument in principle, but in practice it often seems that almost nothing is really controllable—particularly if, in hindsight, it has turned out badly. Of course, when targets are met or exceeded, it is assumed to result entirely because of the excellent management of these same, otherwise "uncontrollable" factors. We would suggest that if truly uncontrollable factors cause the business unit to fall short of its contract targets, generally those same factors will cause competitors to suffer as well, with the result that pay among peers will not be as high as it might have been otherwise. It is much easier to maintain the integrity of the relative pay for relative performance principle if the financial fortunes of managers rise and fall directly with the success of their business strategies.[1]

Another complex question concerns selection of the most appropriate time frame for recognizing and rewarding performance. Almost all U.S. companies, and many in Europe, have so-called short-term plans that are usually designed to provide incentives to managers for meeting and exceeding the business unit's annual plan, or budget, targets. In addition, more and more companies, especially in the United States, are adding "long-term" incentive plans at the business unit level, to reward managers for consistency of performance over two, three, or four years (most have had long-term incentive plans for top corporate managers for some time). This seems to us an unnecessary complication, because if managers are being measured for performance against strategy, the benefits of both short- and long-term plans can be captured in a single plan. The strategic plan itself is a long-term plan, with both short- and long-term milestones. If the chief executive and general manager have agreed, for instance, to a three-year contract for resource and performance commitments, the compensation plan for that business unit should be a single three-year plan, with payouts occurring annually as milestones on the path to superior competitive and financial performance are reached.

As a final note, the structure we propose here ties the entire compensation of business unit management to the performance of the business unit itself, not to the company's overall performance. Is this reasonable? We think it is very reasonable in the sense that if a particular business unit achieves its targets, its management should be well paid, regardless of the performance of other business units. Conversely, if the firm does well overall, but a particular business unit does not perform as expected, there is no reason that its management should expect to receive exceptional pay. To do otherwise runs the risk of introducing still more cross-subsidies into the portfolio, this time from better-performing managers to less successful managers, with no long-term benefit to the company. Once again, Warren Buffett put it best:

> If I had the job of running a football team that was last, but had two outstanding players, I wouldn't pay them less just because they had a lot of clowns around them. Then we'd stay last. Basically, you've got to pay for talent in this world.[2]

Business Unit Compensation: Scaling

The determination of the best mix of fixed and variable compensation and the determination of the maximum total annual compensation, or upside, for performance are two major issues in scaling the compensation plan. They are, of course, closely related. If, for example, it is decided on some basis that upside total compensation for business unit general managers should be a maximum of 120 percent of the peer average total compensation, the level of the general managers' base, or fixed, pay still has to be decided.[3] For example, if the company establishes this base pay at 80 percent of the peer average, the variable component of pay would fall between 0 and 50 percent of the base—a fairly typical range for managers of large business units.

The determination of the best mix of fixed and variable pay and the upside potential for total pay is undoubtedly subject to as much art as science. The numbers we used in the previous example are probably not unreasonable, but there is room for considerable variation. The key point is that we always reference compensation relative to that of peers, while trying to set a reasonable downside—in the form of base pay—for falling well short of the strategic plan targets and a reasonable upside—in the form of maximum total compensation—for *achieving* those targets. Since meeting the targets will mean that the business unit is creating as much value as it possibly can, there is little, if any, need for incentives to do better. If business units regularly exceed their strategic plan targets in a value based company, it probably means that they get a little lucky (e.g., those uncontrollable factors go their way) or the strategies are not really value maximizing or aggressive enough in the first place. In the latter event, the strategies and targets, not necessarily the compensation program, need fixing.

Continuing with the previous example, how should the company scale the variable pay, or bonus, for performance below the strategic plan targets? Again, generalization is difficult, but it is usually possible to agree on what is unacceptable performance, resulting in no bonus and therefore total compensation that is lower than the peer average. From that base, the company can scale rising bonus levels to the "upside" total compensation for managers who achieve their strategic plan targets. If benchmarking with competitors is good enough, it should be possible to set the scale so that over time, average performance compared with peers will mean that only about half of the potential bonus will be paid out, resulting in total compensation of 100 percent of the peer average.

Business Unit Compensation: Funding

In large public companies, we think the uncertainty a manager faces about future bonuses should be limited to whether the targets will be achieved; it should definitely not include any uncertainty about the monetary value the bonus will have. This means that we favor cash or cash equivalents over stock options as the form of bonus payment. Stock options may be an entirely appropriate and desirable form of compensation in start-up companies or in small high-growth companies that are trying to attract top talent without running up their fixed payroll costs. But in large companies, it is virtually impossible to link the future value of an option in the company's stock with the performance of a particular business unit management team. If the business unit does poorly but the stock market rises and the options are "in the money," the wrong signal has been sent to management, and the shareholders have paid for performance they did not get. Conversely, nothing is more disheartening than for managers to do a brilliant job of bringing home a challenging strategy over several years only to find that the value of their bonus, in the form of stock options, is zero because the market averages have fallen.

An alternative approach is to give managers a menu of optional forms of payment at the time the bonus is awarded and let them choose what they like. Some will prefer all cash, some will prefer to receive the company's stock, others will prefer some sort of deferred payment, but most will want a mix. This degree of choice adds some administrative complications (although it would be hard to get more complicated or ingenious than some of the pay plans we have seen). Of course, if simplicity is desired, cash will do nicely.

Compensating Corporate Management

At the corporate level, top management compensation relative to that of peer companies should be determined by the answers to these two questions: Is the company achieving its approved strategies? and Is achievement of these strategies producing positive relative returns for shareholders? To answer the first question, management must look to internal measures of success, but the second question can be answered only by looking at the company's performance in the external capital markets. In our view, the external performance measure is the more important component of the two and should be given a good deal more weight, probably two to three times as much, in determining top management bonuses at the corporate level.

Structure of Performance versus Plan Component

The internal financial measures and targets used to determine business unit and corporate center performance should also used for the compensation plan. As discussed in Chapter Fifteen, these targets are the result of a bottom-up consolidation of the strategies creating the highest warranted value for the company, not a top-down decree. Corporate management must be paid on the basis of the same strategies as the business unit management.

Structure of Performance versus Peers Component

Meeting the company's internal financial and strategic targets but failing to meet its goal of outperforming its peers in the capital markets is not a very appealing outcome for shareholders or management. And the reverse situation, where capital market performance is good but the strategies are not achieved, is probably not sustainable for long. Therefore, linking top management's relative pay directly to relative performance is essential to achieving alignment with the governing objective.

The evidence of linkage between relative pay and relative perform-ance, particularly for chief executives, is rather weak, to put it mildly. In Exhibit 16.1, for example, there appears to be no correlation at all between the 1989–1991 performance for shareholders of companies in

EXHIBIT 16.1

Value Creation vs. Total Compensation for S&P 400[5]

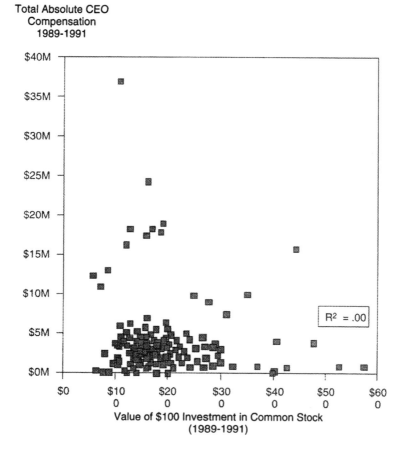

Note: M = millions.

the S&P 400 and the absolute levels of compensation of their chief executives. Many other analyses conducted by academics and journalists confirm this rather puzzling phenomenon.[4] However one interprets all this evidence of the poor relationship between relative performance and relative pay, we conclude, at a minimum, that the compensation committees of corporate boards should be striving to achieve better outcomes than these.

As we proposed in Chapter Sixteen, a straightforward measure of performance for shareholders compares by quartile the company's total return to shareholders against those of an appropriate group of peer companies, both annually and over the long term. Achieving top-quartile performance consistently over time is an immensely impressive and wealth-creating accomplishment, which should result in very high relative total compensation for top management.

Corporate Compensation: Scaling

As with scaling at the business unit level, the issues at the corporate level involve the mix of fixed and variable pay and the upper limit of total compensation. Here again, many factors require considerable exercise of judgment. For discussion purposes, we will stay with our earlier suggestion that base pay be set at about 80 percent of the average total compensation of peer companies (it would probably be difficult to recruit or retain good managers if the downside, as represented by the base pay, were much lower than this). In the case of the chief executive, the upside might be set at 160 percent of the peer average, meaning that his or her single year performance bonus would be between 0 and 100 percent of base pay, a fairly common range in the United States.

The simple matrix in Exhibit 16.2 demonstrates how the chief executive might be compensated under different outcomes. (As the compensation of other senior corporate executives would be tied to the same measures, this example illustrates scaling for the entire group of eligible corporate managers.)

The linkage between relative pay and relative performance is clear, as is the relative importance of beating the competition in the capital markets versus meeting the internal goals. Top management will receive average total compensation by achieving the company's internal

EXHIBIT 16.2

Illustration of Chief Executive Compensation: *One-Year Relative Pay for Relative Performance.*[1]

Company's Relative Shareholder Returns (Bonus 2, weighted at three times the bonus for achieving internal performance targets)		On Track		Off Track	
	Top-Quartile Performance	Base Pay	80	Base Pay	80
		Bonus 1	20	Bonus 1	0
		Bonus 2	60	Bonus 2	60
		Total Compensation Relative to Peer Group Average	160	Total Compensation Relative to Peer Group Average	140
	Second-Quartile Performance	Base Pay	80	Base Pay	80
		Bonus 1	20	Bonus 1	0
		Bonus 2	30	Bonus 2	30
		Total Compensation Relative to Peer Group Average	130	Total Compensation Relative to Peer Group Average	110
	Below-Average Performance	Base Pay	80	Base Pay	80
		Bonus 1	20	Bonus 1	0
		Bonus 2	0	Bonus 2	0
		Total Compensation Relative to Peer Group Average	100	Total Compensation Relative to Peer Group Average	80

Company's Internal Performance Targets (Bonus 1)

Note: All figures are expressed as a percentage of peer group average total compensation.

[1] *These figures do not include a bonus for achieving above-average relative shareholder returns over two or more years, for which additional compensation should be earned. This can be accomplished by applying a multiplier to Bonus 2 for each successive year of above-average performance for shareholders. For example, a multiplier of 1.2 for first-quartile performance would mean that, after four successive years of achievement at that level, the chief executive's Bonus 2 would be 125% of the peer group average total compensation level, so that his or her total pay for the year (assuming internal targets were also on track) would be 225% of the peer group average chief executive's total pay (80 + 20 + 125).*

targets. Above average pay can be earned only by achieving above average performance for shareholders. Since the top managers of the business units depend on achievement of their strategies to receive high bonuses, there is already a lot of incentive in the system to reach the internal targets. Also, there is enough upside potential to provide a very strong incentive to most chief executives.

This example is for compensation in a single year. Often companies want to choose longer time frames as part of a long-term incentive plan. As noted earlier, we see little benefit to this added complexity, which usually means that there are separate short- and long-term plans. As we have shown in Chapter Four, the current price of the company's common stock already reflects very long-term investor expectations of performance, as does investors' pricing of the company's stock relative to that of peers over time. We think a single plan can accommodate the preference of most managers for annual feedback on their performance while also recognizing that sustaining superior performance over longer periods of time is tremendously valuable and should be rewarded accordingly. For instance, as illustrated in the note to Exhibit 16.2, bonus awards can be designed to be a function of the current year's performance as well as the number of consecutive years that the company has been in the first or second quartile of performance.

We believe a compensation plan designed along these lines would benefit many companies, with two provisos. First, the board must not be too flexible about changing the payouts if required performance standards are not met— we have seen this happen more than once under the guise of making adjustments for unforeseen (always negative) events. The shareholders have no such protection. More important, such actions are exactly what causes the zero correlation between relative pay and relative performance that exists in large companies today. Second, performance can be no better than the strategies that produce it, so we emphasize again that changing the compensation process without changing the other institutional value drivers will not ensure consistently better strategies or better performance.

Corporate Compensation: Funding

The form of payment or payment choices for top corporate managers should not necessarily be any different from what is offered to business unit managers. As noted earlier in this chapter we are unpersuaded that stock options provide either good signaling to managers or sufficient benefits to stockholders. The monetary value of bonuses should not be in doubt, only the likelihood of achieving the performance necessary to earn them. Of course, managers' decisions to take the company's stock in lieu of cash or use their cash bonuses to buy options in the company's stock for themselves are good indications of their confidence in the impact their decisions will have on future performance.

Implementing Value Based Compensation Programs

Because expectations of the immediate benefits of changing to value based compensation programs are often so high, many companies are eager to implement them immediately after top management has made a commitment to creating shareholder value. We suggest a somewhat more measured approach. Like physicians, we subscribe to the motto, "First, do no harm."

At the corporate level, we favor designating relative shareholder returns as the primary driver of top management's variable pay as soon as possible. This gets top corporate management focused immediately on the scale and difficulty of its challenge, and also sends the right signal to the rest of top management at the business unit level. However, since we recommend a direct linkage between management pay and achievement of value-maximizing strategies, particularly at the business unit level, it is very important that managers understand the "new game" of governance, strategic planning, resource allocation, and performance management before making too many changes in their compensation programs. Value based management must emphasize development of the right strategies and organizational capabilities, from which financial rewards will follow, rather than focus first on the financial rewards and hope for better strategic and organizational decisions as a result.

Often we suggest a two-phase implementation program for changing the compensation process with respect to the internal targets. In the first phase, the current compensation plans are reviewed and, to the extent possible, modified in order to "do no harm" to the governing objective. In the second phase, after the other institutional value drivers have been changed, top management compensation can be brought fully into line with the objective of maximizing shareholder value. At that point, top management compensation itself joins the ranks as a true value driver of the company.

As a related observation, some boards of directors and institutional shareholders are beginning to ask whether top managers should be required to purchase significant amounts of their company's common stock, thereby increasing their personal financial stake in share price performance over time. We certainly advocate that managers and board members own material amounts of the company's stock and thus have no disagreement with this idea in principle. However, we view stock ownership primarily as a governance technique for better aligning decision making with the governing objective rather than a compensation technique; that is, managers should be compensated appropriately for their performance regardless of the number of company shares they themselves own. The rewards and penalties of stock ownership should be the same for the managers as for any other shareholder and not be confused with relative pay for relative performance.

Concluding Remarks

Perhaps no topic in business is more emotive than compensation for top management, especially for the chief executive. In this chapter we have deliberately avoided any discussion of absolute levels of compensation, that is, whether the right average total compensation for a chief executive in a particular industry should be $1 million or $2 million or some other amount. These average levels vary greatly by industry and by country. It seems to us that this is a matter for shareholders, boards of directors, and top management to work out for themselves. We think, however, that the board of directors and top management should make every effort to ensure that, over time, a company pays its managers proportionally to their success in creating value relative to the compensation of managers of similar companies competing in similar markets. There is no economic justification, or any other justification we can think of, for doing otherwise.

CONCLUSION

Making Value Creation
A Core Competence

A few years ago, in a meeting with a top executive of one of America's largest and best-known companies, the subject of core competences came up for discussion. The company, which had been generating below-average shareholder returns for some time, was just completing a census of all its business units to determine what the firm's "core competences" were. The intention was to develop a vision and strategies built on these purported sources of global competitive advantage, with the attendant hope that this would result in better performance for investors. At one point the executive, who knew us well, commented, "I know your firm doesn't think much of the idea of core competences." "Not so!" we replied, feigning injury at being unfairly accused. We explained that we did not differ about the importance of core competences but about the criteria this company was using to define them. We noted that the management had identified several dozen core competences, mostly in product and process technology and some in marketing.

The question we asked was this: "In that whole long list of core competences, did anyone include making money?" "No," he said, and after a moment of reflection he added, "I see what you mean."

Competitive advantage embodied in strategic assets, such as brands or proprietary manufacturing technology, and in organizational capabilities like superior customer service or just-in-time inventory management, is necessary, of course, to create shareholder value. But competitive advantage alone is insufficient. Great companies like IBM, General Motors, Kodak, Philips Electronics, and Citicorp have all struggled in recent years despite some enormous competitive advantages in assets, technology, and functional skills. Unfortunately, the top managements of these companies not only failed to find the strategies necessary to convert these advantages into new wealth but wasted many resources on strategies that actually destroyed wealth—huge amounts of it. The one core competence they needed most, making money for the shareholders, they did not have.

Chief executives all around the world, faced with intensifying competitive pressures on the outside and costly, sclerotic bureaucracies on the inside, are recognizing the imperative for management to refocus its attention on making money, not only as measured by accountants in higher reported earnings but also as measured by the capital markets in total returns to shareholders. Over the past 20 years, many companies, particularly in North America, Europe, and Australia, have experimented with various approaches to managing for shareholder value. Some, like The Coca-Cola Company, have been able to institutionalize key principles and processes and have achieved great success in both the product markets and the capital markets. The majority are still experimenting. Many feel that they have achieved important gains, particularly at the portfolio level, but they have not transformed their core management beliefs, principles and processes to become value based. In surveys of the largest companies in the United States and the United Kingdom we find that while over 75 percent of the respondents cite "creating shareholder value" as one of their top corporate objectives, fewer than 25 percent claim to have a value based strategic planning process, and fewer than 10 percent claim that value creation is the primary driver of their top management incentive compensation. Thus, while the interest in managing for shareholder value is great, translating that interest into an organizational capability for generating consistently superior performance remains a major management challenge.

Throughout this book we have attempted to show what management can do to make value creation a core competence of the company. In this concluding chapter we discuss some common success factors we observe in the companies that have pioneered the implementation of value based management. The most important of these are:

Strong chief executive leadership;
Ambitious performance goals; and
High expectations for change

Strong Chief Executive Leadership

Maximizing shareholder value will require major strategic and organizational changes. If these changes are to succeed, they must become the chief executive's highest priority. The intensity of the competitive and institutional forces is such that every step forward is threatened with a step or two backward, so the chief executive's commitment to the task cannot be halfhearted or uninformed. The chief executive must be a visible leader of the change process, totally committed to its success, knowledgeable about value based management principles and their applications, and an active participant in the implementation effort. Success is unlikely when the chief executive does not take on this leadership role and level of involvement. Further, the company will be unable to *sustain* superior performance for shareholders unless successive chief executives are equally committed to and capable of achieving the governing objective. Thus, even in companies with excellent performance for shareholders, developing and choosing the right chief executives for the future is essential to maintaining the firm's capacity to create value for shareholders.

The Leader of a Major Change Process

The chief executive has the absolute responsibility to the shareholders, through the board of directors, for managing their investment in the company well. If the chief executive is not perceived by the rest of the organization as the primary "owner" of the initiative to maximize shareholder value, no one else can fulfill this role. It is critical that the chief executive not only supports the required changes but that he or she is the most visible champion of change. In every company we know that has transformed itself from an average to a superior performer, an active, fairly directive chief executive has initiated and led the change. And it was very clear to the entire management team that no other initiative had a higher priority on an ongoing basis.

Totally Committed to Success

There are chief executives who, while they clearly believe in value creation, are not intensely performance driven. On the other hand, we have often found that the chief executives who are most effective at managing for value creation were once equally committed to and successful at managing solely for operating income or earnings-per-share growth. They are intensely performance driven. Achieving the governing objective requires this intensity.

The chief executive must not only be willing to see major strategic and organizational change, he or she must *want* to see that change, to insist on it when necessary. The chief executive can signal this commitment to the organization in many ways, including changes in top management compensation plans, internal communication programs, and his or her own visible participation in the change process. But by far the most effective signal is sent through the changes in the kinds of questions he or she asks and the day-to-day decisions he or she makes. If these questions and decisions are clearly value based, the message will be received by other managers, loud and clear.

Knowledgeable About Principles of Value Based Management

Companies implementing value based management programs often place a high priority on educating hundreds of managers about the principles and even the technical details of measurement and shareholder value analysis. This is a commendable impulse, but while training "the many" is ultimately necessary, it is the wrong place to start. The initial focus should be on "the few"—the chief executive, senior line executives, and the senior staff executives. These members of top management must be entirely comfortable with the key principles and implications of managing for shareholder value. While it is certainly not necessary for the chief executive or all senior managers to be proficient in the measurement techniques and analytical processes, they all must be able to "talk the talk and walk the walk." Otherwise, the top managers' credibility with the rest of the management team will be poor and, worse, they will be unable to make the right decisions for maximizing value.

A Participant in the Change Process

The chief executive must be not only the leader but a player in the change process. Changes in the governance, strategic planning and resource allocation processes, performance management and top management compensation, as well as in major business unit and corporate strategies will require the involvement of the chief executive. His or her input will be critical to the redesign of the institutional value drivers and will always be critical to implementing the changes successfully. If these key management processes are to work well, they must reflect the decision-making requirements and style of the chief executive officer.

Passing the Torch

A final issue in chief executive leadership is succession. In researching the performance of hundreds of companies over many years and, of course, working with many companies that have pioneered the implementation of value based management, it has been our observation that value creation is very "chief executive specific." This, in itself, is not too surprising. But it raises the question of how companies can expect to sustain superior performance by successive chief executives. The importance of this issue is nowhere more vividly documented than in the case of Westinghouse, an early adopter of value based management and a company that, after years of great success, saw its performance for shareholders plummet and its chief executive replaced by the board of directors.

In 1980, when Robert Kirby was chief executive, Westinghouse embarked on a formal program designated by the awkward-sounding acronym, VABASTRAM (VAlue BAsed STRAtegic Management—well, they were engineers, not poets!). The name may have been ungainly, but the program was immensely successful. Value based principles and performance measures were introduced to all business units, and the strategic planning and resource allocation processes were redesigned to incorporate them. Subsequently, the incentive compensation programs were also changed to reward business unit managers for increasing good growth.

There were some immediate and dramatic changes, including divestitures of chronically value-consuming business units like the Lamp division. Internally, profitability standards were raised considerably and business units had to do a much better job—through better strategic plans—of justifying their need for resources. When Douglas Danforth took over as chief executive in 1984, most of the process changes were in place and the company's stock market performance was already showing the impact of the VABASTRAM program. Danforth was a committed and very capable champion of value based management, and the company's performance continued to improve dramatically under his leadership. In fact, from 1980 to 1987, Westinghouse earned one of the highest rates of return for shareholders among the blue-chip companies comprising the Dow Jones 30 Industrials Average Index and was one of the best performing stocks in the United States. Clearly, the capital markets recognized management's concerted efforts to improve warranted value.

By the time Danforth retired in 1987, the company had proved itself very adept at improving performance through aggressive cost-reduction measures and elimination of many bad growth investments. Having done so well on the cost and asset-restructuring side, the new management team under John Marous, chief executive, and Paul Lego, already named his successor, faced the need to find more opportunities for good growth, an admittedly difficult challenge given the many old-line industrial businesses in the Westinghouse portfolio. Unfortunately for the shareholders, a serious mistake was apparently made at this point. The institutional imperative raised its head, and earnings growth became a paramount goal of the company.

For some time, one of the fastest-growing businesses in the portfolio was Westinghouse Credit Company, a subsidiary that was active in commercial real estate finance and lending to leveraged buyouts. There was great demand for real estate and leveraged buyout lending at the time, while accounting practices allowed for substantial loan origination and advisory fees to be reported by Westinghouse as income long before they were actually paid by the borrowers. So the seeds of potential disaster were sown. The Credit Company was able to produce "earnings" literally as fast as it could loan money and charge fees. Since more capable players were already pulling back from the high risk of further construction lending, there were unlimited opportunities to loan money on deals no one else wanted. Indeed, in 1988 and 1989, at the peak of both the real estate and leveraged buyout markets, Westinghouse Credit was widely known as the "lender of last resort." The rest, as they say, is history. Within four years Westinghouse was forced to recognize gigantic losses, totaling over $3 billion, from the bad loans (but great "earnings" producers) written by the credit business. And the preceding decade's hard-won gains for shareholders were entirely reversed as its stock price collapsed.

It may take years to sort out why this shocking lapse of prudent management occurred. That such a mistake could be made in a value based company is, unfortunately, proof that no management process has any natural immunity to the incessant onslaught of the institutional imperative. Good management process can be immensely helpful to a good chief executive, but it cannot survive a less able one for long.

The most important lesson from the Westinghouse experience is that a key concern for any company has to be the development of future chief executives who remain committed to the governing objective and are capable of sustaining the very high levels of strategic and organizational performance needed to create value. As we discussed in Chapter Twelve, it should be one of the board of directors' highest priorities to ensure that every chief executive meets this test. To the extent that a company succeeds in making value creation a core competence, there should be more than enough good candidates inside the organization to choose from.

Ambitious Performance Goals

Management is unlikely to develop value creation as a core competence if expectations of performance improvement are too modest or if maximizing shareholder value is seen as a transient objective. Frequently, chief executives do not know how much improvement in value and shareholder returns is really possible. They may be aware that companies like Coca-Cola, Wal-Mart, and Berkshire Hathaway have achieved superlative performance for their shareholders over long periods of time, but this is often attributed to special industry circumstances, unique competitive advantages, or management techniques that are difficult to transfer to other companies. Thus, while admiring their peers' capabilities and successes, chief executives do not always recognize the lessons for their own companies.

At the outset, simply recognizing the potential for improvement can be more important than knowing how to achieve it. One of the most impressive aspects of the Coca-Cola story is not only the performance the company has actually achieved but the fact that when Roberto Goizueta and Don Keough took over the leadership in 1981, they had the insight that the company still had a very long way to go. After all, Coca-Cola was already the world's largest soft-drink company, with very respectable returns, a high market-to-book value, and the opportunity to still grow rapidly without extraordinary management effort. Many executives in this position could easily have become complacent. Very few would have seen, as Goizueta and Keough did, the still-huge opportunity to increase the company's value, nor would others have pursued it with such determination.

Of course, not every company can achieve shareholder returns as high as 20 to 30 percent per year over long periods of time, although many more could reach this pinnacle than have done so in the past. Performing consistently within the top quartile of comparable companies is itself an extremely ambitious goal. But by setting these kinds of goals, managers soon realize that achieving them will require more improvement than is possible from incremental changes in strategies or operating performance alone. These goals require quantum leaps in performance, year in and year out—performance that is not attainable without special organizational capabilities to create value. If the goals are not set high enough, these capabilities are less likely to be developed.

High Expectations of Change

Many chief executives with high performance ambitions actually have low expectations that managing for shareholder value will be all that helpful, and given their typical initial encounter with various approaches to creating shareholder value, it is not surprising that few executives see the potential to make value creation a core competence.

Most commonly, the conventional approaches to creating shareholder value focus on measurement, not management. The measures are so numerous and so technical (e.g., equity cash flow, free cash flow, warranted value, net present value, terminal value, economic profit, equity spread, EVA, cost of equity, cost of capital, ROE, ROI, ROCE, internal rate of return) that "creating shareholder value" seems like an esoteric financial analysis technique that only three people on the finance or planning staff can possibly understand. Executives might conclude that such analysis could be useful, particularly for making portfolio strategy decisions, but it is hardly the stuff of which great companies are made.

A second concern limiting expectations and acceptance of change is that the words "shareholder value" sometimes inspire fear without hope; that is, shareholder value analysis seems to offer insight mostly into cutting and pruning, not into building the company. Opportunities certainly abound to eliminate bad growth, and it is often easier to spot them (particularly early in the change process) than to identify opportunities to create value through finding new strategies for established businesses or investing in growth initiatives. But it must be emphasized again that maximizing good growth is absolutely essential to creating value. This is harder work and involves more risk than eliminating bad growth, so it may well take the organization longer to find the opportunities and accept the challenges. But over time, most value creation opportunities have to come from increasing profitable growth.

To appreciate the change potential of value based management, executives should focus first on *what* is to be done, rather than *how* it is to be done. The "what" is the achievement of *consistently superior returns* for shareholders. To accomplish this, a company will certainly have to adopt value based profitability measures and use them to help identify and eliminate bad growth strategies. Indeed, these two improvements alone will help managers find many ways to create substantial value for shareholders. Ultimately, however, they are not enough. To perform consistently among the top-tier companies, the organization must also be able to find and implement higher-value growth strategies than its competitors have. Developing this organizational capability should be the ultimate goal of any value based change process. The real changes required to achieve this capability are not in financial measures or portfolio structure. They are in the everyday behavior of the managers themselves—changes in objectives, changes in decision-making skills, and changes in the expectations they have of themselves and of their company to perform with the very best, in both the product markets and the capital markets. To make a large and lasting impact on the company, this is what the change process must accomplish. Chief executives and top management should expect nothing less.

Along with the right expectations, performance goals, and leadership from the chief executive, other factors will influence how well a company is able to establish and sustain value creation as a core competence. Among the more important of these factors are the management champions who help drive implementation of value based management throughout the company and the blueprint for executing the many changes that will be needed to make the governing objective a reality. But even the most committed champions and the best-laid plans will not succeed if the right leadership, performance ambitions, and expectations for change are not in place.

Concluding Remarks

Value creation has always been the ultimate objective of business, not only to create wealth for owners but to stand as the truest measure of how well a company is serving its customers and competing in its chosen markets. With the rise of the modern corporation, serving millions of customers with thousands of products in hundreds of market segments around the world, the virtue of this simple objective has often been forgotten. This is partly because managers see the shareholders as so remote, or even hostile, that the legitimate interests of the owners are subordinated to other institutional objectives. It is partly because the sheer size and complexity of large global corporations have made the task of managing for value much harder than it used to be—it is often difficult for top management to obtain even the most basic information needed to make the right strategic or resource allocation decisions. And partly it is because many executives have become complacent, convincing themselves that objectives other than value creation—such as global market dominance or quality leadership—are the real measures of success. How wrong they are.

Of course, even today value creation is by no means a universally accepted objective at large companies. But few chief executives anywhere in the United States, Canada, Europe, or even Japan are in doubt about the rising expectations of shareholders, especially institutional shareholders, for better performance. The personal consequences for the chief executive who fails to meet these expectations have never been greater. Yet it is unfortunate that so much attention focused on shareholder value in recent years has had a negative connotation. Hostile takeovers and summary dismissals of chief executives are the dark side of value creation, the consequences of disappointment and failure. We much prefer to think of the bright side: the enormous potential for wealth creation everywhere in the world and the vital role that large corporations can and must play in achieving that potential.

Over the past 20 years, there has been a great deal of progress toward improving our understanding of what determines the market value of companies and how management's strategic and organizational decisions will impact that value. There is now enough accumulated knowledge, we believe, for large public companies to undertake serious efforts to make value creation a core competence of the organization. Yet, despite this progress, there is still a great deal to be learned. Managers need not worry about ever exhausting all the possibilities for developing higher-value strategies or building even greater organizational advantages for sustaining superior performance. The forces of competition and the institutional imperative will always provide new challenges, which will stimulate new and better ideas for creating wealth. The process of learning about this most fundamental of management capabilities is really just beginning.

APPENDIX A

Valuation

Basic Valuation Model

The warranted value per share of a company's common stock is determined by the cash it distributes to its shareholders on a per share basis, discounted at the appropriate, risk-adjusted cost of equity capital (K_e). This relationship can be expressed mathematically as follows:

$$\text{Market Value Per Share} = \sum_{t=1}^{\infty} \frac{\text{Cash Distributions Per Share}_t}{(1 + K_e)^t}$$

where cash distributions include dividends and other lump sum distributions of cash but exclude share repurchases. While this approach works well at the company level for valuing securities, it cannot be used at the business unit level because per share data are not available. Consequently, in order to value business unit strategies, one needs a representation of warranted equity value that is not based on per share numbers. Fortunately, cash distributions per share can be translated into the total amount of cash distributed to shareholders—or equity cash flow—and warranted equity value can be derived by discounting future equity cash flow at the cost of equity capital. In almost all cases, cash distributions per share multiplied by the number of shares outstanding will yield the equity cash flow for the entire company. For

299

instance, if a company does not issue or repurchase shares, the number of shares remains constant over time and cash distributions per share multiplied by the number of shares will exactly equal total cash distributions. If, however, the company plans to repurchase shares or issues shares in the future, the equity cash flow valuation will be equivalent to the per share valuation only if the company issues and repurchases its common shares at a value equal to their warranted equity value. Fortunately, this is usually a good assumption unless management believes that the company's warranted value is significantly different from its market value or management intends to treat selected shareholders preferentially (as was the case with "greenmail" schemes used during the 1980s). Because these situations are uncommon, we typically recommend using the same discounted cash flow approach at both the business unit and corporate levels.

There are two approaches to determining the warranted value of a company's (or business unit's) equity capital using discounted cash flow (see Exhibit A.1). In this book, our primary approach has been to estimate this value directly, using what we call the equity approach. However, many companies estimate the warranted value of their com-

EXHIBIT A.1

Two Approaches to Valuation

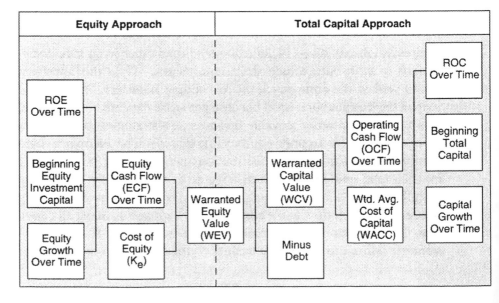

mon stock indirectly, using an alternative valuation model—which we refer to as the total capital approach. Used properly, both of these approaches will produce the same warranted equity value and both can be used to evaluate strategy alternatives. This appendix will focus on some of the issues involved in determining warranted value, using each approach.

The Equity Approach

The warranted equity value (WEV) of a company (or business unit) can be determined directly by discounting its projected equity cash flow back to a present value at the appropriate, risk-adjusted cost of equity capital (K_e). This relationship can be expressed mathematically as:

$$\text{Warranted Equity Value (WEV)} = \sum_{t=1}^{\infty} \frac{\text{Equity Cash Flow}_t}{(1 + K_e)^t}$$

This specification of the discounted cash flow approach is the most direct method for determining the warranted value of a company's equity capital.

The Total Capital Approach

The warranted value of a company's (or business unit's) equity can be derived indirectly by first determining its warranted capital value (WCV)—the intrinsic value of the company's long-term debt and equity capital—and then subtracting the market value of its debt capital (D). This relationship can be expressed arithmetically as:

Warranted Equity Value (WEV) = Warranted Capital Value (WCV) −
Market Value of Debt (D)

where the market value of debt includes the market value of all interest-bearing liabilities, including preferred stock. The warranted value of a company's (or a business unit's) total capital can be determined by discounting its projected operating cash flow (OCF) back to a present value at the appropriate, risk-adjusted, weighted-average cost of capital (WACC). This relationship can be expressed mathematically as:

$$\text{Warranted Capital Value(WCV)} = \sum_{t=1}^{\infty} \frac{\text{Operating Cash Flow}_t}{(1 + \text{WACC})^t}$$

Whether one chooses to use the direct or indirect approach to determining the warranted value of a company's equity, there are two important variables that must be defined: (1) Cash Flow; and (2) the Cost of Capital. We will discuss the approach for estimating each of these variables in turn.

Defining Cash Flow

Equity Cash Flow

Equity cash flow (ECF) is defined as the net cash flow received by all common shareholders. Thus, equity cash flow is equal to dividends paid plus the value of common shares repurchased minus the value of new common shares issued. This relationship can be expressed arithmetically as follows:

Equity Cash Flow (ECF) = Dividends + Share Repurchases −
Share Issuances

In a year in which a company neither issues nor repurchases common stock, equity cash flow is simply the amount of dividends paid to common shareholders.

In its simplest form, equity cash flow represents the portion of earnings not reinvested (or retained) by the company. As long as the company follows "flow-through" accounting, equity cash flow can be defined by using the "short path" (see Exhibit A.2) as earnings less the change in the shareholders' equity account from one year to the next. This relationship can be expressed arithmetically as follows:

Equity Cash Flow (ECF) = Earnings − Δ Equity Invested

Exhibit A.2 also illustrates that the traditional approach to determining cash flow, labeled the "long road," will yield the same result as observing directly cash outflow to shareholders if "flow-through" ac-

EXHIBIT A.2

Defining Equity Cash Flows

Income Statement		
	Year 1	
Revenue	$300	
Cost of Goods Sold	120	
Operating Expenses	60	
Depreciation	30	
Operating Income	$90	
Interest Expense	10	
Taxes	21	(@ 40%)
Earnings After Taxes	$48	
Dividends	$28	

Balance Sheet		
	End of Year 0	**End of Year 1**
Assets		
Cash	$50	$60
A/R	100	120
Inventory	100	120
Gross Fixed Assets	400	440
Accum. Depreciation	150	180
Net Fixed Assets	$250	$260
Total Assets	$500	$560
Liabilities & Equity		
Deferred Taxes	$100	$110
Other Liabilities	200	210
Debt	100	120
Equity	100	120
Total Liab. & Equity	$500	$560

Short Path	
Earnings After Taxes (E)	$48
- Equity Invested (B)	20
= Equity Flow	$28

Long Road	
Earnings After Taxes (E)	$48
+ Depreciation	30
+ Increases in Other Liabilities	30
+ Increases in Deferred Taxes	10
= Sources of Cash	$118
Fixed Capital Investment	$40
+ Increase in A/R	20
+ Increase in Inventory	20
+ Increase in Cash	10
= Uses of Cash	$90
Equity Cash Flow = 118-90=28	

Both Equal to the Direct Method	
Dividends	$28
Share Repurchases	0
Share Issuances	0
Total Equity Cash Flows	$28

counting is used. Therefore, at the corporate level, both the direct and the two indirect approaches can be used. However, at the business unit level, information concerning dividends, share repurchases, and share issuances is generally not available. As a result, the company's internal accounting statements must be used to determine ECF indirectly— using either the short path or the long road. While the long road is more commonly used by accountants, given the potential for mistakes in its use, we strongly recommend that managers employ the short path.

Operating Cash Flow

Operating cash flow (OCF) is defined as the net cash flow received by all investors—including banks, bondholders, preferred stockholders, and common stockholders. Operating cash flow can be measured directly by adding financing cash flow to equity cash flow. This relationship can be expressed arithmetically as follows:

Operating Cash Flow (OCF) = Equity Cash Flow + Financing Cash
Flow

where

Financing Cash Flow = After-tax Interest Payments + Preferred
Stock Dividends – Net Debt Issuances –
Net Preferred Stock Issuances

Like equity cash flow, operating cash flow can be measured by using the company's financial statements. OCF represents the portion of operating income not reinvested by the company (or business unit). Again, as long as the company follows "flow-through" accounting, operating cash flow can be defined as after-tax operating profits less the change in total capital accounts (i.e., interest-bearing debt, preferred stock, and equity invested). This relationship can be expressed arithmetically as:

Operating Cash Flows = NOPAT – Δ Total Capital

EXHIBIT A.3

Defining Operating Cash Flows

Income Statement		Balance Sheet		
	Year 1		**End of Year 0**	**End of Year 1**
Revenue	$300	*Assets*		
Cost of Goods Sold	120	Cash	$50	$60
Operating Expenses	60	A/R	100	120
Depreciation	30	Inventory	100	120
Operating Income	$90	Gross Fixed Assets	400	440
		Accum. Depreciation	150	180
Taxes	36 (@ 40%)	Net Fixed Assets	$250	$260
Net Operating Profits After Taxes	$54	Total Assets	$500	$560
		Liabilities & Equity		
		Deferred Taxes	$100	$110
		Other Liabilities	200	210
		Total Capital	200	240
		Total Liab. & Equity	$500	$560

Short Path	
Net Operating Profits After Taxes (NOPAT)	$54
- Total Capital (Reinvestment)	40
= Operating Cash Flow	$14

Long Road	
NOPAT	$54
+ Depreciation	30
+ Increases in Other Liabilities	10
+ Increases in Deferred Taxes	10
= Sources in Cash	$104
Fixed Capital Investment	$40
+ Increase in A/R	20
+ Increase in Inventory	20
+ Increase in Cash	10
= Uses of Cash	$90
Operating Cash Flow = 104 - 90 = 14	

Both Equal to the Direct Method[1]	
Equity Cash Flows	$28
Financing Cash Flows	
After-tax Interest	6
- Debt Issuance	20
Total Financing	-$14
Operating Cash Flow = 28 - 14 = 14	

[1]*See Exhibit A.2.*

where

$$
\begin{aligned}
\text{NOPAT} &= \text{Net Operating Profit After Taxes} \\
&= \text{Operating Profit} \times (1 - \text{Tax Rate}) \\
\text{Total Capital} &= \text{Interest-bearing Debt} + \text{Preferred Stock} + \\
&\quad\ \text{Equity Invested} \\
&= \text{Total Assets} - \text{Non-interest-bearing Liabilities} \\
&\quad\ (\text{NIBLs})
\end{aligned}
$$

As Exhibit A.3 illustrates, the two indirect methods for determining operating cash flow yield the same result as the direct method. Therefore, at the company level, both the direct and indirect approaches can be used. However, at the business unit level, OCF must be determined indirectly by using the company's internal accounting statements.

Cost of Capital Estimation

Cost of Equity Capital

A company's (or business unit's) cost of equity capital is the minimum acceptable rate of return demanded by shareholders for supplying equity capital. It can also be thought of as the shareholders' expected rate of return (in the form of dividends and share price appreciation) from owning a company's common stock.

The investor's minimum acceptable rate of return is a function of the prevailing level of interest rates and the degree of risk that a particular security is perceived to have. Indeed, as the level of interest rates changes over time, so will a company's cost of equity capital. Because the cost of equity capital varies with perceived risk, the cost of equity for a particular company will vary from that of other companies depending on its perceived risk relative to other firms.

Estimating the cost of equity capital for a company generally involves two steps. First, one must estimate the average cost of equity across all companies, which is commonly termed the market cost of equity capital. Second, one must estimate the relative risk for the company compared with the market average in order to estimate the company's specific cost of equity. For business units, a third step is required, which involves estimating the specific cost of equity for the unit by assessing risk relative to comparable publicly traded companies. We describe each of these steps.

Estimating the Market Cost of Equity Capital

There are two ways to determine the market cost of equity capital (K_m)—the *historical* approach and the *prospective* approach. Results of the two approaches are often quite different. While we address both here, we have a strong preference for the prospective approach.

HISTORICAL APPROACH. The historical approach uses actual realized returns over some specified time period to estimate future expected returns. The historical approach begins by expressing the market cost of equity (K_m) as the sum of two components: the rate of return on "risk-free" investments (K_f) and the "market risk premium" (MRP). This relationship can be expressed mathematically as:

$$K_e = K_f + MRP$$

Typically, for developed countries with stable governments and efficient capital markets, the rate of return on Government securities is considered risk-free. As a result, K_f is usually set equal to the long-term Government bond rate. MRP is estimated by observing historical returns on common stocks and subtracting the risk-free rate. In the United States, the most widely used historical estimate for MRP is 6 to 8 percent.[1] However, the historical estimates are very sensitive to the time period selected, with ranges from under 4 percent to over 8 percent, depending on the years chosen. Even more problematic in the historical approach is the fact that global capital markets have undergone major changes over the past 20 years—changes that could easily cause historical returns to be unrepresentative of future expectations.

PROSPECTIVE APPROACH. While the historical approach is most commonly used for estimating equity costs, it is possible (and we believe preferable) to estimate the cost of equity with a prospective approach. The prospective approach begins with the understanding that a company's stock price is the present value of its future cash distributions per share discounted at some cost of equity capital. With this relationship in mind, the cost of equity capital is simply the internal rate of return (IRR) on the market's forecast of future cash distributions per share that makes the purchase of a company's common stock a zero net present value investment for the average shareholder. This relationship can be expressed mathematically as:

$$\text{Market Value Per Share} = \sum_{t=1}^{\infty} \frac{\text{Cash Distributions Per Share}_t}{(1 + IRR)^t}$$

Of course, in order to apply the prospective approach, one must have an estimate for the market's forecast of cash distributions per share for a particular company. In the United States, we use the forecasts provided by The Value Line Investment Survey combined with other forecasts (taken in perpetuity) as a proxy for the market's forecast and then deduce the appropriate cost of equity capital as the IRR.

Once an estimate for the market rate of return has been developed, an estimate for the prospective market risk premium (MRP) can be derived by simply subtracting the current risk-free rate from the prospective market rate of return. Over the past fifteen years, we have applied this approach regularly to estimate the market risk premium on a universe of more than 1,500 common stocks in the United States. Our analyses indicate that the MRP has averaged between 3.5 and 4.5 percent over long-term Government bonds for most of the last decade—significantly lower than the 6 to 8 percent historical long-term average. Other services that use the prospective approach to estimated expected market returns get results similar to ours.

Estimating a Company's Cost of Equity Capital

The cost of equity capital varies among companies because of differences in business risk and/or financial risk, defined as follows:

Business risk.   The degree of forecast uncertainty that investors perceive concerning the company's future operating cash flow, which cannot be offset by diversified investment in other securities.

Financial risk.   The extent to which the company's use of financial leverage magnifies its business risk relative to the overall market.

A company's risk is typically expressed relative to the risk of the overall market. Thus, if a company is viewed as:

- above average in riskiness, then its risk premium will be the product of the MRP and a multiplier greater than 1,
- below average in riskiness, then its risk premium will be the product of the MRP and a multiplier less than 1, or
- about average in riskiness, then its risk premium will be the product of the MRP and a multiplier of 1.

The most commonly used approaches to estimating a company's risk multiplier are based on the Capital Assets Pricing Model (CAPM). The CAPM refers to the "risk multiplier" (which includes both *business risk* and *financial risk*) as "β"—where β is typically deduced over some historical period by regressing the movements in the company's realized rates of return over the period against co-movements in the market's realized rates of return. Thus, a company's cost of equity capital is typically expressed as a function of the risk-free rate, β, and the market risk premium:

$$K_e = K_f + \beta[MRP]$$

Although the CAPM approach suffers from some of the same deficiencies as the historical approach in estimating the market risk premium, they are less severe. First, the time periods involved in CAPM are much shorter and, therefore, likely to be more representative of future expectations. Second, practitioners typically employ a variety of techniques to get "improved" β estimates that correct some of the historical biases.

In addition to the historical CAPM approach, the prospective approach to determining a company's IRR can be used. However, when the prospective approach is applied to a single company, as opposed to the aggregate of all companies, the method is less reliable because it is typically difficult to find cash flow forecasts for a particular company that are accurate proxies for the market's forecast.

Both the historical and prospective approaches have their respective advantages and disadvantages. In practice, we find that a combination of the historical and prospective approaches works well in estimating a company's relative risk and, thus, its cost of equity capital.

Estimating a Business Unit's Cost of Equity Capital

Five steps are involved in determining the cost of equity capital that is appropriate for an individual business unit. First, "comparable" public companies have to be selected to match the risk characteristics of the particular business unit. "Comparables" should be those public companies that trade in the same capital markets, operate in markets that offer similar or related products, serve the same or similar customers in the same or similar way, and have roughly the same competitive position and strategy as the particular business unit. Second, the cost of equity capital must be estimated for each comparable company (using the approach described above). Third, the effects of leverage should be removed from the cost of equity estimates for each business to determine the "unlevered" cost of equity capital for each comparable company (denoted K_e^*). Fourth, using the comparables as a proxy, the business unit's unleveraged cost of equity capital K_e^* should be estimated, taking into account the business unit's (a) historical variability in cash flow and returns relative to the comparable companies, and (b) competitive position and strategy compared with those companies. Finally, once a target capital structure has been established for the business unit, its unleveraged cost of equity capital should be "levered" to determine the appropriate, risk-adjusted cost of equity (K_e) for the unit.

Weighted-Average Cost of Capital

To ascertain the warranted capital value of a company (or business unit), operating cash flows must be discounted at an appropriate weighted-average cost of capital (WACC). As the name implies, the weighted-average cost of capital represents the average cost of the company's debt and equity capital—weighted by the proportion of the company's capital structure that these two components constitute. This relationship can be expressed mathematically as:

$$\text{WACC} = (1 - L)K_e + L(K_d)(1 - t)$$

where

$$L = \text{Leverage} = \text{Debt}/(\text{Debt} + \text{Equity})$$
$$K_d = \text{Cost of Debt Capital}$$
$$t = \text{Marginal Tax Rate on Debt}$$

(Note: Debt as defined here includes preferred stock)

The cost of debt (K_d) represents the interest rate attached to the next increment of debt added to the company's capital structure. However, since interest expense is tax-deductible in most countries (including the United States), the cost of debt must be adjusted to reflect this tax benefit.

The major difficulty in determining the weighted average cost of capital is defining the proper weights (or leverage). The weights of debt (L) and equity $(1 - L)$ should be calculated by using market values—not book values. However, in most cases where we have seen the total capital approach used, book weights have almost always been used as proxies for market weights. Unfortunately, this is generally an inappropriate method. In fact, since the market value of equity is often quite different from its book value—in most cases, higher—using book weights as a proxy for market weights almost always leads to an inappropriate estimate for WACC.

For example, consider the company illustrated in Exhibit A.4. The weights of equity and debt for this company might look something like this:

EXHIBIT A.4

Determining the Appropriate Weights for Debt and Equity

Book Equity	$150 million	Market Equity	$270 million
Book Debt	$150 million	Market Debt	$130 million
Cost of Equity(K_e)	13%		
Cost of Debt (K_d)	9%		
Marginal Tax Rate	40%		

The weighted-average cost of capital using book weights would be 9.2 percent:

$$WACC = (1 - L)K_e + L(K_d)(1 - t)$$
$$= [(1 - 50\%) \times 13\%] + [50\% \times 9\% \times (1 - 40\%)]$$
$$= 6.5\% + 2.7\%$$
$$= 9.2\%$$

However, the weighted-average cost of capital using the appropriate market weights would be more than 10.5 percent—due to the difference between market and book leverage. The difficulty in determining the appropriate weighted-average cost of capital has caused us to prefer the equity method over the total capital method for valuation—particularly when an exact value is necessary (as in the case of an acquisition or divestiture).

Applying Equity and Total Capital Approaches

The important point to keep in mind is that both the equity and total capital approaches work well when evaluating alternative competitive strategies. While the two approaches should result in the same warranted value for a company, they rarely do, for two related reasons. First, the estimates for weighted average cost of capital are almost always based on book weights rather than market weights. This results in WACC estimates that can differ considerably from a company's actual capital costs. Second, it is difficult to estimate precisely the market value of debt that must be subtracted from a company's warranted capital value in order to obtain the value of its equity. Since most companies have hundreds of different bond issues, it is extremely complicated to determine the market value of these bonds, given prevailing interest rates and call provisions. Thus, in our view, it is easier to use the equity approach in most circumstances.

Finally, in those instances where an exact value for a business or company is needed—as is frequently the case in evaluating acquisition, joint venture, and divestiture strategies—we strongly recommend the equity approach. It is less subject to the measurement biases inherent in the total capital approach and can be tied more directly to transaction prices—which are often based on the purchase or sale of a business unit's or company's equity.

APPENDIX B:

Profitability Measurement

Derivation of Economic Profitability Relationships

We saw in Appendix A that a company's (or business unit's) warranted equity value can be expressed as:

$$\text{Warranted Equity Value (WEV)} = \sum_{t=1}^{\infty} \frac{\text{Equity Cash Flow}_t}{(1 + K_e)^t}$$

We will now demonstrate that equity cash flows can be represented in terms of equity investment, return on equity, and growth in equity investment. Demonstrating this relationship will allow us to derive the warranted value-to-book equation described in Chapter Five.

Linking Cash Flow to Returns and Growth

If a company follows "flow-through" accounting, its equity cash flow (ECF) for any year can be expressed mathematically as:

$$\text{ECF} = \text{Earnings} - \Delta \text{ Equity Invested}$$

Multiplying and dividing the right-hand side of this equation by equity invested gives:

$$\text{ECF}_t = \text{Equity invested}_{t-1} \times \left[\frac{\text{Earnings}_t}{\text{Equity Invested}_{t-1}} - \frac{\Delta \text{ Equity Invested}_t}{\text{Equity Invested}_{t-1}} \right]$$

Since

$$ROE = Earnings_t/Equity\ Invested_{t-1}$$

and

$$Equity\ Growth\ (g) = \Delta\ Equity\ Invested_t/Equity\ Invested_{t-1}$$

equity cash flow can be restated as follows:

$$ECF = B \times (ROE - g)$$

where B represents the amount of equity invested at the beginning of the period.

Deriving the Value-to-Book Equation

If we substitute this specification of equity cash flow in our basic valuation equation, we get:

$$Warranted\ Equity\ Value\ (WEV) = \sum_{t=1}^{\infty} \frac{B_{t-1}(ROE_t - g_t)}{(1 + K_e)^t}$$

If we make the simplifying assumption that both the ROE and the growth of equity capital are roughly constant, or trendless, over time, this version of the valuation equation reduces to:

$$WEV = \frac{B \times (ROE - g)}{K_e - g} \quad when\ g < K_e$$

Dividing both sides by equity investment (B) yields the value-to-book equation outlined in Chapter Five:

$$WEV/B = \frac{ROE - g}{K_e - g} \quad when\ g < K_e$$

While this equation should not be used ordinarily to estimate precisely the value of a company (or business unit), it has three useful roles to play. First, the warranted value-to-book equation can be used to produce a first-cut valuation. For example, assuming a company has equity invested of $5 billion, a ROE of 15 percent, a K_e of 13 percent, and an assumed constant future growth of 8.5 percent, we can derive the WEV of a company as follows:

$$WEV = \frac{B \times (ROE - g)}{K_e - g} = \frac{\$5 \text{ billion} \times (.15 - .085)}{.13 - .085} = \$7.2 \text{ billion}$$

Second, the value-to-book equation draws out the key relationships between equity spread, growth, and the ratio of warranted equity value to book value (and, by implication, the degree of value creation, as measured by the difference between WEV and equity invested):

- A positive equity spread implies a warranted value-to-book ratio greater than 1.0 (and therefore positive value creation); a zero equity spread implies a warranted value-to-book ratio equal to 1.0 (and therefore zero value creation); and a negative equity spread implies a warranted value-to-book ratio less than 1.0 (and therefore negative value creation). These relationships are illustrated in Exhibit B.1.
- Growth works to increase the warranted value-to-book ratio (and therefore value creation) if the equity spread on average is positive; growth does not affect the value-to-book ratio (and therefore value creation) if the equity spread on average is zero; and growth works to decrease the ratio of warranted value to book value (and therefore value creation) if the equity spread on average is negative. These relationships are illustrated in Exhibit B.2.

Third, the value-to-book equation can be used to estimate a company's (or business unit's) value at the end of the planning period.

EXHIBIT B.1

Linking Spread and Value Creation

B	ROE	K_e	Spread	g	WEV	WEV/B	WEB - B
100	13 %	11 %	2 %	6 %	140	1.4	40
100	11	11	0	6	100	1.0	0
100	9	11	-2	6	60	0.6	-40

EXHIBIT B.2

Linking Spread, Growth, and Value Creation

Growth

		5%	6%	7%
	13%	WEV/B = 1.33 WEV-B = 33	WEV/B = 1.4 WEV-B = 40	WEV/B = 1.5 WEV-B = 50
ROE	11%	WEV/B = 1.0 WEV-B = 0	WEV/B = 1.0 WEV-B = 0	WEV/B = 1.0 WEV-B = 0
	9%	WEV/B = 0.67 WEV-B = 33	WEV/B = 0.6 WEV-B = 40	WEV/B = 0.5 WEV-B = 50

$$B = 100$$
$$K_e = 11\%$$

Post-Planning Period or Continuing Values

Although the warranted equity value of a company or business is a function of the equity cash flow it generates in perpetuity, in practice managers rarely (if ever) forecast explicit equity cash flow in perpetuity. Instead, business valuations are usually performed by developing a detailed equity cash flow forecast for some specified planning period—typically five to ten years—and estimating the value of the unit at the end of the planning period. This post-planning period, or continuing, value is the discounted value of all equity cash flow the company (or business unit) will generate beyond the planning period.

Estimating the continuing value requires assumptions concerning the stream of equity cash flow over the post-planning period. As we have shown, this is equivalent to making assumptions concerning the stream of ROE and growth that the unit will generate over the post-planning period. In our experience, it is much easier for management to estimate a company's (or business unit's) ROE and growth than to project equity cash flow directly. For example, long-term ROE assumptions can be linked explicitly to the assessment of long-term market economics and competitive position that are developed as part of the strategic position assessment. In many cases, the appropriate assumption for a unit's performance in the post-planning period is that the ROE and growth will be essentially trendless over time (i.e., that market economics and competitive position will reach some steady state after the planning period ends). This means that the value-to-book equation can be used to estimate the continuing value. In other cases, the expectation is that ROE and growth will trend toward some long-term sustainable level during a transition period (due, for instance, to expectations that the forces of competition will drive equity spreads toward zero over time). This requires a more complex valuation equation, but one that can be modeled easily on a computer.

The key point is that the continuing value can be determined from estimates of ROE and equity growth over the post-planning period, and these assumptions can and should be linked to the strategic characterization of the business.

Economic Profit and Value Creation

Defining Economic Profit (EP)

Economic profit (EP) represents the amount a company or business earns over and above all costs—including capital costs—incurred in the operation of the business. This relationship can be expressed arithmetically as:

$$EP = \text{Earnings} - \text{Capital Charge}$$

where

$$\text{Capital Charge} = \text{Equity Invested}_{t-1} \times K_e$$

Equivalently, for any year, economic profit can be linked directly to a company's (or business unit's) equity investment and its ROE and K_e:

$$EP = \text{Equity Invested}_{t-1} (ROE - K_e)$$

In other words, economic profit depends on the amount of equity capital the business has invested and the equity spread that it generates.

By implication:

$$\text{If, in any year, } ROE > K_e, \text{ then } EP > 0$$

and

$$\text{If } ROE < K_e, \text{ then } EP < 0$$

If, over time, a company or business unit consistently generates a positive spread, it consistently generates positive economic profits. Alternatively, if a company or business consistently generates negative spreads by definition it consistently generates negative economic profits as well.

Linking Economic Profit to Value Creation

Economic profit is extremely useful to making the governing objective operational because it can be linked directly to value creation (warranted equity value less equity invested).

Keeping in mind the basic valuation equation outlined in Chapter Four:

$$\text{Warranted Equity Value (WEV)} = \sum_{t=1}^{\infty} \frac{\text{Equity Cash Flow}_t}{(1 + K_e)^t}$$

and the definition of equity cash flow specified in Appendix A

$$ECF = \text{Earnings} - \Delta \text{ Equity Invested}$$

we can define equity cash flow in terms of economic profit as follows:

$$\begin{aligned} ECF &= E - \Delta B \\ &= E - B_{t-1} \times K_e + B_{t-1} \times K_e - \Delta B \\ &= EP + B_{t-1} \times K_e - \Delta B \\ &= EP + B_{t-1} (1 + K_e) - B_t \end{aligned}$$

If we substitute this specification of equity cash flow in the basic valuation equation, we obtain:

$$\text{Warranted Equity Value (WEV)} = \sum_{t=1}^{\infty} \frac{\text{EP}_t + \text{B}_{t-1}(1 + \text{K}_e) - \text{B}_t}{(1 + \text{K}_e)^t}$$

By simplifying this equation, we can show that the warranted equity value of a company (or business unit) is equal to the present value of its future stream of economic profits plus the beginning equity investment:

$$\text{WEV} = \sum_{t=1}^{\infty} \frac{\text{Economic Profit}_t}{(1 + \text{K}_e)^t} + \sum_{t=1}^{\infty} \frac{\text{B}_{t-1}(1 + \text{K}_e)}{(1 + \text{K}_e)^t} + \sum_{t=1}^{\infty} \frac{\text{B}_t}{(1 + \text{K}_e)^t}$$

$$= \sum_{t=1}^{\infty} \frac{\text{Economic Profit}_t}{(1 + \text{K}_e)^t} + \text{B}_{(t=0)} + \sum_{t=1}^{\infty} \frac{\text{B}_t}{(1 + \text{K}_e)^t} - \sum_{t=1}^{\infty} \frac{\text{B}_t}{(1 + \text{K}_e)^t}$$

$$= \sum_{t=1}^{\infty} \frac{\text{Economic Profit}_t}{(1 + \text{K}_e)^t} + \text{B}$$

Therefore, the warranted equity value of a company (or business unit) can be determined not only by discounting its future equity cash flow (ECF) at the cost of equity capital (K_e), but also by discounting its future economic profit (EP) at the cost of equity capital (K_e) and adding the company's (or business unit's) current amount of equity invested (B).

Alternatively, value creation (WEV – B) can be determined directly by discounting a company's (or business unit's) future economic profit stream back to a present value at the appropriate cost of equity capital (K_e):

$$\text{Value Creation} = \sum_{t=1}^{\infty} \frac{\text{Economic Profit}_t}{(1 + \text{K}_e)^t}$$

If economic profits are expected to grow at a constant rate over time, this formula can be simplified to:

$$\text{Value Creation} = \frac{\text{Economic Profit}}{K_e - g} \quad \text{when } g < K_e$$

Using the information from Exhibit B.1, we can now illustrate the linkage between economic profit and value creation, as shown in Exhibit B.3.

EXHIBIT B.3

Linking Economic Profit and Value Creation

B	ROE	Spread	K_e	g	EP	WEB - B
100	13 %	2 %	11 %	6 %	2	40
100	11	0	11	6	0	0
100	9	-2	11	6	-2	-40

Because economic profit is so closely tied to value creation, a number of companies have chosen to use EP as a key performance measure at all levels in the company.

Proper Uses of Performance Measures

Since performance measures play a central role in the management of most companies, it is important to understand clearly how they should be used and which measures are most appropriate.

When to Use Performance Measures

In essence, there are two fundamental uses for performance measures: (1) as an aid to strategy development (i.e., to inform one's judgment about which alternative strategies for a company, business unit, or product market unit have potentially higher value than the current strategy); and (2) as an aid to monitoring and rewarding performance (i.e., to inform one's judgment about how well a company, business unit, or product market unit has performed).

Aid to Strategy Development

The first use for performance measures is to aid the development of value-maximizing strategies. This application can be thought of as providing management with an "economic signal" about performance. For example, if one business unit has been earning a return on equity that is five percentage points less than its cost of equity capital and another business has been earning five percentage points more than its cost of equity, management has a strong signal that the first business has been destroying value and the second business has been creating value. These economic signals are important because they stimulate questions and options for improvement. However, no decision should ever be made on the basis of these signals alone. For example, it would be foolhardy to decide to divest the business unit earning five percentage points less than its cost of equity capital solely on the basis of the profitability signal in a single period. If the business is pursuing a viable turnaround strategy, its operating value might be significantly higher than its divestment value, so that divestiture would not be the highest-value option.

What is the best economic signal? Without hesitation, the answer must be either the ratio of warranted equity value to equity investment (i.e., warranted value-to-book ratio) or the difference between the warranted equity value and equity investment (i.e., warranted value minus book). A warranted value greater than investment signals that the current strategy of the business or company creates value, while a value less than investment signals that the current strategy destroys value. This measure has the great advantage of capturing the projected performance over the long term (technically, an infinite term), so that any near-term distortions from nonrecurring events or large-scale investment in plant or research and development are offset by expected benefits over time. Its only potential drawback is its reliance on the book value of equity capital as a proxy for how much has been invested so far. Since book values are subject to accounting distortions, in some instances it may be necessary to make adjustments (for example, adding back write-offs) so that the denominator of the ratio more accurately reflects the amount of capital that has been invested by shareholders over time. Moreover, under no circumstances do we recommend that the warranted value-to-book ratio be used for strategic decision making. Nevertheless, in most businesses, the economic signal provided by comparing warranted equity value to book equity invested can be extremely useful for assessing the desirability of growth-focused versus return-focused strategy alternatives.

In many instances, it is not practical to conduct a thorough valuation in order to get a performance signal as an aid to strategy development. This is especially true for individual product market units within a business, where management must usually rely on measures of performance during a single period. What is the best single-period measure? While there are several candidates for this honor, we believe economic profit is the best. We have two reasons for this contention. First, economic profit has a direct link to value creation. Positive EP in any period signals a contribution to value creation, while negative EP signals a contribution to value destruction. Moreover, the present value of an economic profit stream is equal to warranted equity value less the equity investment. Our second reason for preferring EP as a single-period measure is that it provides a sense of magnitude or scale, since it is a dollar-based (or local-currency-based) measure. It also provides several other benefits. For instance, by dividing EP by units of output (e.g., pounds, square feet, cars sold), EP per unit can be expressed by subtracting economic cost per unit (operating costs plus a capital charge) from price, a formulation that is very useful for line managers. For example, an economic cost per unit of $1.20 when prices are averaging $1.15 (or an economic loss of 5¢ per unit) sends a different signal from an operating cost per unit of $1.00 and an operating margin of 15 percent. In addition, we've observed that a business unit reporting an economic loss for the year is more motivated to improve than a unit reporting an average ROI of 10 percent (despite the fact that both pieces of information may describe the same business unit). Finally, it is typically much easier to perform trade-off analysis with EP than with any other measure. For example, the longer-term impact on EP of investing in fixed capital to reduce operating costs or cutting price to build market share sends a much better signal about likely value creation than any other performance measure provides.

What about other, more traditional measures? The second choice would be the measure of profitability spread—ROE less the cost of equity capital (K_e). This measure provides a directional signal about value creation although not about its magnitude. One cannot tell, for example, whether a spread of 5 percent in a given year is better than a spread of 3 percent, since the latter may create more value if growth potential or investment opportunities are much larger than in the former case. After these two measures, the choices go downhill quickly. An ROE or ROI taken alone suffers from the absence of a standard— i.e., is an ROE of 12 percent profitable or not? Similarly, there is no standard when we use profit margins, earnings per share impact, sales growth, market share and most other traditional measures to gauge profitability or value creation. There is no question that many of these measures can be very useful and informative—especially when tracked over time and relative to competitors. Nevertheless, none of these measures can provide by itself the all-important profitability signal that ties directly to the governing objective of value creation. That role goes to economic profit alone.

Aid in Monitoring and Rewarding Performance

Of course, one of the most important uses of performance measures is to monitor and reward performance. As we noted in Chapter Fifteen, no single performance measure suffices to determine whether a business unit's performance is in line with its value-maximizing strategy. Properly monitoring and rewarding performance requires a combination of different measures—both strategic and financial. Nevertheless, if management is forced to choose only one financial performance measure at the business unit level, we recommend economic profit. It is the best single-period measure of value creation. Moreover, it works well at all levels (business unit and corporate) in an organization. Economic profit is also excellent for tracking performance over time, since it incorporates both equity spread and growth. In short, while economic profit is an incomplete measure, it can be tremendously useful in monitoring a business unit's performance and rewarding managers for superior performance.

When Performance Measures Should *Not* Be Used

Single- or multiperiod performance measures (even economic profit and warranted value-to-book) should never be used for making strategic investment decisions. For a company with the governing objective of maximizing value for shareholders, relative value is the only test that should be used for evaluating strategic alternatives. The only way to assure that an investment will likely create value is to compare the value of the business with the investment to the value of the business without the investment. For example, when deciding whether an aggressive strategy to build market share is better than the current strategy of pricing for higher returns, one must compare the relative values of these two, mutually exclusive options. Likewise, when deciding whether to build a new manufacturing plant, one must compare the value of the business with and without the new facility, not merely estimate the net present value or internal rate of return on the project itself. Finally, when deciding whether to make an acquisition, one must compare the value of the acquisition, including all combination benefits (or synergies), with the purchase price. We don't know of any other means to measure performance for strategic decision making that is not somehow biased or flawed. The bottom line: Comparing relative values directly is the only way to properly evaluate strategic decisions.

"Flow-Through" Accounting

Throughout both Appendices to this book we have stressed the importance of what we call "flow-through" accounting. It is a system of bookkeeping that forces all transactions to flow through both the income statement and the balance sheet. For example, if a plant shutdown results in a write-off, the asset write-off on the balance sheet flows through as a loss on the income statement. Similarly, if an asset is revalued upward on the balance sheet, the upward adjustment flows through as a gain on the income statement. Under this method of accounting, the only transactions that should not flow through the income statement are dividend payments, new share issuances, and share repurchases. Thus, charges to the shareholders' equity account will result only from retained earnings, share issuances, and share repurchases. Therefore, equity cash flow can be reasonably approximated as earnings less the change in book equity invested.

With a few notable exceptions, in the United States Generally Accepted Accounting Principles (GAAP) are largely a "flow-through" method of accounting.[1] However, not all countries follow this type of accounting system. For example, in the United Kingdom, goodwill amortization on the balance sheet does not flow through the income statement; and asset revaluations, which are made periodically on the balance sheet, do not flow through the income statement. As a result, equity cash flow cannot be approximated easily from the publicly available accounting statements. Nevertheless, in those countries that do not use flow-through accounting for the purpose of generating financial statements, management accounting statements can and should follow these procedures. In this book, all the financial relationships assume this type of flow-through effect. Without flow-through accounting, it is difficult to measure performance from a value perspective because accounting measures cannot be linked to cash flow and value. Thus, in companies that do not use flow-through accounting, we strongly recommend the adaptation of management accounting procedures to follow such practices before attempting to measure and track performance.

Management Accounts

In order to measure profitability correctly, each business must have a common set of financial information—including full income statements and balance sheets. Exhibit B.4 illustrates a standard set of management accounts that must be developed for each business unit or product market where management wishes to track performance. The specific accounts will vary from company to company but should always provide enough information to determine economic profits.

Most business units have the necessary income statement information needed for valuation and profitability measures. Few companies, however, have complete balance sheets at the business unit level, and even fewer companies have developed information concerning the economic profitability of marketing individual products and serving specific markets. In general, we find it is necessary to deal with three issues in developing this information: (1) shared costs and assets; (2)

EXHIBIT B.4

Standard Management Accounts

Income Statement	Balance Sheet	
[1] Revenue	[8] Operating Cash	[14] Accounts Payable
[2] Cost of Goods Sold	[9] Accounts Receivable	[15] Other Non-Interest-Bearing
Gross Margin	[10] Inventory	Liabilities
[3] Selling	Current Assets	[16] Deferred Taxes
[4] Administration	[11] Gross Fixed Assets	Non-Interest-Bearing
[5] R&D Expense	[12] Accumulated Depreciation	Liabilities
Operating Income	Net Fixed Assets	[17] Debt
[6] Interest Expense	[13] Other Assets	Equity (Plug)
Pre-tax Income		
[7] Taxes	Total Assets	Total Liabilities and Equity
Net Income		

Total Capital = Debt plus Equity
      = Total Assets minus Non Interest-Bearing-Liabilities

transfers between business units within the corporation; and (3) allocation of debt to the business units.

Shared Costs and Assets

To the extent possible, all shared costs and assets should be allocated on the basis of usage. For example, a shared purchasing department might allocate costs based on the number of orders processed per business, the volume of purchases, the number of order lines entered, etc. The task of allocating shared costs and assets can be made much easier if an activity-based costing system is in place. Nonetheless, even in companies that do not have activity-based costing systems, some general breakdown of costs and assets by product and market is typically feasible.

For example, some costs are naturally driven by product—namely, manufacturing costs, some research and development expenditures, and usually property, plant and equipment costs. Others, however, are influenced more by the business unit's market participation—namely, direct selling costs, after-sale support costs and working capital. Ultimately, in order to assign these shared costs and assets to specific products, management must determine the fundamental drivers of each cost and asset, then determine each product or market segments usage based on these drivers.

Some companies prefer to pool costs and assets that are difficult to allocate directly to individual product markets at the business unit or corporate level, valuing them instead as a separate unit (with a negative warranted equity value). We strongly discourage this approach except for selected corporate costs and assets that do not support the existing business units (e.g., excess cash and, in some cases, centralized research). Our experience indicates that it is best to allocate all costs fully to the business units, so that the sum of business unit values is equal to the value of the entire company. This process provides line managers with more complete profitability information than if shared costs and assets are pooled at a more aggregated level, and its use can greatly enhance the quality of day-to-day operating decisions—particularly in the areas of resource allocation and product pricing.

Transfers Between Business Units

In vertically integrated companies, managers must deal with the issue of raw material and other transfers between units in the extended activity chain. It is vitally important that these transfers be "priced" to provide the best economic signal to both the upstream and downstream business units.

As we noted briefly in Chapter Twelve, we believe that in most cases where an appropriate market price is available, transfers between value centers—or strategically independent business units—should reflect market prices. Market-based transfer prices provide the downstream unit important information about the advisability of continuing to source the input internally versus purchasing it from an external vendor. At the same time, market-based transfer prices provide the upstream unit with the information management needs in order to assess different capacity options. Thus, in most cases, market-based transfer prices will be most appropriate between different value centers within a vertically integrated company.

Between cost centers and value centers, where market-based proxies are not available or are inappropriate because the external market is small relative to the internal market, transfers should be made at their full economic costs—all operating costs plus a charge for capital. This will enable managers of the value centers to assess the value created or destroyed at each stage of the activity chain. It should be noted that in this case, strategy decisions will always require close coordination between the value centers and the cost center.

Allocating Debt to Business Units

If management chooses the equity approach to valuation, each business must be allocated a portion of the company's borrowing in order to calculate its equity cash flow and, thus, its warranted equity value.[2] The simplest approach to debt allocation is to assign the company's overall capital structure to each business unit. This works well for companies that have little debt. However, for many companies, assigning a uniform capital structure across all business units can produce cross-subsidies within the portfolio, causing those businesses with high debt capacity to be undervalued and those with low debt capacity to be significantly overvalued. Furthermore, in some businesses (e.g., financial services), capital structure decisions can meaningfully affect competitive position since higher leverage can produce lower total economic costs. Thus, in many cases, it is important to assign different capital structures to different business units within the company.

We have found that the best way to allocate debt to business units is to assign either the current corporate credit rating or a target credit rating to each business unit, then use this rating to set a capital structure target for each unit. For example, the dominant credit rating determinant for many businesses is the interest coverage ratio (or pretax operating income divided by interest expense). For a single-A credit, for example, an interest coverage ratio of six times might be appropriate (given the expected variability in the business unit's pretax operating income over time). This implies that the interest expense of each business unit would average one-sixth of its pretax operating income, and its capital structure would be set so that the level of debt generates the target level of interest over time. This relationship can be expressed mathematically as follows:

$$\text{Target Interest Expense} = \frac{\text{Expected Pretax Operating Income}}{\text{Target Interest Coverage}}$$

and

$$\text{Target Debt} = \text{Target Interest Expense}/K_d$$
$$\text{(where } K_d \text{ equals the cost of debt)}$$

and

$$\text{Target Leverage} = \text{Target Debt/Expected Total Capital}$$

While a more complex methodology using multiple ratios would be warranted for some companies, particularly those with volatile business units or units engaged in real estate or financial services, for most companies the allocation of debt using a uniform interest coverage ratio works reasonably well.

Once debt has been allocated to a business unit, equity capital is merely the residual. The portion of the business unit's total assets that is not financed by non-interest-bearing liabilities (such as accounts payable, deferred taxes, etc.) or debt must, of necessity, come from the shareholders. Equity investment from year to year is represented by changes in this residual value. In years when the equity account has increased, additional funds have been supplied by the shareholders. Conversely, in years when the equity account has decreased, the business had paid out a portion of its equity to the shareholders either in the form of dividends or share repurchases.

Notes

Chapter One: The Governing Objective

1. Herbert V. Prochnow, and Herbert V. Prochnow, Jr., *The Toastmaster's Treasure Chest,* Harper & Row, New York, 1979, p. 135.
2. Excerpted from the Indian Head Mills Co. Manual in "The Chief Shows Them How at Indian Head," *Fortune,* May 1962, pp. 129–130.
3. Oren Harari, "You're Not in Business to Make a Profit," *Management Review,* July 1992, pp. 53–55.
4. Judith H. Dobrznyski, "More Than Ever, It's Management for the Short Term," *Business Week,* November 24, 1986, pp. 92–93.
5. Theodore Levitt, *The Marketing Imagination,* The Free Press, New York, 1983.
6. Oren Harari, "You're Not in Business to Make a Profit," *Management Review,* July 1992, pp. 53–55.
7. *NCR 1990 Annual Report,* p. 2.
8. Jia Wang and H. Dudley Dewhirst, "Boards of Directors and Stakeholder Orientation," *Journal of Business Ethics,* Vol. 11.2, February 1992, pp. 115–123.

Chapter Two: The Potential for Value Creation

1. This analysis assumes that all dividends are reinvested.
2. In certain industries, like computers, the top-tier company's total shareholder returns were below the average S&P 500 company; in other industries, like the food and beverage industry, the bottom-tier performer actually outperformed the S&P 500 average. This highlights the importance of comparing performance with that of the appropriate peer group before reaching conclusions about management's performance.

3. Edmund Faltermayer, "The Deal Decade: Verdict on the '80s," *Fortune,* August 26, 1991, p. 60.

4. U.S. Congress Joint Committee on Taxation, *Federal Income Tax Aspects of Corporate Financial Structures,* U.S. Government Printing Office, Washington, D.C., 1989, cited in Steven Kaplan, "The Effects of Management Buyouts on Operating Performance and Value," *Journal of Financial Economics,* Vol. 24, 1989, pp. 217–254.

5. See Kaplan, pp. 217–254. Kaplan tests three important findings: (1) performance improvements were not the result of employment reductions; (2) value increases were not the result of "insider information" exploited to the detriment of other shareholders; and (3) value increases were the result of aligning management incentives with the interests of the company's shareholders.

6. Warren Buffett, "Letter to the Shareholders of Berkshire Hathaway," *Berkshire Hathaway Annual Report,* March 1, 1993, pp. 2–3. Note that these same principles have been published several times between 1984 and 1992.

7. Ibid., p. 2.

8. Ibid., February 29, 1988, p. 6.

9. *Fortune,* January 29, 1990, p. 46.

10. *The Coca-Cola Company 1991 Annual Report,* pp. 48–49.

11. *PepsiCo. Inc. 1991 Annual Report,* pp. 5–6.

12. Charles F. Knight, "Emerson Electric: Consistent Profits, Consistently," *Harvard Business Review,* January-February 1992, p. 57.

13. Ibid., p. 62.

14. Ibid.

15. Geraldine E. Willigan, "The Value-Adding CFO: An Interview with Gary Wilson," *Harvard Business Review,* January-February 1990, p. 93.

16. "Reality Intrudes Into the Magic Kingdom," *The Economist,* April 21, 1990, p. 71.

17. Ibid.

18. *The Walt Disney Company 1991 Annual Report,* p. 47.

19. David J. Collis, "The Walt Disney Company," *Harvard Business School Case N2–388–147,* 1988, p. 20.

20. *Financial World,* July 20, 1993, p. 45.

21. Ibid.

22. Lloyds Bank Plc, *Short Report to Shareholders,* 1991, p. 5.

Chapter Three: Value Based Management

1. "Capitalism's Creative Destruction," *The Economist,* April 4, 1992, p. 15.

2. Ibid.

3. We acknowledge our debt to Warren Buffett, who coined the term "institu-

tional imperative" in a characteristically witty and informative letter to the shareholders in the *Berkshire Hathaway 1989 Annual Report,* p. 22.

4. As the term "process" is currently widely used in the business world, we find it helpful to establish three broad classifications: decision-making processes like strategic planning; enabling processes like management education; and general business processes like customer order fulfillment. We refer to each type of process at various points in the book, but we are concerned principally with the decision-making processes at the corporate center and in the business units.

Chapter Four: Linking Market and Management Values

1. The price of the 3M bond would be calculated as follows:

$$\$950.92 = \sum_{i=1}^{30} \frac{\$45.00}{(1.048)^i} + \frac{\$1000}{(1.048)^{30}}$$

2. For more information on standard techniques for pricing bonds, see Richard A. Brealey and Stewart C. Myers, *Principles of Corporate Finance,* McGraw-Hill, New York, 1988, Chapter 23.

3. See Appendix A for a more detailed elaboration of some important aspects of common stock valuation.

4. See Appendix A for a detailed description of equity cash flow determination.

5. See Appendix B for a description of continuing values.

6. See Appendix A for a detailed explanation of cost-of-equity capital estimation.

7. Value Line Investment Survey, March 6, 1992, p. 1894. Reinvestment computed as the change in book value per share. Resale value in 1996 calculated as the forecast P/E ratio (16) multiplied by the anticipated earnings per share ($9.00), for a total of $144.00 resale in 1996.

8. Predicted value was calculated using the same methodology as in the 3M example (see note 5). The correlation coefficient of .8 (and a coefficient of determination of .64) is not uncommon. In our experience, the correlation coefficient has ranged from .70 to .95 (with coefficient of determination ranging from .50 to .90).

9. In analyzing the pricing of common stocks in countries outside the United States, including Europe, Japan, and Australia, we find that they all reflect fairly accurately the prices predicted by the dividend discount model, although the quality of capital market information is often not as good as one would like. This result is not surprising, given the relatively free movement

of capital around the world, and will be even more pronounced in the future as global capital markets become more integrated.

10. See Appendix A for a description of cash flow valuation using both the equity approach and the total capital approach.
11. See Appendix A for a definition of equity cash flow at the business unit level.

Chapter Five: Financial Determinants of Value Creation

1. See Appendix B for the derivation.
2. See Appendix B for derivations of the value-to-book equation.
3. While the value-to-book relationship provides a quick-and-dirty method of estimating the investor's valuation of a company's equity, it should be noted that there are several inherent limitations to using the value-to-book equation for valuations:
   (a) Use of the value-to-book equation requires specification of constant values for growth, return on equity capital, and cost of equity capital (the "book" value of equity is a constant and doesn't affect the valuation). For businesses that have not reached "steady-state" conditions, it can be problematic to use near-term forecasts for growth and ROE as proxies for very long-term trends.
   (b) The accuracy of the value-to-book equation for valuation purposes will also be compromised in situations where accounting practices allow certain events to be recorded on the balance sheet without recording them at the same time on the income statement. Outside the United States this is a significant issue, as accounting practices often make reported book values, ROEs, and growth unreliable indicators of cash flow. However, in all cases, internal management accounts should be designed to provide easy and reliable equity cash flow measures at the business unit level and the company level and avoid the distortion sometimes contained in reported financial statements. See Appendix B for a discussion of "flow through" accounting.

   While these limitations affect the use of the value-to-book equation for valuation purposes, the fundamental economic relationships revealed by the equation still hold.
4. Some readers may be familiar with the concept of residual income—or earnings less a capital charge—that General Electric, among others, developed in the 1950s and 1960s to measure profit center performance. Economic profit is a precise form of residual income, where residual income is equal to earnings less all interest charges, taxes, and a capital charge consisting of the cost of equity multiplied by the magnitude of equity invested.

   One of the most intriguing aspects of economic profit occurs when it is projected in time and discounted to its present value. The result is equal to the value of the business, or company, less the amount of equity capital invested. In other words, the present value of the economic profit stream from a business unit's strategic plan is equal to its warranted value minus its book equity, a direct measure of the value created by the business. This relationship is derived in Appendix B.

5. In 1992, among the Dow Jones Industrials, only GM had a market value less than book value. Given this, one would expect GM's forecast equity spread to be negative. One possible reason why GM "misplots" is simply that Value Line's forecast ROE is more bullish than the consensus forecast made by investors.

6. Historically, market value-to-book ratios have been considerably lower than they were at year-end 1992. In fact, between 1983 and 1993, the average market value-to-book ratio for the Dow Jones Industrials was 1.6, with anywhere from 5 to 25 percent of the companies trading at market value-to-book ratios of less than 1.0. The high market value-to-book ratios in 1992 stem largely from record-low interest rates combined with a forecast turnaround in the economy boosting forecast equity spreads.

Chapter Six: Strategic Determinants of Value Creation

1. We used Value Line's earnings and book value data to calculate the return on equity for each company and then estimated the cost of equity for each on the basis of data compiled by Marakon Associates.

2. They do not impact the average equity spread except in certain special situations, such as government price controls, which dictate the level of profitability in a market or industry.

3. There are other determinants; however, we have found these four to be the most important drivers of profitability in most markets.

4. See Michael E. Porter, *Competitive Advantage,* The Free Press, New York, 1985, pp. 119–163.

Chapter Eight: Competitive Strategy

1. Maria Mallory, "Heinz's New Recipe: Take a Dollop of Dollars . . . ," *Business Week,* September 30, 1991, p. 86.

2. Hans Becherer, quoted in Steve Weiner, "Staying on Top in a Tough Business in a Tough Year," *Forbes,* May 27, 1991, pp. 46–67.

Chapter Nine: Participation Strategy

1. Market economics should be attractive over time, *given entry.* We often see businesses enter new markets and, in doing so, dramatically reduce market profitability.

2. Surmountable means feasible and at a cost that is low enough to be economically attractive.
3. See Chip Johnson, "Clorox is Stained With Pretax Charge of $125 Million to End Detergent Line," *The Wall Street Journal,* May 20, 1991, p. B7.
4. Joseph H. Kozloff, quoted in Johnson, p. B7.
5. Clorox management, quoted in Johnson, p. B7.

Chapter Ten: Corporate Strategy

1. C.K. Prahalad and Gary Hamel, "The Core Competence of the Corporation," *Harvard Business Review,* May-June 1990, pp. 86–89.
2. A reasonably effective summary of the academic research can be found in Alan Auerbach, ed., *Corporate Takeovers: Causes and Consequences,* University of Chicago Press, Chicago, 1988.
3. Each "peer group" was defined by U.S. Government Standard Industrial Classifications using COMPUSTAT data on stock returns for the two weeks prior and two weeks following the date of each announcement.
4. Much has been written about this subject in the past few years. For example, C.K. Prahalad and Gary Hamel in their article, "The Core Competence of the Corporation," *Harvard Business Review,* May-June 1990, pp. 79–91, advocated identifying and exploiting the company's "core competencies" as a means to enter new markets, describing core competencies as the "collective learning of the organization." In their article, "Competing on Capabilities: The New Rules of Corporate Strategy," *Harvard Business Review,* March-April 1992, p. 57, George Stalk, Philip Evans, and Lawrence Shulman used a similar but expanded methodology that they called "Capabilities-Based Competition" to illustrate how organizational capabilities can be used to create sustainable competitive advantage and enter new markets as well.

Chapter Twelve: Governance

1. Louis Kehoe, "Gerstner Sees No Place for a 'Vision' at IBM," *The Financial Times,* July 28, 1993, p. 24.
2. Bart Ziegler, "AT&T's Bold Bet," *Business Week,* August 30, 1993, p. 26.
3. If tax minimization can be achieved using transfer prices that do not distort the true economics for the "seller" or the "buyer" unit, they should certainly be taken into account. But if tax management practices result in degrading the company's economic profitability measures, it is almost certainly better to pay more tax in order to preserve the integrity of these vital profitability signals.

Chapter Fourteen: Resource Allocation

1. The "sunk" $800 million less some depreciation, the new $150 million, and additional working capital to support sales growth over the three years.
2. William W. Alberts and James M. McTaggart, "The Difference Between Evaluating Investment Projects and Evaluating Business Strategies," *Commentary,* Marakon Associates, October 1981.
3. Andrew Pollack, "Japanese Consortium Backs Motorola on Satellite Phones," *The New York Times,* April 3, 1993, p. 43, and Ken Yamada, "Technology: Motorola Signs up Some Investors in Iridium Satellite Phone System," *The Wall Street Journal,* December 23, 1992, p. B6.
4. Stock price was well below the initial offering in 1993.
5. Christopher Power, "Flops," *Business Week,* August 16, 1993, p. 77.
6. Ibid.
7. The business dissolution rate is over 50 percent for businesses five years old and less. Business dissolution includes businesses that disappear for any reason at all, including failure, bankruptcy, owner retirement, owner health, or the desire to enter a more profitable market. Source: Bruce D. Phillips, U.S. Small Business Administration Office of Advocacy, January 1992.

Chapter Sixteen: Top Management Compensation

1. One big exception is if corporate management breaks the contract either by making measurement changes in the middle of the plan period or by pulling back on resource commitments even when the business unit is on target. In that case, of course, adjustments should be made.
2. Warren Buffett, Letter to the Shareholders of Berkshire Hathaway, *Berkshire Hathaway Annual Report,* March 4, 1986, p. 11.
3. We are assuming here that the company has reasonably good information on the pay practices of its peers.
4. Michael C. Jensen and Kevin J. Murphy, "CEO Incentives: It's Not *How Much* You Pay, But *How*", *Harvard Business Review,* May-June 1990, pp. 138–153.
5. Graef S. Crystal, "How Much CEOs Really Make," *Fortune,* June 17, 1991, pp. 72–80.

Appendix A: Valuation

1. Roger G. Ibbotson and Rex A. Sinquefield, *Stocks, Bonds, Bills and Inflation: 1926–82,* Financial Analysts Research Foundation, Charlottesville, VA, 1983.

Appendix B: Profitability Measurement

1. FASB 52, for example, which deals with gains and losses resulting from foreign currency translations, requires that translations adjustments not flow through the income statement but be made as adjustments to the shareholders' equity account directly. While these adjustments are typically made only at the corporate level—and therefore do not usually interfere with business unit valuations—they do violate the notion of flow-through accounting.

2. We should note that even if management chooses to use the total capital approach to valuation, it will be implicitly allocating debt to the business units since the weighted-average cost of capital (WACC) incorporates implicit assumptions about the proportion of debt and equity in each unit's capital structure.

Glossary

Attractive Market. A product market in which the annual weighted average equity spread of all competitors is positive over time.

Book Equity (B). Invested equity capital including share issuances and reinvested earnings (also referred to as net worth, equity investment, and shareholders' equity).

Business Strategy. A predetermined sequence of business unit actions designed to change the competitive environment in a way that achieves the company's governing objective (i.e. creates the highest possible value).

Capital Charge. The amount of capital employed in a business unit (or product market unit) multiplied by the pretax cost of capital.

Cash Flow. At the corporate level, the net value of funds distributed to the shareholders (referred to as equity cash flow) or to the shareholders and bondholders (referred to as operating cash flow). At the business unit level, cash flow is the net value of funds generated by the business that are available for distribution to the parent company.

Competitive Position. The economic profitability and growth rate of a particular business unit relative to that of the average competitor in its product market, produced by its differentiation position and relative economic cost position.

Competitive Strategy. The element of business strategy that addresses the question of how the business should compete in each market segment it serves. Competitive strategy comprises product offering strategy, cost and asset strategy, and pricing strategy.

Continuing Value. The value of the business at the end of the planning period—or the time period for which financial performance is explicitly forecast (sometimes referred to as post-planning period value).

Core Business Processes. Activities such as procurement, logistics, manufacturing, marketing, selling and customer service in which the organization engages every day to supply products and services to its customers. "Core" is used to identify only those processes that enable the business to differentiate its offering profitably and/or achieve a favorable economic cost position.

Corporate Center. The organizational unit (or units) that performs all activities not carried out by the business units themselves.

Corporate Strategy. A predetermined sequence of corporate center actions designed to achieve the company's governing objective (i.e. to create the highest value possible). Typically, corporate strategy entails three general activities: portfolio strategy (profitably adding and subtracting businesses from the portfolio); the management of shared strategic value drivers; and the development of organizational capabilities.

Corporate Value Assessment. An objective appraisal of the value created and destroyed by each business unit in a company's portfolio and assessment of the underlying drivers of value creation within the company.

Cost Center. An organizational unit that performs activities or services for more than one business unit and is not itself a business unit because it has a limited external market for its services, or the company's strategy precludes it from selling its services outside the company.

Cost of Equity Capital (K_e). The minimum annual rate of return required by the company's shareholders for supplying equity capital. Also, the discount rate used to determine the warranted equity value of a company or business unit.

Creating Value. Generating a return on equity that is consistently above the cost of equity capital or a consistent stream of economic profit. Alternatively, producing a warranted equity value in excess of the shareholders' equity investment.

Differentiation. Customer perceptions of a superior product or service offering that make them willing to pay a higher price.

Direct Forces. The two forces that combine with the four limiting forces to determine the economic profitability of a particular product market. Specifically, the intensity of direct competition and customer pressures.

Economic Cost. Total operating costs plus a charge for capital—where the capital charge represents the amount of capital employed in the business unit (or product) multiplied by the pretax cost of capital.

Economic Profitability. A company or business unit is economically profitable if its equity spread or economic profit is positive on average, over time. A company or business unit is economically unprofitable if its equity spread or economic profit is negative on average, over time.

Economic Profit (EP). Income earned by a company or business unit over and above the dollar cost of the equity capital required to finance its operations—this dollar cost of equity capital is obtained by multiplying the cost of equity by the amount of equity invested in the company.

Equity Cash Flow (ECF). At the corporate level, the portion of earnings that is paid out to investors rather than reinvested (or retained), or dividends plus share repurchases minus share issurances. In a year when the company neither issues nor repurchases common stock, equity cash flow is the dividend paid to the stockholders. At the business unit level, it is earnings less the amount of equity reinvestment.

Equity Invested. Book equity, net worth or shareholders' equity.

Equity Spread. A company's or business unit's return on equity (ROE) minus its cost of equity capital (K_e). If (ROE $- K_e$) > 0, the company or business unit is generating a positive equity spread. Alternatively, if (ROE $- K_e$) < 0, the company or business unit is generating a negative equity spread.

Financial Characterization. The second phase of the strategic position assessment, when management's understanding of the business unit's strategic position in the product markets is translated into credible financial forecasts (including full income statements and balance sheets) for the business unit.

Governance. The roles and responsibilities of the shareholders, the board of directors, and the chief executive officer in managing the legal and economic relationships between the company and its owners and other stakeholders. Also includes the roles and responsibilities of business unit general managers and top managers in the corporate center, including the chief financial officer and the heads of the human resources, corporate planning, and legal functions.

Grounded Forecasts. Financial forecasts that are consistent with management's best assessment of the long-term attractiveness of the markets in which a business participates as well as the business unit's long-term competitive position in these markets.

Growth Rate (g). Usually refers to annual growth in equity capital.

Institutional Imperative. The unyielding tendency toward growth—irrespective of its consequences for the value of a company or business to the shareholders—that drives management behavior in many companies.

Institutional Value Drivers. Key management processes that can enable a company to build an organizational advantage for achieving superior performance for shareholders over time.

Limiting Forces. The four forces, along with the two direct forces, that determine the profitability of a particular product market—the intensity of indirect competition, the threat of competitor entry, supplier pressures, and regulatory pressures. Limiting forces usually place a ceiling on the level of returns a market can earn over time.

Management Processes. Processes that enable management to develop better information, make better choices, and execute strategies more effectively than competitors: strategic planning, resource allocation, performance management, and incentive compensation.

Market Economics. The average economic profitability and growth rate for all competitors in a particular product market.

Market Value of Equity (M). The company's current stock price multiplied by the number of common shares outstanding. Also referred to as market capitalization.

Market Value-to-Book Ratio (M/B). The market value of equity divided by equity invested.

Net Divestment Value (NDV). The present value of after-tax proceeds from selling, liquidating, or spinning off a business unit.

Net Worth. Book equity, equity invested, or shareholders' equity.

Operating Cash Flow (OCF). At the corporate level, the portion of after-tax operating profit that is paid out to all creditors (shareholders, bondholders, banks, etc.) in the form of dividends, interest payments, share repurchases, or debt prepayments. At the business unit level, after-tax operating profit less reinvestment of total capital.

Participation Strategy. The element of business strategy that states which product markets the business plans to serve and how it plans to enter new markets or exit markets.

Post-Planning Period Value. The value of the business at the end of the time period for which financial performance is explicitly forecast (also referred to as continuing value).

Relative Shareholder Returns. The total return (in the form of both dividends and share price appreciation) earned by the company's shareholders in relation to the shareholder returns generated by similar companies over any given time period.

Return on Equity (ROE). Net earnings (or net income) divided by book equity at the end of the preceding year.

Return on Investment (ROI). Net operating profits after taxes divided by total capital at the end of the preceding year.

Shareholder Value. The market value of common stock. For a public company, this can be directly observed as the product of share price and number of shares outstanding. Also referred to as the market value of equity.

Spread. The difference between return on equity and the cost of equity capital (ROE-K_e). Business units that earn positive spreads over time are economically profitable; business units that earn negative spreads over time are economically unprofitable.

Strategic Alternatives (Options). The specification of participation strategy choices and competitive strategy choices that differ from those currently pursued at the business unit level, or the specification of alternative corporate strategy choices to those currently pursued at the corporate level.

Strategic Characterization. An objective diagnosis of the economic profitability and growth of a business unit's product markets as well as its differentiation and relative economic cost position in these markets.

Strategic Position Assessment. An objective diagnosis of a business unit's strategic position, including a fact-based strategic characterization of its product markets, a grounded financial characterization of these markets and a valuation of the current strategy. The strategic position assessment is the first step in a value-based strategy development process.

Strategic Value Drivers. The organization capabilities that are controllable by management and have the largest impact on the business unit's future competitive position and potential for value creation.

Total Capital. Invested capital, including all interest-bearing debt, preferred stock and common stock. Also, total assets minus all non-interest-bearing liabilities.

Total Shareholder Returns. The total return (in the form of both dividends and share price appreciation) earned by the company's shareholders.

Unattractive Market. A product market in which the average equity spread of all competitors is negative over time.

Value Based Management (VBM). A formal, or systematic, approach to managing companies to achieve the governing objective of maximizing wealth creation and shareholder value over time.

Value Contribution. The contribution that a product line, customer group or product market makes to the overall value of a business or group of businesses.

Value Creation. Warranted value over and above the shareholders' investment in a business or company (warranted value minus investment). Also referred to as capital gain.

Warranted Capital Value (WCV). An internal valuation of a business unit or company based on management's own best estimate of the future operating cash flow it will generate over time, discounted at the weighted-average cost of capital.

Warranted Equity Value (WEV). An internal valuation of a business unit or company based on management's own best estimate of the future equity cash flow it will generate over time, discounted at the cost of equity capital.

Warranted Value-to-Book Ratio (WEV/B). Warranted equity value divided by equity invested, or warranted capital value divided by total capital invested.

Weighted-Average Cost of Capital (WACC). The minimum annual rate of return required by a company's shareholders and bondholders for supplying debt and equity capital.

Wealth. The worth of a company—used as a synonym for value.

Bibliography

Alberts, William, W., "Do Oligopolists Earn 'Non-Competitive' Rates of Return," *American Economic Review,* September 1984.

———, "Have Interstate Acquisitions Been Profitable?" *American Banker,* September 18, 1986.

———, "Pricing a Loan Product Profitably," *Commercial Lending Review,* Spring 1988.

———, "A New Look At Calculating ROE," *The Bankers Magazine,* March-April 1989.

———, "Assessing The Profitability Of Growth By Acquisition, A Premium Recapture Approach," *International Journal of Industrial Organization,* May 1989.

———, "The Experience Curve Doctrine Reconsidered," *Journal of Marketing,* July 1989.

———, "Mergers and Acquisitions: Strategies For Growth," J. L. Livingstone, Editor, *The Portable MBA In Finance And Accounting,* New York: John Wiley, 1992.

Alberts, William W. and James M. McTaggart, "The Short-Term Earnings Per Share Standard for Evaluating Prospective Acquisitions," *Mergers & Acquisitions,* Fall 1978.

———, "The Divestiture Decision: An Introduction," *Mergers & Acquisitions,* Fall 1979.

———, "Strategic Investment Planning and the Relationships between Growth, Cash Flow, and Profitability," presented at The Financial Management Association, Boston, MA, October 1979.

347

_____, "Value Based Strategic Investment Planning," *Interfaces,* January-February 1984.

Auerbach, Alan, ed., *Corporate Takeovers: Causes and Consequences,* Chicago: University of Chicago Press, 1988.

Brealey, Richard A. and Stewart C. Myers, *Principles of Corporate Finance,* New York: McGraw-Hill, 1988.

Collis, David J., "The Walt Disney Company," *Harvard Business School Case N2–388–147,* 1988.

Copeland, Tom, Tim Koller, and Jack Murrin, *Valuation,* New York: John Wiley, 1990.

Day, George S. and Liam Fahey, "Putting Strategy into Shareholder Value Analysis," *Harvard Business Review,* March-April 1990.

Hax, Arnold C. and Nicolas S. Majluf, *Strategic Management: An Integrative Perspective,* New York: Prentice-Hall, 1984.

Jensen, Michael C. and Kevin J. Murphy, "CEO Incentives: It's Not *How Much* You Pay, but *How,*" *Harvard Business Review,* May-June, 1990.

Kaplan, Steven, "The Effects of Management Buyouts on Operating Performance and Value," *Journal of Financial Economics,* Vol. 24, 1989.

Knight, Charles F., "Emerson Electric: Consistent Profits, Consistently," *Harvard Business Review,* January-February 1992.

Levitt, Theodore, *The Marketing Imagination,* New York: The Free Press, 1983.

Marakon Associates, *Commentary* series:

"The Major Financial Objective of Strategic Planning," February, 1979.

"Capital Allocation," April 1979.

"Establishing Hurdle Rates—Part One: The Company's Overall Cost of Equity Capital," July 1979.

"Establishing Hurdle Rates—Part Two: Divisional Costs of Equity Capital," November 1979.

"Strategic Investment Planning in A Multi-Business Company," June 1980.

"The Evolution of Value Based Management," Fall 1990.

"The Divestiture Decision," October 1980.

"The Marakon Profitability Matrix," April 1981.

"The Difference Between Evaluating Investment Projects and Evaluating Business Strategies," October 1981.

"Winning," November 1981.

"Growing Profitably by Acquisition," June 1982.

"Balancing Near-Term and Long-Term Perspectives in Business Unit Planning," June 1983.

"Competing in Multinational Markets: The Temptation to 'Go Global,'" October 1984.

"Business Strategy: Managing the ROI-Growth Tradeoff," Winter 1986.

"The Ultimate Poison Pill: Closing the Value Gap," Spring 1986.

"Gaining Advantage Through Global Financing," Summer 1986.

"Measuring Value Contribution—A Key to Profitable Strategic Management," Fall 1986.

"Beating the Odds: The Challenge of Making Profitable Acquisitions," Winter 1987.

"The Cost of Capital in the U.S. and Japan," Fall 1989.

"The Management of Shareholder Value (Part I)," Fall 1989.

"Premium Recapture in the Pharmaceutical Industry," Fall 1989.

"Avoiding the Raiders: Lessons for the U.S. Experience," Spring 1990.

"The Management of Shareholder Value (Part II): Application to Business Strategy," Spring 1990.

"Managing to Create Value—Four Lessons Learned," Fall 1990.

"Does the Stock Market Penalize Long-Term Thinking? The Case of Apple Computer," Summer 1991.

"Short-Termism: A Contrary View," Summer 1991.

"The Dangers of Strategic Intent," April 1992.

"Total Quality and Value Creation," June 1992.

"The Governing Corporate Objective: Shareholders versus Stakeholders," June 1993.

McTaggart, James M., "The Impact of Restructuring on Shareholder Value" (Chapter 5), *Corporate Restructuring: A Guide to Creating the Premium Valued Company,* Milton L. Rock & Robert H. Rock, New York: McGraw-Hill, 1990.

McTaggart, James M., "The Ultimate Takeover Defense: Closing the Value Gap," *Planning Review,* January-February 1988.

Miller, M.H. and F. Modigliani, "Dividend Policy, Growth and the Valuation of Shares," *Journal of Business,* October 1961.

Modigliani, F. and M.H. Miller, "The Cost of Capital, Corporation Finance and the Theory of Investment," *American Economic Review,* June 1958.

———, "Corporate Income Taxes and the Cost of Capital: A Correction," *American Economic Review,* June 1963.

———, "Some Estimates of the Cost of Capital to the Electric Utility Industry, 1954–57," *American Economic Review,* June 1966.

Ohmae, Kenichi, *The Mind of the Strategist,* New York: McGraw-Hill, 1982.

Porter, Michael E., *Competitive Advantage,* New York: The Free Press, 1985.

Porter, Michael E., *Competitive Strategy,* New York: The Free Press, 1980.

Prahalad, C.K. and Gary Hamel, "The Core Competence of the Corporation," *Harvard Business Review,* May-June 1990.

Rappaport, Alfred, *Creating Shareholder Value,* New York: The Free Press, 1986.

Stalk, George, Philip Evans, and Lawrence E. Shulman, "Competing on Capabilities: The New Rules of Corporate Strategy," *Harvard Business Review,* March-April 1992.

Stewart, G. Bennett, III, *The Quest for Value,* New York: Harper Business, 1991.

Wang, Jia and H. Dudley Dewhirst, "Boards of Directors and Stakeholder Orientation," *Journal of Business Ethics,* February 1992.

Willigan, Geraldine E., "The Value-Adding CFO: An Interview with Gary Wilson," *Harvard Business Review,* January-February 1990.

Index

351

About the Authors

JAMES M. McTAGGART and PETER W. KONTES are, respectively, the chairman and president of Marakon Associates, an international management consulting firm they founded in 1978. MICHAEL C. MANKINS is vice president of Marakon Associates and manages the firm's Stamford, Connecticut, office.

LaVergne, TN USA
03 March 2010
174616LV00002B/5/A